PSALMS 1-89

Eric Lane

'A commentator of yesteryear once said that he never wrote a commentary on a Bible book before he had read the book through at least fifty times. Eric Lane shows the same extensive direct contact with the text and this gives his work an attractive and stimulating freshness. His views on the chronological order of the psalms are somewhat controversial but will likewise stimulate the reader.'

Dr Geoffrey Grogan

PSALMS 1-89

The Lord saves

Eric Lane

CHRISTIAN FOCUS

Copyright © Eric Lane 2006

ISBN 1-84550-180-2
ISBN 978-1-84550-180-8

10 9 8 7 6 5 4 3 2 1

Published in 2006
in the
Focus on the Bible Commentary Series
by
Christian Focus Publications Ltd.,
Geanies House ,Fearn, Ross-shire,
IV20 1TW, Scotland, UK

www.christianfocus.com

Cover design by Danie Van Straaten

Printed and bound by
J. H. Haynes, Sparkford

Contents

Notes

Abbreviations:

f	the following verse
cf	compare
MT	Masoretic Text, i.e. the Hebrew text of the Old Testament
LXX	Septuagint, i.e. the Greek translation of the Old Testament, from the 3rd century BC
OT	Old Testament
NT	New Testament
Mg	Margin, i.e. the notes at the bottom of the page in the NIV
KJV	The King James Version of 1611
NKJV	The New King James Version of 1982
GNB	The Good News Bible of 1971
ESV	The English Standard Version of 2001

Books consulted:

J. A. Alexander: *The Psalms Translated and Explained* (Zondervan)

C. C. Broyles: *The Psalms: New International Biblical Commentary* (Hendriksen/Paternoster)

J. M. Good: *Historical Outline of the Book of Psalms* (London: W. H. Dalton, 1842). Out of print

Allan Harman: *The Psalms – a Mentor Commentary* (Mentor/Christian Focus)

G. W. Grogan: *Prayer, Praise and Prophecy* (Mentor/Christian Focus)

F. D. Kidner: *The Psalms* (IVP)

H. C. Leupold: *Exposition of the Psalms* (Evangelical Press)

C. S. Lewis: *Reflections on the Psalms* (Collins Fontana)

W. S. Plumer: *The Psalms* (Banner of Truth)

Introduction

For those desiring further information on the points covered here, references are given to the relevant passages in the books listed above. Particularly valuable is Geoffrey Grogan's recent book 'Prayer, Praise and Prophecy', which is virtually an extended introduction to the Psalms.

1. THE NATURE OF A PSALM

A psalm is basically a poem set to music and sung. This sets the Book of Psalms apart from the other books of Scripture. While there are a few other songs scattered through the books of the Bible (Harman, p. 8), the style of writing in the rest of Scripture tends to be either narrative or didactic. While this might make the Psalms seem less important than other books, and even expendable, it is probably true that for many centuries the Psalms would have been the most familiar part of Scripture to people who had no access to the other books (Broyles, p. 7). Even today, psalms or parts of them are known to people who have never read the rest of the Bible.

Many of the Psalms extol God for his personal greatness and his deeds in history. Others express commitment to his covenant and law, and yet others hope for the coming of the Messianic kingdom (Harman, pp. 9-10) Many are in the form of prayers, complaints and even curses. Nevertheless, praise predominates, so that the title in the Hebrew Bible is SEPHER TEHILLIM – 'Book of Praise-psalms' (Leupold, p. 1).

All this shows the difficulty of generalising about the Psalms. Many were clearly composed to be sung by the people of God gathered together, and these take on a liturgical pattern (Broyles, p. 2, under 'Fourth'). Others are very private and personal, such as those written by David when he was on the run from Saul or cornered by Absalom. Yet even these appear to have been retained and later issued for congregational use, as the inclusion of the words 'for the director of music' in the titles indicates. We therefore have to treat each psalm on its own merits.

2. THE STRUCTURE AND COMPILATION OF THE PSALMS

When we look at the Psalter as a whole, we observe that it is divided into five books, each of which is rounded off with a doxology: at 41:13, 72:18-19, 89:52, 106:48 and 150, the whole of which is a doxology and thus appropriately closes the whole collection.

This arrangement is ancient, for it is found in the Greek translation (the 'Septuagint', or LXX for short) made in the second or third centuries BC. But it has proved impossible to discover for certain the principles on which the divisions were made, if there are any. Clearly it is not **chronological**, for the earliest psalm, by Moses, is number 90 (in Book III), and David's last psalm appears as 72, ahead of earlier ones which are numbered 138 and 145.

Neither is it possible to trace any **theological** development. There are blocks which have a common theme: God's universal kingship in 93–99 , the 'Hallels' in 113–118 and 146 to 150, and the 'Songs of Ascents' in 120–134, but that is the most we can say. There are also some groupings by **author**: 'Psalms of the sons of Korah' in 42–49, and 'of Asaph' in 73–83. But none of this explains the whole structure.

Some have suggested that the books are distinguished by the particular name of God that is preferred. But this only applies to Books I: 'Yahweh' and II: 'Elohim' (Kidner, p. 5; Harman, p. 24; Leupold, p. 3). According to Josephus, the first century Jewish historian, collections were made by godly kings such as David, Jehoshaphat and Hezekiah, and by Ezra, who was the final editor. These men may have been guided by whatever psalms came to hand at various times, and so added a fresh collection to the existing ones. This appears to be how the book of Proverbs was compiled.

It may be that we shall never know the history of the structure of the book. We must remember that Psalms is the longest book of the Bible, and therefore could not be written on one scroll. This purely pragmatic consideration may explain a great deal, as it does with the length of the Gospels. Also, in days when few copies would be available, it is possible that each synagogue was rationed to one scroll. It would therefore be desirable that a representative selection of psalms, covering different subjects, activities and experiences of the godly life, should comprise each scroll. Although we have the whole Psalter, it is no bad method to follow this scheme of a book at a time in personal Bible study and preaching. The origin of the structure then need not bother us too much.

3. AUTHORSHIP

Many psalms claim to have been written by David and others. Some even refer to the specific event which occasioned a psalm. In our English Bibles these superscriptions are not seen as part of the text and are therefore not given a verse number. In the Hebrew Bible they are, which explains why our verse numbering is out of kilter with the Hebrew Bible. This doesn't mean they were inserted by the authors themselves, since they are written in the third person; for example, Psalm 3 reads: 'A psalm of David when **he** fled from **his** son Absalom' (emphasis mine). They must therefore have been added by a later editor, although who and when is not known. They were there before the third century BC, since they feature in LXX.

This is partly why many modern scholars reject them as unhistorical – 'conjectures made by the collectors'. They also point out that the preposition translated 'of' (Hebrew Le) does not necessarily mean 'by', but can mean 'to ... for ... about' (Broyles, pp. 27-28). They also point to anachronisms such as the term 'temple', which did not exist in David's time. They claim that in many cases the situation in the superscription doesn't fit the subject matter.

Conservative scholars tend to be more cautious. They believe that the NT use of the psalms confirms their authorship. For example, Psalm 16 is clearly attributed to the historical David in Acts 2:29, following the quotation of the closing verses of the psalm (Kidner, p. 33). The fact that they were added by an editor does not necessarily invalidate them. They were preserving 'a valuable and well-authenticated tradition which they felt should not be lost and could be of use to readers in centuries to come' (Leupold, p. 6). Broyles has a rather more complex explanation (p. 29).

No doubt psalms which were composed in connection with a particular incident were later edited for use in congregational worship. This would involve some updating to bring them into line with current events or experiences. But the editors felt they should not abandon all reference to their origin. The study of this background throws a great deal of light on the meaning and value of the psalms. This applies not merely to individual psalms but to the whole collection. David is not the only author to whom psalms are attributed (Kidner, pp. 35–36). Those not attributed to anyone or to a particular situation must have been written by someone in connection with a particular event or period. Put together they give us a different approach to the history of Israel from that recorded by the Biblical authors. The histories are purely factual but in the psalms we see how people felt about what was happening, and particularly how they prayed or praised.

This approach has been developed in the Appendix to my commentary on Psalms 90–150 by suggesting an historical order.

4. POETRY

Much of the Bible is written in poetry. There are fragments almost from the beginning, the earliest being Adam's words on seeing Eve for the first time:

This is now bone of my bones
and flesh of my flesh;
She shall be called 'woman'
For she was taken out of man (2:23).

Evidently the sight of her so struck Adam that he burst into verse and gave us the first love poem! There are also whole books in verse, such as Job and Proverbs, plus many passages in the prophets. This may not be immediately obvious to readers, since Hebrew poetry is very different from English. Our poetry is far more complex, with a number of different styles, from 'blank verse' to the elaborate sonnet form, both used by Shakespeare. We also have a number of different meters in which the accents fall on the syllables, and frequently rhyme is used. Hebrew poetry is much simpler: the accents are on the words rather than the syllables, which makes the rhythm more difficult to detect, and there are no rhymes. The nearest equivalent in English poetry would be the 'sprung' rhythm of Gerald Manley Hopkins.

The chief feature of Hebrew poetry is **parallelism**, in which the thought of one line is repeated in the next in different words. For example:

> He does not treat us as our sins deserve,
> or repay us according to our iniquities (103:10).

This is called 'synonymous parallelism'. There is also 'synthetic parallelism', where the second line adds something to the first, for example:

> The LORD is near to all who call on him ,
> to all who call on him in truth (145:18).

Lastly, there is 'antithetic parallelism', in which the second line contrasts with the first, for example:

> The wicked borrow and do not repay,
> but the righteous give generously (37:21).

This latter form is used in many of the Proverbs. It is important to bear this in mind in interpreting the psalms, especially in the case of 'synonymous parallelism'. We should not try to find a different meaning in the second part of a verse where it is simply repeating the thought of the first line.

All the psalms are poems for the simple reason that they were designed for singing. The music of the words easily lent itself to melodies which enabled the congregation to sing the psalms together. What these melodies were like will probably never be known. Possibly they were not completely unlike the 'chants' used by churches which sing the psalms in their original form.

5. TECHNICAL TERMS

There are several technical terms (mostly found in the titles or superscriptions) of which the meaning cannot be precisely determined.

Selah is the most frequent, occurring seventy-one times. It appears to be derived from a Hebrew word meaning 'to lift up'. This may indicate an interlude in which the musicians took up their instruments, or simply an increase in volume, like our term 'crescendo'.

Higgaion occurs in 9:16 along with *Selah*, and may mean that the quieter instruments were to be used for this interlude. The term means 'meditation' and is found in Psalms 19:14 and 92:3 as part of the text itself.

Psalm (Hebrew **MIZMOR**) is used frequently and *Song* (Hebrew **SIR**) occasionally. The difference seems to be that the former was composed for a particular occasion and the latter was a more generally known piece.

Other terms are *Shiggaion, Miktam, Maskil, A Prayer, A Praise* and will be commented on in the book as they appear. Kidner gives all these a thorough discussion in his introduction pages 32-46.

The phrase *To the Choirmaster* or *Director of Music*, used fifty-five times, shows that, whatever the particular incident which prompted the psalm, it was passed to the music director to be included in the collection he was compiling or editing. At this point some alterations may have taken place to make it suitable for congregational singing. This would explain how a psalm composed at a time of crisis acquired a complex literary form, such as an acrostic.

Phrases beginning **According to ...** seem to refer to the tune and are commented on in the book as they appear.

6. TYPES OF PSALM

The Psalms have been a happy hunting ground for those whose approach to Scripture is to take well-known verses and isolate them from their context, giving them individualistic and even erroneous interpretations. But it will not only save us from going wrong but also open up these texts more meaningfully if we treat them in accordance with their particular type. For, while we cannot rigidly categorise all the psalms infallibly, we can detect some common forms. The chief ones are the following.

(a) **Hymns**. (Harman, pp. 32, 46-47; Broyles p. 13). These are psalms addressed to God himself in praise and worship. Examples are 92, 103, 113. They tend to begin with a call to worship, addressed either to the writer's own soul (103:1) or to the assembled people by a priest or Levite (113:1). They specify what God has done to merit this praise (103:2-19) and end with a repetition of the call to praise, often extended not merely to all Israel, but to the nations of the earth (96:7-13) and even the inhabitants of heaven (103:20-22).

(b) **Prayers** (Harman, pp. 32, 48; Broyles 16). Many psalms are in the form of earnest petitions to God for help in need. Most come from the pen of David and date from the time of his sufferings at the hand of Saul or other enemies. Such a one is Psalm 4, where he seeks relief from (his) distress (v. 1). Some of these include laments over the degree of suffering being endured. Psalm 13 is a good example, since it not only bewails the trials but complains about their seeming unending duration. How long? is thrice repeated. Often the struggle in prayer is resolved in an assurance that God has heard: 4:7f, 6:8f.

(c) **Thanksgivings**. (Harman, pp. 32, 50; Broyles, p. 18). These are frequently connected with the prayers and laments, and are acknowledgements that God has answered prayer. For example, Psalm 18 is a long recital of God's deliverances, for it comes late in David's life and takes account of his many sufferings and escapes, both from Saul, the neighbouring nations and from Absalom. Others are 32 and 34. But such psalms are not confined to the individual; some are offered by the whole community: for material blessings (65), victories (75), deliverances (107) and their whole history (136).

(d) **Remembrance** (Harman, pp. 33, 52-54). Some of this type can easily be included under 'Thanksgivings', for they are recollections of God's mighty works for Israel down its history, which prompted the response of thanksgiving. Examples are 78, 105, 106. The likelihood is that these were composed for use on great occasions such as the dedication of the Temple or the major feasts: Passover, Tabernacles, etc.

(e) **Wisdom** (Harman pp. 33, 52; Broyles 21). The main Wisdom literature of the OT lies outside the Psalms – in Job, Proverbs and Ecclesiastes. But some psalms are in the style of those books and tackle the issues they raise: guidance in how to live, understanding of the types of people in the world, especially the 'righteous' and the 'wicked', and the problems thrown up by the clash of these types. These psalms vary considerably. There are those which dwell upon the practicalities of normal life, such as 25, and those which wrestle with the great ethical issues such as why the wicked seem to thrive at the expense of the righteous. Psalms 37 and 73 are the most extensive treatments of this subject. Psalms such as these would be more for personal use than singing in services.

Under this heading we may include psalms which glory in the Law of God (Harman p. 44). In the OT 'law' means more than the code of regulations for personal conduct, government and worship, for the term TORAH approximates to what we call 'the Word of God', that is, divine teaching. So when the psalmists are exulting in their love for the Law, they are rejoicing in the fact that they have a God who teaches them about himself, his world, his special dealings with them and his guidance on how to live. The chief psalms of this type are 1, 19 and 119.

(f) **Kingship**. (Harman, pp. 38-42). Many psalms are addressed to or written about 'the King'. Some of these are about David or his successors on the throne: 20, 21, 89, 132. To address praises and prayers to a mortal man, even if he is in a position of supreme power, sounds almost blasphemous. We have to remember that the king of Israel was God's representative and therefore what was said to or about him was said to or about God.

But there are also psalms in which God is acknowledged as King in his own right without reference to any human monarch. Israel was a theocracy and the Lord alone was its King. This was why it was only with reluctance that he allowed them to have a human King in the first place. It could be interpreted as a rejection of his own rule (1 Sam. 8:1-9). The only safeguard against this was to keep in view that, whoever occupied the throne of Israel, God was its true King. By singing the psalms regularly they would never be able to forget this: 'The LORD reigns' is a not infrequent phrase. The chief psalms on the Lord's Kingship are 48, 93, 96-99.

But the psalms go beyond this. Israel's God was the only God; all others were man-made idols, so that, whether people acknowledge him or not, he is *King of all the earth* (47:7). That psalm is probably the best one in which to see his universal sovereignty, but there are many other references, e.g. 11:4, 29:10, 50:1-4, 66:1-7, 74:12-17, 96.

(g) **The Messianic Hope** (Leupold, pp. 20-22; Kidner, pp. 18-25). We are probably all familiar with the idea that a Messiah to redeem the human race is promised and predicted in the OT from the fall of man through to the last prophet. The psalms are not excluded from this prophetic note, which is chiefly seen in those psalms which contain the theme of Kingship. One of the best psalms in which to see this idea is one of the earliest (Ps. 2). The occasion appears to be a rebellion of some local kings against Israel's king (vv. 1-3). The psalmist looks beyond this to the universal King (vv. 4-5), who has personally *installed* Israel's king (v. 6), referred to in verse 2 as *his anointed one*, literally MASIAH, from which the word 'Messiah' (Greek 'Christ') comes. The king then pronounces the words with which God inaugurated him (vv. 7-9). The words 'you are my Son' echo what God said to

Samuel in 2 Samuel 7:14, but the kingdom he promised his
Son far exceeds what David and his successors possessed; in
fact it is universal. The verse in which he is called God's Son
is quoted of Jesus in the NT (Matt. 3:17; Acts 13:33; Heb. 1:5),
and Jesus himself proclaimed his universal kingdom when
he sent his disciples 'into all the world to make disciples
of all the nations' (Matt. 28:19; Mark 16:15). Since the reign
of Israel's king is undergirded by the King of all the earth,
these rebellious kings are advised to make peace with him
(vv. 10-12).

Psalm 110 is in similar vein and is also quoted several
times in the NT (Matt. 22:44; Acts 2:34-35; Heb. 1:12-13, etc.).
Psalm 72, originally written to celebrate Solomon's accession,
goes far beyond anything ever achieved in that glorious reign,
which never extended 'from the river (Euphrates) to the ends
of the earth', nor did 'all kings bow down to him', as Christ is
promised they will do to him (Phil. 2:9-11). The psalm begins
with a prayer that he will be a righteous man who will reign
justly. Although Solomon did not go as far into evil as some
of the later kings and approximated to David more than most,
he scarcely lived up to this standard (1 Kings 11:6).

The way in which Jesus would come into his kingdom by
way of suffering is also to be found in the psalms. Of this David
is himself the example, for he suffered much at the hands of
Saul in his early days and of Absalom in later ones. He writes
of these sufferings in such psalms as 22 and 69. However, they
go far beyond anything David ever experienced, and were
fulfilled in Jesus down to the last detail: 'they have pierced
my hands and my feet' (22:6).

In addition to these the NT applies to Christ several of the
less obvious passages in the Psalms, such as Hebrews 2:13
quoting Psalm 22:22, and Romans 15:9 quoting Psalm 18:49.
This should not surprise us, since Christ spent the time taken
by a seven-mile walk going through the OT Scriptures to bring
out *what was said ... concerning himself* (Luke 24:27).

(h) **Covenant** (Harman, pp. 25-29). The nation from which
the Psalms came and which sang them in its gatherings was a
nation in a particular relationship with God. He had made a

covenant with them by which he declared them 'his people'. This was made with Abraham and his descendants through Isaac (Gen. 17:2, 7) and formally ratifed at Sinai through Moses (Exod. 19:5-6). This covenant assured Israel that God would protect them from their enemies who would be 'cursed' if they 'cursed' Israel (Gen. 12:2-3.) At the same time Israel could be 'cursed' if she broke the laws of the covenant (Lev. 26:14-39). On the other hand, obedience to the covenant guaranteed that God would continue to provide for and protect them (Lev. 26:1-13, 40-45). Later God made a covenant with David to the effect that his descendants would always occupy the throne of Judah (2 Sam. 7:11-16).

Although it would be going too far to speak of specific 'covenant psalms', these covenants are clearly the background to a number of them. Psalm 105:8-11 alludes to the covenant with Abraham; in fact the whole psalm celebrates the works of God down to the time the descendants of Abraham were in Egypt as being in fulfilment of that covenant. For after summarizing the history of Israel up to their journey from Sinai, it gives as the reason 'for he remembered his holy promise given to his servant Abraham' (v. 42). Psalm 106 virtually takes over where 105 leaves off and thus recalls the Mosaic covenant. Its blessings are celebrated in the first part (vv. 1-12), for their deliverance from Pharaoh at the Red Sea was due to God's promise to protect and deliver his people from their enemies. However, verse 13 goes on to speak of how they 'forgot what he had done and did not wait for his counsel', that is, they did not act on the terms of the covenant. The consequence was that the curses of the covenant came on them. Psalm 78 is similar, showing how God dealt with Israel according to whether or not they obeyed the conditions of the covenant.

The covenant with David is mentioned at the end of Psalm 78 (vv. 70-72), but has more extended treatment in Psalm 89, especially from verse 19. Psalm 132 is also based on God's covenant with David, but more from the point of view of his choice of Zion than of David and his descendants. Although the use of the term 'covenant' may not be frequent (only twenty-one times) the idea permeates the entire book. Wherever psalms refer to Israel as 'the people of God' the covenant is in view, because this was its chief clause (Gen. 17:7). 95:7 is a typical example of this: *he is our God and we are the people of his pasture.* Such sentiments can be found all over the psalms. The same applies to the idea of being *chosen* (33:1; 135:4), as it does to the use of the term *servant* (31:16; 89:3). The language of the psalms echoes the covenant all the way through.

We must not overlook those psalms which call on 'the nations' to acknowledge God, and even speak of how they will do so. Look, for example, at 67 and 117. Such passages are not infrequent. Also they are allusions to God's covenant with Abraham, which not only promised to curse Israel's enemies but to bless those who befriended them (Gen. 12:2-3). Indeed it predicted a time when 'all peoples of the earth' would come into this relationship. This great hope is confirmed by the prophets (Isa. 2:2-4) and celebrated in the psalms. When Paul is exulting in the universality of his gospel in Romans 15 he quotes two psalms: 18:49 in verse 9, and 117 in verse 11.

(i) **Imprecations** (Kidner, pp. 25-32; Leupold, pp. 18-20; Harman, pp. 58-52). It does not escape most people's notice that there are passages in the psalms which they find difficult if not impossible to sing, or even read, with a cheerful spirit. These are the passages in which the writer calls down curses on his enemies. The chief culprits are 55, 59, 69, 79, 109 and 137. The latter is particularly notorious, for though it begins with the famous words *By the rivers of Babylon we sat and wept* and continues in most poignant words which evoke our sympathy, it suddenly ends with about the most vindictive curse that anyone ever made (v. 9). How can anyone sing those words in a Christian service praising God? How could they even sing them in the synagogue or temple before Christ? Modern attempts to make them singable only succeed in sanitizing them: 'be warned of judgment on you and your children', goes Michael Perry's version of the verse in Jubilate Hymns. This of course raises the whole question of how far the psalms of the old covenant are appropriate for worship under the new covenant. Which ones? In what way? We will defer this matter to our last section and now simply try to explain why such language is present in the Bible. There are two ways of answering this:

1. The curses of the psalms are in line with the nature of the covenant considered above. God's covenant with Israel included curses on those who broke its terms of obedience to God's laws. Some of the psalms were written at times of great wickedness among the people of God, which sometimes went to the length of ill-treatment of the righteous by the wicked. For the psalmists to call down curses on these persecutors was simply to pronounce the judgment of God on them; it was to do in poetry what the prophets did in preaching. Most imprecatory psalms arose out of this kind of situation, especially in connection with David's persecution by Saul and his men. Psalm 59 relates to such an occasion. Psalm 55 probably refers to David's betrayal by Ahithophel, who went over to Absalom, and to all the suffering that followed that. Hence David's prayer of verse 15.

Psalm 69 has a more extended curse (vv. 22-28), and probably refers to Absalom and his followers. Psalm 109 has a similarly long imprecation and again is against Ahithophel. In all this David was not speaking out of turn, but simply echoing what God himself had said. Nor was he saying these words to the people themselves, or to his own friends; they were for God's ears alone, they were prayers. Are we not told not to take vengeance ourselves but put it into God's hands (Deut. 32:35; Rom. 12:19)?

Psalm 137:8-9 is different, for it refers to another nation – Babylon. It sounds vindictive, like 'I'll get you for that!' or 'You did it to me, I'll do it to you!'. But the answer again lies in the covenant: *whoever curses you I will curse* (Gen. 12:3). God's curse is not vindictive language but just judgment. God repays people and nations in proportion to their crimes. He did this repeatedly in the OT and on some occasions Israel herself was his instrument in punishing them. He himself authorised them to destroy wicked and corrupt nations like the Amalekites and Amorites. He authorised the prophets to declare this: Isaiah 13 announced the judgment of Babylon and includes the words: *their infants will be dashed in pieces before their eyes* (v. 16). The

psalmist was simply concurring in the judgment of God. The
Babylonians had done such things to others (2 Kings 25:7),
and God would requite them: *Do to her as she has done to others*
was Jeremiah's call to the nations to gang up against Babylon
(Jer. 50:15). If we have problems with these cursing passages
they are not really with the writers and their words, but with
God and his judgment. This is not the place to justify God's
judgment, but we should remember that it has a place in the
New Testament and the teaching of Jesus, as well as in the Old
Testament (e.g. Matt. 7:21-23; 13:40-45; 21:44; 24:51; John 5:22;
9:39; Rom. 2:16; 2 Thess. 1:6-10; 2 Peter 3:7-10).

2. The whole Old Testament is prophetic. That is what it
means to call it 'the Word of God'. It declares his thoughts
and proclaims his acts. These concern not only the past and
present but the future too. This prophetic note is found not
just in the official prophets but the narrative passages and even
the Psalms. Those who spoke and wrote what now forms the
Old Testament did so by the Spirit of God, as Christ and his
apostles recognised (Matt. 22:43; 2 Pet. 1:21). This is another
way of saying they spoke prophetically.

We have seen how many passages in the Psalms go
far beyond the experiences of the writers and point to
Christ. His salvation was not to be a physical or political
deliverance, but a deliverance from sin, the devil and hell.
It was to be for all nations as well as for Israel. Psalm 110 is
a case in point, as the NT confirms. In the same way as the
psalms prophesy salvation they also prophesy judgment.
In these cursing passages the writers are speaking not in
their own name but God's. They therefore had authority
to pronounce guilt and punishment on sinners. Augustine
wrote of such passages: 'these are not the words of one
wishing mischief may happen to his enemies; they are the
words of a prophet, of one who is foretelling in Scripture
language the evil that must befall them on account of their
sins'.

These points in no way lessen the severity of the language,
but they do free it from personal vindictiveness and put
it in the context of the whole word of God. We can at least

understand why they are there. Further remarks will be found in the commentary on the particular psalms.

7. SPIRITUAL VALUE

What is the Bible? What is about? Is it a **story**, telling the history of the human race, particularly of one nation up to the coming into the world of the Redeemer, after which the story expands again to the whole race, culminating in the end of the world. Yes, it is clearly that; but is that its main theme and value?

Or is it a book of **doctrine**? Does its value lie in what it teaches about the nature of God, about humanity, about the earth and the universe, about human behaviour, sin and salvation, the creation of the universe and its end? Yes, there is much teaching in the Bible. Indeed it is possible to write 'a theology of the Psalms', as Geoffrey Grogan has recently done. But is that what they are mainly about?

It is possible to know both these aspects in great depth, yet to miss the main point: a personal relationship between man and God. It is to this that both the story and the teaching are designed to lead us. This is where the book of Psalms comes into its own. That is not to say there is no story running through the Psalms. The Appendix to this commentary shows it is possible to link them with the history of Israel from Moses to Ezra. Some psalms are virtual summaries of parts of Israel's history (78, 105, 106). Again, the psalms are full of doctrine. This is why the NT appeals to them when expounding such matters as the divine nature of the Messiah (Matt. 22:41-45; Heb. 1, where five psalms are quoted) or justification by faith (Rom. 4:6-8). The Psalms are linked with the whole teaching of Scripture.

But there is an important difference between the Psalms and the other books of the Bible: their constant use of the first person singular or plural: 'I ... we'. They come out of the life-situations of these historical figures; they describe how these people **experienced** the God who had revealed himself in history, law and prophecy. 'The Psalms are not abstract writings about theology or anything approaching a philosophical discussion of religious themes. They are really an expression of the knowledge about God and his ways, which is rooted in personal experience of a vital relationship with him' (Harman, p. 19).

This is their real value. You find here flesh and blood people in real life situations facing up to the depravity within them (51), finding forgiveness with God (32), going on to rejoice in him (116), committing themselves to obeying and serving him (25), struggling with prevailing wickedness (37, 73), experiencing spiritual barrenness, doubt and rejection (77), and even facing death (39, 88).

There is no experience common to man that is not echoed in one or more psalms. Moreover, these experiences are not spoken of in a detached clinical way, but are full of emotion, so that whether we are exhilarated or depressed, encouraged or fearful, we will find an echo of our feelings in the psalms. Perhaps there are parts of Scripture that can be managed without; but the Book of Psalms is not one of them. The best way to use them is to meditate on one or part of one every day alongside your daily Bible reading. This will help you to a balanced Christian life.

In order to keep this book within reasonable bounds, theological, ethical and spiritual applications have not been discussed. These are left to the reader to work out, but 'questions' are raised after each Psalm, to indicate the main lines on which you should be thinking.

Psalm 1

Meditating on the Law

The psalm chosen to open the collection roots it firmly in the whole tradition of God's revealed truth, for it is the conviction of one whose *delight is in the law of the LORD*. The Scriptures, or those which existed at the time, were known as *the law of the LORD*, for the word TORAH means more than a code of rules; it is the instruction or knowledge that God has revealed, which is contained in history and wisdom books as well as laws. The psalms are part of this tradition. Although many are personal reflections about individual experience, they are still the word of God.

The justification for this claim lies in the spiritual standing of their writers, who are **the righteous**, so-called because they **delight in** the word of a righteous God. They are clearly distinguished from **the wicked**, who do not. The prayers and complaints come from those who because of their righteousness are opposed by the wicked. The praises are addressed to a righteous God who steps in on behalf of the righteous.

Although written in the third person, we may take this as the writer's personal testimony. He finds his happiness in avoiding the company of the wicked, for the reasons he gives here.

Verse 1: he is rejoicing in his isolation from society. Far from being boring, he finds it a **blessing**. For although Israel was 'God's people', there was little true godliness among them. Many were **wicked, sinners** and even **mockers** at the godly. The writer was glad not to have to put up with their company, and counsels anyone who might hear his song to beware of such.

Verse 2: tells us how he spent his time when there was no one to converse with, possibly because of the nature of his occupation; he spent his time **meditating on the law of the Lord**, which he had been taught as a boy. Since education was done orally by memorization, he would have no difficulty recalling this. Far from being tedious, he found it a **delight**, even when his work kept him awake at **night**.

Verse 3: suggests he was composing his psalm under a **tree by a stream**, which may only have been an irrigation ditch. Nevertheless it kept the tree's **leaf** from scorching in the sun and even enabled it to **yield fruit**. This to him is a good illustration of the character of one who avoids bad company and spends his time thinking about the word of God.

Verse 4 shows him observing agricultural operations, in which he may himself have taken part – the cutting of the corn, or its threshing. What he notices is how easily **the wind blows away the chaff**. This is a good picture of the lives of those whose company he disdains (v. 1) – they are useless and unstable.

Verse 5 goes further: it is a preview of their final appearance before God, when they will be swept away from his presence.

Verse 6 ends on a positive note: he encourages himself and any others who hear or read his words (down to the present time and company) to hold fast to their faith and their faithfulness to God. However difficult this is, they will be glad at the end of the day – and sorry if they follow **the way of the wicked**.

Consider:

(1) How does the psalm help us relate our faith to our daily life, and use our daily routine for the good of our soul?

(2) What does the psalm teach us about the uses of solitude, showing us that loneliness is not the worst thing in the world?

(3) How do verses 4-6 compare with Matthew 7:23?

Psalm 2

Installed as King on Zion

Although it has no title the psalm is ascribed to David in Acts 4:25 in very specific terms: 'You spoke by the Holy Spirit through the mouth of your servant our father David'. Apparently his tenure of the throne had come under threat, but victory has confirmed it. The psalm is used in the NT in relation to Christ's sonship and resurrection (Matt. 3:17; Acts 13:33; Heb. 1:5). It breathes an air of confidence which is well suited to the exaltation of Jesus to his kingdom.

Verses 1-3: Rebellious nations challenge David

The background here is that David is established on his throne in Jerusalem by *the* LORD as *his Anointed One*. The ceremony of anointing by the High Priest has taken place, symbolically transferring authority and power to the King. To protect his kingdom from further attacks by these nations, David has apparently imposed some kind of vassalage on them (v. 3). Angered by this they get together to *plot* how they can escape (v. 1). In this their *kings ... and ... rulers* take the lead, seeing David as a common threat (v. 2). They pass a resolution to break the terms of peace imposed on them (v. 3), which may be economic sanctions, disarmament or the closing of their borders.

But the key word is the first one: *Why?* (v. 1). This is not so much a request for information as an exclamation of astonishment that these mere mortals should set themselves up against the one chosen by God. This explains its use by the early church in their prayer of Acts 4:18-31. The apostles had been threatened with death if they continued to teach in the name of Jesus, but saw this as fulfilling the nations' defiance of David, as they say in verse 27. But how can it succeed when it is God's Son they are opposing and God's word they are refusing (v. 28)? It is all *in vain* as the psalmist says in verse 1.

Verses 4-6: God responds to the challenge

David's bold *Why?* is justified, for he speaks on God's behalf. As his *Anointed One* he is not only king but prophet and can report the reaction of *the One enthroned in heaven*. At first God is merely amused at the insolence of these feeble mortals (v. 4). But when they persist he grows angry (v. 5) and thunders out that David's installation in Jerusalem was his will and deed (v. 6). This both silences the nations and emboldens David, as the next three verses show.

Verses 7-9: David declares God's will

David's prophetic insight into the mind of God enables him to go even further and *proclaim the decree of the* LORD. He did this again later in Psalm 110:1 when he made known what the Father ('the LORD') said to the Son ('my Lord') in eternity concerning his Son's appointment as King of the universe. Here David declares that his own appointment as king is similarly God's *decree*, and constitutes a special relationship with him as *Son* to a *Father*. Further, it entitles him to an *inheritance – the nations* of the earth, over whom he has authority to govern powerfully, and if they rebel to destroy them totally (v. 9).

This was – indeed **could** only be – true in a limited way of David and his successors. It is really prophesying Messiah's kingdom, as the NT writers bring out. The Father himself addressed the words of verse 7 to Jesus on his baptism (Matt. 3:17) and transfiguration (Matt. 17:5). Paul preached in Pisidian Antioch that the resurrection of Christ established that he was the Father's Son and quoted verse 7 (Acts 13:32-33). Hebrews 1:5 applies it to Christ's exaltation to the throne of heaven with authority over all the powers of heaven and earth. Verses 8-9 are referred to in Revelation 2:26, where the church too is given a share in Christ's kingdom. This *decree* was soon to be set down in the form of a covenant between God and the line of Davidic kings (2 Sam. 7).

Verses 10-12: David challenges the nations

Fortified by God's decree, David is able to reply to the challenge of verses 1-3 with his own challenge. It is a gracious rather than an aggressive response, for it combines an invitation to join him in worshipping God (v. 11) with a warning against the folly of continuing in opposition (v. 10), lest the Lord's patience runs out, with dire consequences (v. 12a). If they do this, they too will find blessing (v. 12b). It will therefore *be wise* (v. 10) for them to *Kiss the Son*, that is, to acknowledge David's appointment sincerely.

In New Testament fulfilment, the gospel comes to us with the same two notes: of **gracious invitation**, offering us blessing if we *kiss the Son* (Jesus, that is), accept him as Saviour and Lord, and of **serious warning** of the consequences of refusing the One God has appointed to rule, who will, if we persist, 'put us under his feet' with all his other 'enemies' (1 Cor. 15:25).

Questions:
(1) Do verses 1-3 help explain why the church frequently finds herself opposed and attacked by political authorities? Look again at Acts 4:18-31.

(2) How has Christ been fulfilling verses 8-9 since his return to heaven?

(3) How should the church respond to opposition according to verses 10-12? (See Matt. 5:9-16, 43-48; Rom. 12:17-21; 1 Pet. 3:13-17.)

Psalm 3

The First Night of David's Flight from Absalom

This psalm is attributed to *David, when he fled from his son, Absalom*. The background may be the arrival of David and his colleagues at Bahurim after a long day's march (2 Sam. 16:5, 14). Here they rest for the night and David reflects on the events of the day in this and the next psalm. Whether he composed them at that time or later when looking back it is pointless to argue. He certainly composed them to be sung, for each is entitled *a psalm*, or literally 'a song' – a different word from that used for the title of the whole collection and for some individual ones, which means 'praises'. Thus the book as a whole is for the praise of God, though particular compositions could be prayers, reminiscences or even imprecations in the form of 'songs'.

Verses 1-2: The gravity of the situation
Things look blackest during the blackness of night and David was no exception to this human weakness. What he is most conscious of is the size of the opposition: *how many are my foes!* (v. 1). Some are in active rebellion, they *rise up against me*. Those who are not taking up arms are speaking harsh words, accusing him of being forsaken by God (v. 2). To David the second was worse than the first, for he could never forget God's warning to him after the Bathsheba episode: 'out of your own household I am going to bring calamity upon you'

(2 Sam. 12:11). No doubt this had been what prompted him to accept Shimei's curses submissively (2 Sam. 16:5-14), and the thought was preying on his mind as he lay down to sleep. The *Selah* interval emphasises the radical change of direction the psalm is to take.

Verses 3-4: The greatness of God

We get the impression that David is lying awake overwhelmed by the thoughts expressed in verses 1-2. Suddenly a shaft of light from heaven shines upon him. A vast army with swords and spears is pursuing him. What defence has he? Of course!: *you are a shield ... O LORD*, and a better one than a soldier's, for *you are ... AROUND me*, so that I am protected on all sides (v. 3). And how could God have forsaken him, since he is *my Glorious One* (literally 'my glory' mg.)? It was God alone who had honoured him with the throne; he had no right of inheritance and was not even popularly elected, as Saul had been. God had honoured him, so that he might honour God. So how could God now forsake him? No, he will 'deliver' (v. 1), he will *lift up my head*, which will no longer hang in shame before his accusers.

Thus 'lifted up' by God, he himself now *lifts up*, not his *head* only but his voice, *to cry aloud to the LORD* (v. 4). Nor is this just 'singing in the rain' or whistling in the dark, it is purposeful, effective. He will have *answers from his holy hill*. He had returned the ark to its place on Zion (2 Sam. 15:24-26) and had frequently prayed there and been heard. But his absence from it now in no way limited God. The ark only **symbolized** his sovereignty and his covenant with David and Israel. Whatever Absalom decrees, God will have his way.

Verses 5-6: The presence of God

So David can return to bed, *lie down* and rest his head on the promise and power of God, and thus *sleep*. There may be a suggestion that he was afraid to shut his eyes for fear of assasssination, since he says *I woke again, BECAUSE the LORD sustains me* (v. 5). God's 'shield' had been around him while he slept, so that he did not die. This thought took away all *fear* (v. 6). He could now face the opposition, even if their number multiplied again, and instead of just pursuing him, surrounded him *on every side*. He had the answer: the Lord surrounded him like a shield (v. 3).

Verses 7-8: The deliverance of God

But peace and fearlessness were not enough. He must have victory, otherwise God's declared will would be frustrated. So in answer to his 'many foes' who 'rise against' him (v. 1), he calls on God to arise against them and do for him what they said God would not do – *deliver* him (v. 2). His lurid language in verse 7 is metaphorical,meaning 'render them harmless', like a toothless lion with a broken *jaw*. Now let them say what they like about God forsaking him – he will prove the opposite, for *from the* LORD *comes deliverance*. Nor is his concern and euphoria just for himself; the well-being of the whole nation was tied up with his safety. The same God who covenanted with him had covenanted with his people. With David's deliverance came the *blessing* of his people.

Questions:
(1) Does the psalm help you with the problem of sleeplessness through anxiety or overtiredness? (See Lev. 26:6; Luke 8:23.)

(2) Does it make any difference to your fellowhip with God whether you are away from your usual place for prayer and your usual church for worship (v. 4)?

(3) Can you see any ways in which David here:
    a) anticipated Christ's struggle against his supernatural foes? (See Luke 22:53; John 12:31.)
    b) is thus a pattern for the believer? (See 2 Cor. 4:8.)

Psalm 4

David's Evening Meditation

The verbal similarities between this psalm and the previous one point to the same occasion, so that the title of 3 may be said to do duty for both psalms. The word for distress (v. 1) is the same as that for 'foes' in 3:1 (Hebrew TSAR). *Answer* (v. 1) is used in 3:4, and *call* in the same verse is identical with 'cry' in 3:4. *Glory* in verse 2 occurs in 3:3, and verse 8 is very similar to 3:5. So this is David still probably reflecting on the whole situation on his first night away from Jerusalem.

Verse 1: His prayer to God
This continues the thought of 3:7, that God would hear his prayer for deliverance. His appeal is similar – to his covenant relationship with God, except that 'my God' becomes *my righteous God*, the One who will certainly honour his covenant promise. There is some word play here, for it reads literally 'in a narrow place make for me a wide place'. The corner into which he was being driven symbolised his loss of freedom, and to this he prays to be restored.

Verses 2-5: His challenge to his enemies
There are two possible interpretations of verse 2. One is that the reference is to idolatry on the part of his enemies, who were turning his *Glorious One* (NIV mg) that is, God, *into shame* by *loving and seeking false gods*. The other is that he is speaking

of their depriving David of the *glory* of being king of Israel by spreading *delusions and lies* (NIV mg) about him. Since there is no evidence that Absalom was idolatrous and since the campaign was all about 'Who rules?' the second interpretation seems the likelier.

There is a pause or musical interlude (*Selah*) before he follows this up with the challenge to them to recognise that his being *set apart* for the throne was the will of *the Lord*, who would therefore *hear (his) call*, both for his own relief (v. 1) and for their defeat (3:7). He develops this in verse 4 which reads literally 'Tremble and do not sin', that is, 'tremble before God, go away, reflect on your words when you lie down, then you will give up your sinful rebellion, which is really against him and his will'.

In your anger is the Septuagint translation, the one used by the apostles, hence Paul's quotation of it in Ephesians 4:26 in connection with righteous anger. Absalom and his companions however had no grounds for such anger. What follows confirms this. Let them first acknowledge their sin before God, then come and be reconciled to him through the appropriate *(right) sacrifices* (v. 5). This will restore them to the life of faith, so that they will *trust in the Lord* and abandon their enterprise.

Verses 6-8: His encouragement to his friends

David then turns his attention to his faithful followers, who were near despair, questioning whether any good could come out of this dire situation. David's answer is to turn to God again, this time on their behalf rather than his own. What better words can he use than the old Aaronic blessing (v. 6b) first given during the desert journey (Num. 6:25)? If God gave them a vision of himself, would this not make all the difference? It certainly had done so for him (v. 7). He might not be enjoying the abundance of the harvest *grain and new wine* that some were, but his *heart was filled with greater joy* than theirs. With this assurance he can *lie down and sleep in peace* (v. 8) for however strong and near his enemy may be, *the Lord (will) make me dwell in safety*.

Questions:

(1) Make verses 4-5 into a mini-Gospel sermon, using *anger* in the sense of 'tremble' (before God).

(2) Is verse 6b true for you? Do you have such a vision of God? Or is your mind more like verse 6a than verses 7-8?

Psalm 5

The Morning After

References to *the morning* (v. 3) suggest that after the struggles of the night (Ps. 3) David has collected his thoughts and is bringing them to God in prayer. It is therefore likely that the occasion of this psalm is the same as that of Psalm 3.

Verses 1-3: David asks God to hear him
The title contains the instruction *for flutes*, which is probably explained by the *sighing* with which David is now coming to God (v. 1). Whereas trumpets accompany praise and rejoicing, and strings form a background to peaceful meditation, the more plaintive, even mournful, sound of *flutes* on their own is appropriate to a heart in anguish. In our Lord's time flutes were still used to accompany mourning for the dead (Matt. 9:23).

However, David's appeal to God to *give ear to (his) words ... (and) ... listen to his cry for help* is based not only on his anguish but on God's sovereignty and faithfulness: *my King and my God* (v. 2). He is calling on the One who, after releasing them from Egypt, took over from Pharaoh as their ruler: Exodus 15:18, and who subsequently entered into covenant, first with the whole people (Exod. 19) and then with David (2 Sam. 7; Ps. 89:3-4), so that David could justifiably call him *MY God*.

This made all the difference: now he could say, not *give ear* but *you hear my voice* (v. 3). Although he cannot physically express this in the morning sacrifice at the tabernacle, he regards his prayer as a substitute for this, for the word *lay* is that used of the priest laying the fire for the burnt offering and arranging the sacrifice on it: Leviticus 17:8; Psalm 141:2. This elevates the whole spirit of his prayer: now he can *wait in expectation* that the Lord will work for him. This sets the tone for the rest of the psalm.

Verses 4-6: David distances himself from his enemies

Now he is sure that God is hearing him, David's thoughts of his enemies are different from what they were in Psalm 3. Then he was thinking of the strength of their numbers (3:1), now he is thinking of the weakness of their position before God. God cannot *dwell with* them because they are *wicked* and God *takes no pleasure in evil* (v. 4) in fact he *hates* such (v. 5). Since God is not with them, they will not *stand*. When he appears among them it will not be to prosper but to *destroy* them.

For God is just, and their charges against David have no basis in fact but are lies (v. 6). Absalom and his party were acting against him out of sheer deceit and cruelty; they are *bloodthirsty and deceitful men*. This is the truth behind Absalom and his campaign. It is sufficient ground for David to believe they will not succeed and that he will return, as he goes on to say.

Verses 7-8: David hopes for restoration

Although Absalom and his followers possess Jerusalem, they are not fit to enter the *house* of God, where he 'dwells' and his 'presence' is revealed (vv. 4-5). But David is acceptable and believes he will return there, not because he is different from others, but *by your great mercy*, for it was only God's *mercy* that kept him in the path of *righteousness* which was essential for those who want to *come into (your) house* (v. 7).

This assurance was at least partly connected with his decision to return the ark to Jerusalem with Zadok and the Levites, which he did, saying, 'Take the ark of God back into the city. If I find favour in the Lord's eyes he will bring me back and let me see his dwelling-place again' (2 Sam. 15:25). He now believes he has found favour with God, that he is the object of his *mercy* and even visualises the scene when he will once again *bow down towards (his) holy temple*. Meanwhile he is just as close to God as if he were there.

This does not make him complacent (v. 8). His *enemies* are still very real and he could easily give up and let them have their way. But this would dishonour God, who has not only pledged himself to David but has heard David's vows to him (Ps. 101, etc). So he prays that God will keep him on the right path: *make straight your way before me*.

Verses 9-10: David still suffers at the hands of his enemy

Having prayed for himself David now turns to his enemies. Though it has not yet come to blows, for they have not caught up with him, their propaganda campaign has done great damage to him and his people. Their method of proaganda is to use *deceit … words that cannot be trusted*. For their intention is *destruction* – character assassination. The *open grave* would be a hole in the rock rather than in the ground, thus resembling a huge *throat* waiting to swallow him up. Since God 'abhors those who tell lies' (v. 6) David is justified in calling on God to pass judgment on them (v. 10). So the motivation is God's honour not personal spite.

This is the first of a number of 'imprecatory' passages, as they are called. The strong language, as in other imprecatory psalms, is that of one speaking in God's name. This gives him authority to pronounce both verdict: *guilty*, and sentence: *banish*. In a way they are their own undoing: *Let their intrigues be their downfall*. Sin brings its own punishment, as surely as reaping follows sowing (Rom. 6:23; Gal. 6:7). For a fuller discussion on the imprecatory psalms, see the Introduction, page 20.

Verses 11-12: David encourages the righteous

David is speaking not only for himself but as king of God's people. He encourages them to do as he does and *take refuge in* him and thus be free from care. He prays that God will protect them in this time of danger as a mother hen does her chicks and *spread protection* over them (v. 11) (cf. Matt. 23:37). Since this might seem a feeble comparison in the face of a huge army at their heels, David changes to a military metaphor in verse 12: *surround them with your favour as with a shield.* An army may be closing in on them, but it must break through God's own armour to get at them! Of this, David is persuaded: *SURELY you will bless the righteous.* He has come a long way in a dozen verses: from 'sighing' (v. 1) to sureness.

Questions:
(1) When you come to God in prayer, are you able to balance your current mood with a sense of the sovereignty and faithfulness of God? (See vv. 1-3, cf. Isa. 37:14-20.)

(2) Do you take personally opposition to you as a Christian, or are you able to look at it objectively as against God rather than yourself? (See vv. 4-6, 9-10, cf. 1 Sam. 8:7.)

(3) Does it make any difference to you *where* you are when you seek God's face? Do unfamiliar locations lessen your sense of God's presence? (See Ps. 139:7-12.)

(4) Do you use your experiences to encourage others by sharing your blessings with them? (Vv. 11-12, Heb. 10:25.)

Psalm 6

David Crosses the Jordan

This psalm fits well with the rebellion of Absalom, shortly after Pss. 3–5. David is able to get to the other side of the Jordan, thus putting the river between him and his enemy (2 Sam. 17:24). But Absalom soon musters his forces and is in swift pursuit. David is aware of this (vv. 7-10) and, whatever his outward bearing before his men, here is how he felt in himself. This is reflected in the musical directions: the use of *stringed instruments* to give a subdued, even melancholy, atmosphere, enhanced by the sheminith. In 1 Chronicles 15:20-21 we are told of eight Levites playing 'according to Alamoth' and six 'according to *Sheminith*'. The best interpretation seems to be that the former are treble and the latter bass notes, which would make the music even more sombre.

Verses 1-3: David cries to God
He cries in *agony* (v. 2) and *anguish* (v. 3 – the same word in Hebrew). His whole being (*soul* is 'life', not just 'spirit') down to his very *bones,* was afflicted. This is not necessarily physical illness, but more likely fear, which can have a similar effect and make a person feel *faint* (v. 2). The worst thing to David was that this may all be due to God's *anger ... wrath*, his *rebuke ... discipline*. David knows that his own sins, if not the immediate, are the ultimate cause of all this (2 Sam. 12:9-10).

David had always accepted that he must be punished, but *how long* must it go on for? Has God not punished him enough over the years? Will he not now *be merciful* to him?

Verses 4-5: David prays God to deliver him

If God will only do this it will end his suffering. Not because he is innocent but *because of your unfailing love* which triumphs over wrath. God has unconditionally promised this in his covenant, which he made, not only with all his people generally, but with David individually. While this was made before his great sin (2 Sam. 7), it was renewed at the same time as he passed sentence on him (2 Sam. 12:13). This gives David the boldness to ask what benefit God would derive from his death, for he would no longer be alive to *praise* him. This is precisely the argument Heman had used, perhaps was using at this very moment, if as a friend of David he had been imprisoned by Absalom (Ps. 88:10-12)! Neither knew what the other was feeling, yet both felt the same!

Verses 6-7: David returns to his woes

This intense pleading, on top of his hasty flight, had made him feel *worn out*. Yet he cannot sleep, but spends all night *weeping* until his eyes are sore and weak. It is all because his family and friends have become his *foes*.

Verses 8-10: David recovers his confidence

Some think that at this point David received a word of encouragement from a prophet; others that God spoke directly to him. Be that as it may, it is a surprising and complete reversal. Fear has gone and he who felt rebuked and banished by God now challenges his enemies: *away from me!* For it is they who are *evildoers* not he. What is the justification for this? *The Lord has heard!* This does not mean God has recovered from his hearing loss, but that he was now listening favourably, first to his *weeping*, then to his *cry*, and finally to his *prayer*. So it is not merely David shouting 'Go away!' but God driving them away *ashamed and dismayed*. The latter word is the same as that used for 'agony' and 'anguish' in verses 2-3. The tables have been turned right round. He even recovers the spirit of prophecy as he concludes: *they will turn back in sudden disgrace.* He did not know at the time how this would happen, but subsequent events are to bear it out.

Questions:
(1) How do verses 1-3 bring out the serious and debilitating effects of the fear of man? (Cf. Prov. 29:25; Luke 12:4-7.)

(2) Do verses 3b and 5 encourage you to question and even argue with God? (cf. Mark 7:24-30.)

(3) How do verses 8-10 anticipate the Christian's victory over his enemies? (cf. 2 Thess. 1:5-10; 1 Pet. 5:8-9.)

Psalm 7

David Finds Refuge From His Enemies in God

Cush may be Saul, whose father was Kish, or it may refer to Saul's character, since *Cush* implies 'perfidious'. Alternatively it may refer to one of David's enemies from the tribe of Benjamin such as Shimei, who blamed David for the deaths of members of Saul's family. As David fled from Jerusalem Shimei followed him with a string of curses and a shower of stones (2 Sam. 16:5-14). David receives this treatment calmly and will not allow Abishai to silence him, since he sees it as a reproach from God. However, underlying this are feelings which come out in this psalm. *Shiggaion* probably describes the passionate nature of the composition or the type of tune to which he wanted it set – one with a strong and wild rhythm. Notwithstanding this the thought of the psalm is very God-centred.

Verses 1-2: God is David's safe refuge

David is being pursued by Absalom as by a *lion* who threatens to *rip (him) to pieces*. Having only a small band of followers there is *no one to rescue* him. He must do what all hunted animals do in such cases – go into hiding, find a *refuge*. But where is there that is safe? He has been through all this with Saul. What had he done then? Trusted God, put himself in God's hands (Ps. 27, etc.). This is what he does now.

Verses 3-5: God is David's judge

David is not assuming he is in the right and is quite prepared for God to show him he deserves *this* treatment (v. 3). He had said as much in 2 Samuel 16:11-12. Has he failed in his duty to his loyal people (v. 4a)? Has he been unjust to his enemies (v. 4b)? Are Shimei's charges correct that he is responsible for all the blood shed in the household of Saul (2 Sam. 16:8) and that God is 'repaying' him for it? If this is how God sees him he will submit to it, even though it may mean defeat and death (v. 5). The dramatic pause or musical interval (*Selah*) is very appropriate here before he turns the tables.

Verses 6-9: God as David's vindicator

God has not convicted David of having *guilt on (his) hands* (v. 3), so now comes a big change: from the frightened hunted animal of verses 1-2 and the penitent figure of verses 3-5 to the bold petitioner of the God he claims as *my God* (v. 6). His boldness knows no bounds: let God meet the *rage* of his enemies with his own fierce *anger* (v. 6). He goes further as he calls for God to set up his tribunal against his *enemies*. Let God *decree justice*, that is, set up a court at which all are gathered, as at the final judgment day, with God himself ruling *over them from on high* (v. 7), that is, taking his seat on the judgment throne, so that he might *judge the peoples*. The thought is that if God has appointed a day to judge all (Acts 17:31), he will certainly include those who have rebelled against the anointed King of his people.

David realises he himself is part of this, that he too must be judged. However, in view of his openness to inspection now (vv. 3-5) he believes he will be vindicated and proved to be a man of righteousness and integrity (v. 8). The *righteous God* knows the truth about us all, for he sees *minds and hearts*. He will put things right and *bring to an end the violence of the wicked and make the righteous secure* (v. 9). If he is going to do this in the long term he will surely do it in the present situation.

Verses 10-16: God is David's Saviour

In the light of the foregoing David is no longer **asking** for deliverance, he is **experiencing** it. God is for him his *shield*, he is the *God Most High*, whom Melchizedek served and by whom Abraham swore (Gen. 14:18-19). His justice is eminently plain – he *saves the upright* continually (v. 10), and just as often, *every day, expresses his wrath* (v. 11), on the one who *does not relent*, so that the hunter (vv. 1-2) becomes the hunted, with God himself in pursuit (vv. 12-13). How much fiercer is he than the most savage lion (cf. v. 2)!

But most of the time he does not have to take action personally; he only has to leave the wicked to their wickedness. For sin contains within it the seed of its own undoing, somewhat like the seed implanted in the womb (v. 14, cf. Jas. 1:15). David gives the usual example of the man who lays a trap falling into it himself (vv. 15-16). Most of the time therefore God does not need to intervene directly but reveals his wrath simply by 'giving us up' to our own chosen ways (Rom. 1:24, 26, 28).

Verse 17: God is worthy of praise

What can anyone, not only David, do but *thank* and *praise* him? What more can God do to prove his *righteousness* than save those who do his will from those who, because they cross swords with God, also oppress his people? This is one of the big themes of Scripture, which reaches its climax in the Book of the Revelation.

Questions:
(1) Apply David's experience in verses 1-2 to Satan's attacks on believers in 1 Peter 5:8.

(2) When criticised do we proudly justify ourselves and feel hurt by accusations, or humbly examine ourselves before God to see if these things are true? (See Matt. 5:3-5, 7:1-5; Gal. 6:1.)

(3) How does David teach us to see current injustices in the light of God's final universal judgement (vv. 6-9), and how does the New Testament enlarge on this? (See Acts 17:31; 1 Pet. 2:18-23.)

Psalm 8

David Meditates Under the Stars

David could have composed this psalm while, like some later shepherds, 'keeping his flock by night', lying on the ground and looking up at *the moon and the stars* (v. 3). David admires the patterns they form, for *set in place* has the sense of 'arranged', like a bowl of flowers. Since it was the LORD *our* LORD who did this, he must be that much greater. So David is led on to similar profound thoughts to those suggested by the sun in Psalm 19.

Verses 1–2 ask questions about the universe
(1) **What is it?** It is the expression of God's *name* – his *majesty* and *glory* (v. 1). This is similar to Psalm 19:1-6 but has great significance for us in this evolutionary age. For it explains:

a) **the unity of the universe**, which comes not from its evolution from a single organism but its creation by the one God;
b) **its diversity** – its many and varied elements harmonize because they are modelled on a God who is three Persons in perfect harmony.

(2) **Why is it?** To reveal a God whose *glory* is greater than it (*above the heavens*, v. 1b). This he did so that he might receive

praise from his creatures (v. 2, Rev. 4:11). This *praise* is rendered by all things as they perform their functions. Even *children and infants praise* him, for though their noises are unintelligent and inarticulate they show they are alive (and how!). Even the inanimate *praise* him just by existing (Ps. 148). How much more do the conscious articulate praises of men and women set forth his *glory!*

This *praise* is also a bastion against the forces of evil (v. 2b), hence Jesus' use of it on encountering his enemies when entering Jerusalem (Matt. 21:16). The fall of the angels deprived God of some of his worshippers; they drew man after them and nature too revolted. But God's reply was to enable the universe to continue to function as an expression of his *glory* (v. 1). Then he raised a special people to be 'a kingdom of priests' (Exod. 19:6) and this was only a trailer for the church of Christ (1 Pet. 2:9), who would spread his praises over the earth until the time comes finally to *silence the foe and the avenger.*

Verses 3-9 ask questions about *man*
(1) **What is man?** (vv. 3-4). Compared with even the small part of the universe that David can see as he looks up (v. 3), *man* seems insignificant in size, glory and durability, for *the moon and stars* have outlasted countless generations of *man*, who is ENOSH (v. 4a), that is, weak; and BEN ADAM, that is, 'son of the ground', from which he was made (Gen. 2:7) and to which he soon returns (Gen. 3:19).

The answer is that *man* has a special relationship with God, who takes particular notice of him (*mindful*, see Matt. 6:25-30; 10:29-31) and takes particular *care* of him – literally he 'visits him' (KJV), as we do our friends, seeking personal communion (Luke 15:1-2, 19:10; John 4:24). This is why he modelled us on himself (Gen.1:26-27) and gave us a spiritual nature (Prov. 20:27; 1 Cor. 2:11). This sets us apart from all his other creatures.

(2) **What is man's place in the universe?** (vv. 5-9)
　　a) he ranks **next to God** (v. 5), literally 'you made him lack little of God'. Originally he was superior to the angels

who, in God's provision, serve man as well as God (Heb. 1:13-14), which may have provoked the angels to jealousy and led them to rebel against God and attack Adam and Eve. Temporarily we are inferior because we are sinful and they (the unfallen ones) are holy. But as they served the Son of Man (Matt. 4:11; 28:2; Luke 22:43) so they aid his disciples (Matt. 18:10). Ultimately angels and redeemed people will unite in the praise of God (Eph. 1:10; Rev. 4). This is the *glory and honour* with which man is *crowned*;

b) he is **sovereign over all other creatures** (vv. 6-8). He was endowed with God's nature in order to be his representative on earth (Gen. 1:26-28) – to cultivate it (v. 6, Gen. 1:29; 2:15-16) and rule the living creatures (vv. 7-8, Gen. 2:19-20). The fall interrupted this process (Heb. 2:8) so that there is now fear between men and animals (Gen. 9:2); the elements of nature are often hostile and will ultimately bring us down to their level (Gen. 2:19-20). We are 'for a little while lower than the angels' (Heb. 2:7) and subject to oppression from the evil ones (Eph. 6:12). Those in Christ are partially restored to sovereignty, since Christ reigns (Matt. 28:18) and we reign with him (2 Tim. 2:12), and we will be fully restored hereafter (Matt. 19:28).

c) he is always **subject to God** (v. 9) in this world and the next, so that worship is our perpetual duty and privilege (Rom. 1:21; Rev. 1:6; 4:8-11).

This psalm seems to have been re-issued by David in the days of his kingdom *for the Director of music* to use in Temple worship. Leupold translates *Gittith* 'after the tune of the treaders of the winepress' which may be the Feast of Trumpets, a harvest festival in September, for which the theme of the psalm is appropriate.

Question:
How does this view of the universe and man contrast with and answer current non-Christian views on these matters?

Psalm 9

David Celebrates Victory

This psalm is celebrating a victory, probably over the Philistine confederacy, recorded in 2 Samuel 5:22-25. Clearly David is back in Jerusalem, as the references to *Zion* show (vs. 11, 14), *Zion* being the hill on which David set up his palace. But he is very conscious that it is really the Lord who reigned there; David is only his representative (vv. 4, 7, 11). This God had shown he also ruled the nations of the world (vv. 5, 8, 11), which is perhaps the outstanding feature of this psalm.

Psalm 9 is one of the so-called 'acrostic' psalms, in which each verse or group of verses begins with a different Hebrew letter in alphabetical order. This psalm covers only half of the alphabet (the first eleven letters), it omits DALETH (the fourth letter) and does not stick rigidly to the pattern in some places. Some say it should be combined with Psalm 10, but this only has the last four letters in verses 12-18, and is very different in subject and tone.

The title of the tune has also caused problems – there are almost as many interpretations as there are commentators! For a run-down of those prior to 1867 see the commentary by W. S. Plumer. If *The Death of the Son* is correct, *Son* might be used in the sense of 'Chosen One' or 'Champion'. It may have been composed to celebrate the slaughter of Goliath, the

Philistines' chosen champion. David thought it appropriate to use it here to celebrate this decisive victory over the Philistines and their allies.

Verses 1-2 both begin with the letter ALEPH, which begins verbs in the first person singular: *I will* ... David is praising God both for himself (*you ... your name*) and his *wonders*, a word used frequently in the psalms sometimes rendered as 'miracles' particularly to describe God's redemptive miracles (106:7, 22). The victory over the Philistines had been all God's.

Verses 3-4 combine under the letter BETH which begins verse 3. They specify the way in which God has displayed his *wonders* in recent events – by causing their enemies to *turn back ... stumble and perish*, which David and his army could never have achieved alone. In this way God has proved David's *cause* was *right* and that he, God, has the authority to destroy nations (v. 4).

Verse 5, beginning with the letter GIMEL, develops this claim that God has a moral right to inflict defeat on David's enemies, since they are *wicked*. The conflict had been over whose *name* would prevail – the Lord's or that of the Philistine gods. This was a victory over Satan and all his worshippers.

Verse 6 omits DALETH and moves on to HE, describing the extent of the devastation inflicted on those nations. It is of course true that the Philistines and the other nations were not finished for ever and were to continue to harass Israel. But the past tense used here is 'the prophetic perfect', which refers to something that will so certainly happen it can be spoken of as if it already has. This decisive victory is the proof of what will surely come (see Matt. 25:31-33).

Verses 7-10 begin with WAW, which is the conjunction 'and'. It is not translated here but indicates the logical consequences of these events and the deductions to be drawn from them. They have proved who is in charge (v. 7) and that what he has done on this occasion is a model of what he will do universally (v. 8). This bears out the remark on verse 6 about the 'prophetic perfect'. This verse thus looks forward to the Kingdom of Christ (cf. Ps. 72:1-2 and Isa. 32:1-2, both considered to be 'Messianic').

But retribution is only one aspect of God's justice. There is also remuneration: those who **know** (and) **trust** him will be protected (vv. 9-10) especially when they are under threat from the wicked. Putting both these aspects of God's justice together and emphasising them by beginning each with the same Hebrew letter is a lesson for us in good theology.

Verses 11-12 combine under the letter ZAYIN which begins verse 11. These verses take up the thought of verses 8-10 and call for the appropriate response of praise to God for the way he has proved he is the ruler and judge of all nations (v. 11), and shows he does this with justice, both 'retributive' and 'remunerative'.

Verses 13-14 begin with HETH and appear at first to run contrary to the triumphal spirit of the psalm. This is because David is well aware that he has not seen the last of his *enemies*, who will continue to *persecute* him. Nor is he totally safe in his own land, as subsequent events will show. *The gates of death*, that is, its powers[1], would strive to bring him into their domain. So he calls on God to *lift* (him) *up* and bring him into *the gates of the daughter of Zion*. The thought is that Israel is God's pure virgin daughter, untarnished by the gods of other nations. He sees the Lord's *daughter* at the *gates* of his new capital, not to hear the sentence of death but the proclamation of victory.

Verses 15-16, beginning with TETH, enlarge on the subject of God's justice, which usually works indirectly as the wicked become victims of their own wickedness (v. 15). 'All who draw the sword will die by the sword' (Matt. 26:52), 'a man reaps what he sows' (Gal. 6:7). But it is no less the work of God than is his direct intervention. Here follows a pause for meditation (*Selah*) with accompanying soft music (Higgaion).

---

[1] The city gate was the place where cases were tried and judgement passed. Thus it came to symbolise the power of life and death, cf. Matthew 16:18.

Verse 17, beginning with YOD, brings out the main feature of what it means to be *wicked*, that is, to *forget God*. It is our alienation from him that is the root of all sin and the cause of our condemnation (Rom. 1:18-21).

Verse 18, although beginning with the next letter CAPH, is closely connected with verse 17 through the repetition of *forget*. The wicked may *forget* who is the true God, but *the needy and afflicted* who cry to him, not to other gods, and place their *hope* in him, *will not always be forgotten*, nor will they *ever perish....*

Verses 19-20 leave the acrostic form aside for the final cry to God to assert his authority over the *nations. Man* here is ENOSH which refers to his frailty (as in 8:4). *Nations* are made up of frail creatures and if they successfully resist God then it will look as if man is superior to him (v. 19). They need a good fright to show them *they are but men*, creatures of the dust (v. 20).

Questions:
(1) What evidence can you see in recent events that God still judges the world righteously (v. 8)?

(2) How does Christ use the idea of *the gates of death* (vv. 13-14) to forecast the history of the church in Matthew 16:18?

(3) Is God's justice a fitting subject for praise and rejoicing for Christians? Do you do it? If not, is it a lack of understanding of its place in our salvation? (See Rom. 3:21-26.)

Psalm 10

Why Does God Not Intervene?

This psalm comes from a time when the wicked were in the ascendant in Israel and God was apparently doing nothing about it. This was a not infrequent occurrence, so the precise period cannot be located with certainty.

Verse 1: The psalmist cries to God in anguish
His problem was not just the corruption of his people, but the inactivity of God. It was a problem with which Habakkuk was to wrestle (his name means 'wrestler') centuries later, when God not only appeared to tolerate the sins of Israel but allowed them to be punished by a much worse nation, the Babylonians.

Verses 2-11: The psalmist justifies his question
It was not just that the people had departed from God and his ways, but that they did it so arrogantly. This is shown in many ways:
1. *They bullied the faithful* (v. 2). Like all bullies they targeted those *weaker* than themselves – those who remained loyal to God, who were in a minority and therefore an easy prey for *the arrogant*, who *hunt* (them) *down* as a pack of hounds does a fox. It is not agreed whether the second line refers to *the weak* (as NIV translates) or to *the arrogant* (as most others

translations understand it). Even if the latter are right it is not clear whether it is a prediction: they shall be *caught in the schemes* they devise, or a prayer: let them be *caught....* Verses 8-10 develop this and picture vividly the details of the *hunt*. In verse 8 they are compared to an assassin jumping out of a dark place away from human habitation. In verses 9-10 they are like a lion waiting to pounce on a *helpless* creature, who stands no chance of escape, nor is shown any mercy. This does not necessarily mean the faithless were actually murdering the faithful; rather that they were taking advantage of their weakness, perhaps enslaving them or running protection rackets.

2. *They boasted about their sins* (v. 3). Instead of being ashamed of their behaviour they gloried in parading their lustful feelings and congratulated each other on the greed which drove them to bully the weak. As for God! He did not even enter into the matter!

3. *They blasphemed God* (v. 4). This follows from the end of verse 3: God would have corrected their misbehaviour, but they do not *seek him*, in fact *there is no room* for him even in their *thoughts* – he never enters their minds.

4. *They gloated over their good fortune* (vv. 5-6). They justify their attitude to God on the grounds that they are doing fine without him. Since they are *prosperous* there must be something special about them that exempts them from his *laws*. From their lofty perch they can *sneer at all* their *enemies*. Not only is this so in the present but it will go on always – they will *never have trouble*.

5. *They are unrestrained in their language* (v. 7). Their minds dwell on *trouble and evil* and they make no attempt to restrain the words with which they clothe their thoughts, so that they come out with *curses and lies and threats*. As with Psalm 14:1-3 Paul uses this verse to describe universal sinfulness in Romans 3:14.

6. *They live with no reference to God at all* (v. 11). This sums up why they speak and act in this way. It is their whole attitude to God which lies behind it. God to them is like someone who has lost his memory or keeps his head under the bed covers, so that he *never sees* – he has no idea what people are doing.

Verses 12-15: The psalmist appeals to God

Although God seemed to be ignoring all this, to whom else could a man turn? There was no one else who could deal adequately with such wickedness, no one else who cared for his faithful sufferers. The writer uses all three of God's basic names to add force to his appeal: YAHWEH ('LORD', v. 12), EL ('God', v. 12) and ELOHIM ('God', v. 13). Since God seemed to be lying dormant, his first call is for him to *Arise*, to wake up to what is going on. Then he must act: *lift up your hand*, both to punish the troublemakers and to rescue their victims, especially the latter: *do not forget the helpless*, as you seem to be doing at present.

Then he turns to *the wicked*. Surely God cannot just let them go on when they do not merely persecute *the helpless* but *revile God* (v. 13a) and disclaim all accountability to him (v. 13b). After this outburst he begins to collect his thoughts and realises he is in danger of dishonouring God – not in the way *the wicked* were, but by doubting him. So he firsts reassures himself of God's full knowledge: *you ... do see trouble and grief*, you are not hiding yourself away (v. 1). Then he reminds himself of his righteousness, which means that what God knows he must deal with: *consider* and *take ... in hand*.

If this is so, he will first rescue his suffering people – *the victim* who *commits himself to you* – on the ground that he has promised to be *the helper of the fatherless*. Then he will deal with their oppressors. The prayer in verse 15 breathes a sense of assurance that these things will happen. He will destroy their power *(break the arm)* and *call* (them) *to account*, those who thought they would not be *found out* (see v. 11).

Verses 16-18: The psalmist glorifies God

Having cast off his doubts and come to grips with the situation, he now dons the prophet's mantle again and sees this incident as a model of how God would establish his righteous rule over whole *nations* of unbelievers (v. 16). This looks on to the Kingdom of Christ which his gospel would set up across the earth. The point here is that if God can impose his will and establish his power over all *nations*, he can certainly do that with the troublemakers among his own people. So he will show that he hears ... *the desire of the afflicted* (v. 17), and will come to their aid (v. 18a). The second line hints at the way he will do this: by removing the oppressors from the scene. Those who *terrify* others will themselves be terrified.

Questions:

(1) What is the New Testament's answer to the Old Testament's problem: why does God tolerate wickedness so long? Why does he not do something about it? (See 2 Pet. 3:8-9.)

(2) In what ways would you say non-Christians correspond to those about whom David complains here? Does this include the way they treat Christians? (See Rom. 3:9-20.)

(3) Have there been times when you have been frustrated because you thought God was doing nothing, when in fact it was you who hadn't been praying, or not praying rightly? (See James 4:2-3.) Do you pray in the light of God's universal sovereignty? (See Jer. 32:16-25.)

Psalm 11

The Realism of Faith

This psalm comes from a time when David was in dire straits and being advised to take refuge in the mountains, which he frequently did when Saul was pursuing him (1 Sam. 24:2; 26:1). But here he has other plans – perhaps to seek asylum with the Philistines in Gath. So he refuses the advice.

Verses 1-3: David disdains advice
If this psalm comes from the time of David's flight to the Philistines (1 Sam. 27:1-2), then verse 1b refers to those who were challenging that decision. Their advice was 'Go back to *your mountain* refuge', probably 'the hill of Hakilah' from which he had retreated to 'the desert' when he heard of Saul's approach (1 Sam. 26:1-4). Saul had now left that area after his encounter with David (1 Sam. 26:25).

David's reasons for rejecting this advice are:
1. *It was unrealistic* – he would be an easy target. His advisors used the *bird* illustration (v. 1) to mean 'Go there directly and swiftly'; David saw another meaning – he would be as vulnerable as a bird, a 'sitting duck'. He had already described himself as 'a partridge in the mountains' (1 Sam. 26:20 – a good reason for associating this psalm with that incident). Indeed, says David, Saul's men are probably

already waiting in *the shadows* with their *bows* bent and their *arrows against the strings* (v. 2). Moreover, since Saul had broken his promise the previous time David had him at his mercy, how could he trust it this time? Relationships are built on truth; promises kept are their *foundations* (v. 3). No truth, no trust, *the foundations are ... destroyed*. Nor was this just a matter between David and Saul. Saul was king and his injustice and unfaithfulness were destroying the whole fabric of society. In such an atmosphere David was not safe anywhere. The fact that he was *righteous* counted for nothing.

2. *It was untrusting.* David had a *refuge in the LORD* (v. 1a). He had kept him safe until now and he would not break his promises. It might seem the height of foolishness to put himself in the hands of the Philistines, but God's hand was not so short it couldn't reach the lands beyond Israel. David's escape to Gath was therefore not a lack of faith but a protest against the ungodliness of his own nation (1 Sam. 26:19).

Verses 4-7: David's confidence in God

These verses contrast strongly with verses 1-2. In Israel the anointed king (David) is in flight and the rejected king (Saul) is out pursuing him; but *the LORD* is in residence *in his holy temple* (or 'palace' – the same word in Hebrew) and seated *on his heavenly throne* in his city which is built on the *foundations* of truth and righteousness (v. 7 and see Ps. 87:1, Heb. 11:10). Habakkuk found this word a great assurance at a time when the foundations of society were again crumbling and even worse judgments were threatened (Hab. 2:20).

But the Lord is no mere figurehead monarch:

1. *He observes* (v. 4b). Whereas from (his) *mountain* David could only see the immediate vicinity and Saul was dependent on informers, the Lord from his throne in heaven *observes the sons of men*, not merely out of interest but to *examine them*, both the *righteous* and *wicked* (v. 5).

2. *He reacts* (v. 5). Passing over his reaction to the righteous, which comes more into verse 7, he is moved to *hate* by those who act deceitfully and violently without cause merely out of *love* (for) *violence*, because it is in their nature. The depth of

his anger is brought out in the unusual reference to *his soul*, showing he hates this behaviour with his whole being.

3. *He acts* (v. 6). The Lord the King does not just sit and fume. He has power to deal with the wicked. The description is drawn from the judgement of Sodom and Gomorrah (Gen. 19:24) and a *scorching wind* blasted the Egyptian grain in Pharaoh's dream (Gen. 41:6). *Fire and burning sulphur* occur in Revelation 9:17-18, showing the language goes beyond the overthrow of Saul to a total, universal and final judgment. Saul and his men are classed with all whom God will destroy at the last day.

Finally, verse 7 sets down the *foundations* of God's *throne*, which are his *righteous* nature and *love* (of) *justice*. Only those whose lives are built on the same foundation, that is, *upright men* will want to have anything to do with such a God. They will be attracted to him, they will not be afraid because *his eyes examine them*; in fact they will want to *see HIS face* (emphasis mine).

Questions:
(1) How can we combine *realism* (vv. 1b–3) with *faith* (v. 1a)?

(2) From verses 4-7, on what should we base our faith, prayer and action when experiencing opposition?

(3) What do you understand by 'the vision of God' (v. 7 and Matt. 5:8)?

Psalm 12

David Under Pressure

This psalm comes from a time when David felt isolated and in danger, even from his own people because they had forsaken godly principles. It fits well with his fleeing into hiding from Saul (1 Sam. 19:9-10).

Verses 1-4: David brings his situation to God
The word translated *help* is literally 'save' or 'send a Saviour'. It would normally have an object – 'me' or 'us'. Possibly David originally said 'me', but dropped this when he edited it *for the director of music* (title) to use in congregational worship. Before making his actual petition he draws the attention of *the* LORD to two aspects of his situation:

1) he is *isolated* (v. 1) from other *godly* and *faithful* people. These are covenant terms which indicate the people he is having trouble with are Israelites – in covenant with God – but in breach of his covenant. It was not strictly true that *the faithful have vanished* and *are no more*, just as it was not true for Elijah that he was the only prophet left (1 Kings 19:10). It means that because David was cut off from them, as far as he was concerned they were *no more*.

2) he is the object of their *false accusations* (v. 2). This was how they were being unfaithful to the covenant – they were lying and deceiving people about him, which was very serious since it was a flagrant breach of the Ninth Commandment, for

the Ten Commandments were at the very heart of the covenant between God and Israel.

His prayer (vv. 3-4) is the logical response to this situation, for *cut off* means *cut off* from the covenant, which God threatened to do with all who broke it (Gen. 17:14). David strengthens his request by pointing out the arrogant way in which his enemies were spreading their malicious rumours (v. 4). They are sure of success, for they cannot be stopped and are answerable to no-one (cf. Ps. 36:1-4). How can God tolerate such behaviour?

Verse 5: God answers him

David's complaint was so right. It brings an immediate answer from God. As in 5:10 David again speaks as God's prophet declaring what God has revealed to him. This lays down an important principle, worthy of expression in a congregational song. God might not act swiftly just to deal with the arrogant, but when they cause suffering to *the weak ... and needy*, when they oppress and make them groan, God steps in: *I will arise*, or 'shine forth', as he did at Sinai, striking terror into the beholders. Moreover, his intervention is a direct answer to the original prayer, which was for *help* or to 'save', for *protect* is from the same root as *save* and can be translated 'put in safety'.

Verses 6-8: David responds to God's answer

The contrast between verses 6 and 2 cannot be accidental. Sinners tell lies to and about each other. But what God says is as free from deceit as silver which has been fired seven times is free from dross. The number seven symbolizes perfection, therefore *the words of the LORD are flawless*. This means that the promise he made in verse 5 can be relied on – he will *keep us safe* by protecting us *from such people*. Although the words are not from the same root as *help* (v. 1) and *protect* (v. 5), the idea is similar. In fact they develop the idea, containing the assurance that what God does once he does again and *for ever*. This will therefore be a prayer he can repeat whenever necessary.

Even if the situation worsened and reached the extreme of verse 8, even if moral values are turned on their head and *what is vile is honoured* and the wicked operate without restraint, God's promises would still hold. David and the godly were going to face such times; indeed it may have been when things were at their lowest and the nation rose up against him under Absalom, that he issued this psalm for public use. Its solemn tone was to be expressed in the music: *sheminith* (title) means an octave, which may refer either to a low accompaniment or to low voices; Leupold translates it 'by the basses', whose deep voices would set the mood of the psalm.

Questions:
(1) What do you learn from this psalm about our salvation in Christ?

   (2) What does this teach you about the relationship between prayer and the Word of God?

Psalm 13

David Forsaken by God

David's troubles with his persecutors are clearly still dragging on. But why isn't God helping him? This is the dilemma he faces here – and resolves.

Verses 1-2: David is back in his pit

David is in an even lower state than in the previous psalm, for not only was the persecution continuing but God was apparently doing nothing. *Forget ... hide your face* are not words to be taken literally, but to mean that God was inactive. Conversely, to *remember* and *see* describes God springing into action, e.g. Exodus 2:24-25. Since God is doing nothing David must spend his nights wrestling with his thoughts, that is, making plans, only to spend *every day* in *sorrow* because his plans did not work out. Meanwhile, Saul his *enemy* remained in the driving seat.

David's thrice repeated *How long?* shows a man on the verge of despair – he can see no end to this. Nothing he did, planned or prayed changed anything – except for the worse.

Verses 3-4: David begins to climb out

The path from despair to victory is called Prayer, for it is a path which elevates our thoughts from ourselves up to God. So we notice how, although he had indeed been addressing God in verses 1-2, he changes from the interrogative to the imperative mood – a change which is not just grammatical but spiritual and moral (cf. Ps. 86 where vv. 1-4 and several others are in the imperative). This is true prayer. So he simply asks God to do the things he was complaining he was not doing: to *look on* him and listen to him (*answer*), that is, come into action.

He has good grounds for his requests: first, that he is likely to die (v. 3b) – the Hebrew represents the approach of death as the dimming of the **eyes**. If his *eyes* closed it would be in the sleep of death. It is not possible to say whether David was exaggerating his condition or whether he was physically and critically ill at this time. The second reason follows from this – that his death would be welcomed by his *foes*. This would be more than a personal problem – it would mean that injustice had triumphed. His third reason, however, lies in the word *my* before *God*. It was this covenant relationship he was in with *the* LORD, both as an Israelite and the anointed king, that chiefly entitled him to be remembered by God.

Verses 5-6: David reaches the summit

The *I* is emphatic here; not as it was in verses 1-2 – the *I* of self-pity – but now as the *I* who is in covenant with God. This explains the outburst of covenant language: *unfailing love ... salvation*. How different everything looks at the top of a mountain from what it does in a hole at the bottom! There David had been conscious only of his present woes. Now he can look back and see the ways *he has been good to me* – not least in again 'lifting him from the slimy pit' and putting another 'new song in his mouth' (40:2-3).

How has this been achieved? By trust – it is faith that gives the energy to climb the path of prayer. A formal remembering of God and calling on him is ineffective. We have to believe him (Heb. 11:6).

Questions:
(1) Can you see Christ in the way people treated David and in its effect on him? (See Luke 17:11-19, 22:4.)

(2) How should we react to those who repay our good with their evil? (Try Rom. 12:17-21.)

(3) Could you cope with spiritual depression and despair? Learn how to while you are still thinking straight. (See Ps. 94:19; 1 Pet. 5:5-7.) Pray specifically that this will be clear to you if and when the time comes.

Psalm 14

David's Desperate Appeal
for God's Intervention

David's experiences – with Saul in his early life and later as head of a large family and king of a nation – have opened his eyes to the real state of the human heart. Mankind, even the holy nation, is so corrupt that only God can deal with it.

Verses 1-3: The truth about the state of the people
The NIV follows those who think the Hebrew verbs (which are in the past or 'perfect' tense) should be translated as presents. This is probably to bring the psalm into line with Paul's use of it in Romans 3:10-12, where he applies it to the depravity of the whole human race in all ages. However, there is good reason why the past tense is used – that it refers to a particular historical situation. This may have been when he witnessed the depravity that was not only in the nation but even his own family. Here the underlying cause is revealed: renunciation of belief in God (v. 1). Since wisdom begins with the fear of God, folly means rejecting him.

The consequences of this are dire: they become corrupt, so that they only do vile deeds and not good ones. Nor is it the case that their lack of belief is due to genuine problems, intellectual or practical. They simply do not understand (v. 2), they have no awareness of God, and do not even want it; they do not seek God. Having turned from God's way they have turned aside to their own way (v. 3), which is the essence of sin (Isa. 53:6; Eccles. 7:29) . So they have become rotten (corrupt – a different word from that used in v. 1, with the sense of milk turning sour). This leaves no room for anything good.

Verses 4-6: The oppression of the righteous remnant

The words **not even one** seem to suggest the whole nation is thus, or even the whole of mankind, which is how Paul takes it in Romans 3:10-12. But since he goes on to speak of *my people ... the righteous* this cannot be so. We need to look at the psalm first of all in its historical context, considering what it meant at the time, not as it came to be used in the New Testament. The latter comes after (see Question 1). Here it obviously means a large section of the nation, perhaps the majority. This explains verses 4-6: those who have reneged against God's covenant are persecuting those few who remain loyal. They *devour my people as men eat bread*, or, as Leupold renders it, 'they devour my people to feed themselves' – they prey on them. They make them poor (v. 6) and frustrate (their) plans to better themselves.

But it will be worse for them in the end. They should know from their history and recent experience that God is on the side of the righteous poor, his own people, and against the wicked. But they never learn, because they are fools who do not understand the ways of God. So they will have to learn by experience, for it is they who will be over-whelmed with dread, while their victims will enjoy the presence of God (v. 5), who will be their refuge (v. 6).

Verse 7: David's cry on behalf of the oppressed remnant

All this seems afar off at the time of writing. Hence the cry goes up for the Lord to bring about his salvation. After all, there he is now in his place in Zion, seated on the ark between the cherubim (80:1). Will he not come out and restore the fortunes of his people, his spiritual Jacob, his true Israel, and make them glad again?

Questions:
(1) Viewing this psalm in the light of Romans 3:10-12 what do we learn about human nature?

(2) What connection does this psalm establish between belief and behaviour? Cf. Romans 1:28.

(3) What does the psalm teach us about the need for and means of 'revival'? Cf. Isaiah 64.

Psalm 15

Who May Live With God?

This psalm appears to be connected with the setting up of the Tabernacle on Mount Zion and the bringing in of the ark which symbolised the presence of God there. It considers the conditions, not just for entering the tabernacle but for DWELLING in your sanctuary ... LIVING on your holy hill (v. 1).[1] But no one, even the high priest, ever did this. There were priests' rooms around the sanctuary when the temple was built, but these were only occupied during the period of duty. So we are obviously to view this spiritually as referring to fellowship with the God whose presence was revealed on the ark in the Tabernacle.

The conditions specified (2-5a) show the superiority of Old Testament religion to that of the nations around. They too had conditions for approaching and entering the sanctuary of their gods, but these were wholly ritualistic, whereas the psalm's are ethical. The New Testament moves up a gear and sees such virtues not as works of the flesh but fruits of the Spirit (Gal. 5:22-23).

---

1. The terms used are interesting: **sanctuary** is OHEL, one of the words used of the Tabernacle; **Live** is from the same root as the other word for Tabernacle: MISHKAN: 'Who shall tabernacle in your tabernacle?' cf. John 1:14, where 'made his dwelling' is the Greek equivalent of MISHKAN.

Verse 2a-b: true in character

The first two parts of the verse are two ways of saying the same thing: the way to live (walk) a blameless life is to do what is righteous. This is the general word for Old Testament morality, aspects of which are spelt out in what follows.

Verses 2c-3: restrained in language

The Biblical concept of truth-speaking is not so much factual accuracy (which on occasions may be impossible or even wrong) as trustworthiness. This is shown here in the example given which amounts to 'don't spread malicious rumours about your neighbour which will do (him) wrong by casting a slur on him.' Bear in mind that the context is that of coming into God's presence to worship him. How can the tongue that has slandered another praise God? (See James 3:11-12.)

Verse 4a: clearcut in allegiance

The previous point is not to be taken to mean that we shut our eyes to another's sin. Glaring faults are to be noticed and detested. In the same way true godliness will be evident and esteemed. It is where sins are only rumoured that we are to be restrained.

Verses 4b-5a: honourable in dealing

Two examples are given here: First: KEEPING PROMISES even when it hurts. This does not mean oaths cannot be repudiated when they are plainly seen to be mistaken, as with Jephthah's. Proverbs 6:1-6 (on standing surety) indicates that this was allowed. It is going back on a good promise because it is found inconvenient that is condemned here. Second: MONEY MATTERS. The Old Testament is strongly opposed to the two things referred to here: lending on interest and accepting bribes. The reason was that a fellow-Israelite who comes to you for a loan does so because he is destitute, and you will only add to this if you charge interest. But this was permitted in the case of foreigners, since the loan would be to build up a business that was already flourishing. This distinction carries over into the New Testament. Accepting a bribe against the innocent is connected with giving evidence or making judgements in court.

The New Testament would classify all this under the heading of 'Love your neighbour as yourself', which if you do you will fulfill these conditions. Such a person, says verse 5, gains what he sought in verse 1: security in God. It does not mean he will not be upset by changed circumstances, but he will not be shaken from his secure dwelling place in God – see 91:1. As the New Testament puts it, one who loves his neighbour loves God first and dwells in him (1 John 4:16).

Questions:

(1) What has put 'dwelling in God' on a higher plane for New Testament believers? (See John 14:15-24.)

(2) In the light of verse 3 and Christ's words in Matthew 7:1-2 when is it right to pass judgment on another and when is it wrong? (See Lev. 19:17; 1 Tim. 5:19-20.)

(3) Consider how it is that love is the key to all these ethical conditions (1 Cor. 13:4-7).

Psalm 16

David Faces Trouble in Family and Nation

In spite of David's resolution to be an example of godliness to the people (Ps. 101), there was clearly a lack of it in the nation he governed. There is evidence of strife, immorality and even idolatry. In fact corruption broke out in David's own family. 2 Samuel 13 tells the sad story of the rape of Tamar (David's daughter by Maacah and sister of Absalom) by Amnon (his son by Ahinoam). This was partly God's judgment on David himself, as God had warned in 2 Samuel 12:10-12, beginning the train of events which led to Absalom's rebellion; but also a reflection of the state of society generally. David's awareness of this comes out in some of his psalms, which show him bringing these burdens to the Lord and seeking to encourage the godly remnant.

Of the different views on the meaning of *Miktam* (title), the most likely is 'engraving' or 'inscription'. Some take this literally for the epitaph David wanted inscribed on his monument because of a near-death experience alluded to in verse 10. Others would take it metaphorically to mean he wanted these thoughts inscribed on his memory as something to hold on to in turbulent times.

Verse 1: David seeks God's protection
David brings to God first his concern for himself. 'Keep me safe from going down the road some of the people are going

down, even my own family. Keep me safe from the threat of
the assassin'. He encourages himself by remembering how in
the past God had been his refuge, especially from the hand of
Saul. Now he takes refuge in him again.

Verses 2-4: David re-affirms his resolutions

When he first came to the throne he made certain promises
about his life, his reign and the company and the colleagues
he would choose (Ps. 101). He is still of this mind (v. 2). I is
literally 'you', but is in the feminine and probably refers to
his soul or mind, which had said to the Lord, 'you are my
lord' (e.g. 31:14), you are the one from whom and whom alone
comes all my good'.

In Psalm 101 he had vowed to associate himself with the
godly and this he re-affirms in verse 3. This shows there was
much ungodliness in Israel at this time in spite of his best
efforts in organisation. This stemmed from the idolatry which
had either crept back or never been expurgated (v. 4). People
were still running after other gods – *run* denoting eagerness
or desperation. They were taking part in blood-sacrifices and
uttering the names of the Baals with their lips.The Canaanites
had ascribed the land's fertility to Baal, but Israel claimed to
believe it was the Lord who blessed the land with milk and
honey, grain and fruit. Yet here they were ascribing it all to
Baal! This was to recur in Hosea's time (Hos. 2:17). But David is
clear that this is the road to disaster: their sorrows will increase,
a phrase used of the punishment of Eve in Genesis 3:16.

Verses 5-11: David's assurance increases

God honours David's trust in him (v. 1) and his firm stand
against idolatry (vv. 2-4) by increasing David's assurance of
his favour.

Firstly, he gives him a sense of contentment (vv. 5-6). Since there
is no verb such as in *you have assigned* (NIV), some translate this
'you are my portion' (v. 5). He is contrasting himself with the
idolators. Because they ascribe their well-being to Baal they
have no portion in the blessings of God. After the conquest
the land was portioned out by lot and shared among the tribes

(v. 6). Idolators have no right to this. It is those who like David renounce idols and are faithful to the Lord who enjoy the pleasant places and delightful inheritance of the land. David, unlike the idolators, was content with this.

Secondly, he assures him of his guidance and protection. David was facing problems in his private and public life (see introduction). But now he is trusting God. These do not lessen his love for him, rather they increase it and fill him with praise, for God counsels and instructs him. Even at night, though he may lie awake, he is not tossing and turning with worry, but meditating on the wisdom with which God has filled his heart (v. 7). Nor is this merely mental or emotional. God is before him and beside him, like his right-hand man, coming between him and his enemies. So even under attack he can say I shall not be shaken (v. 8).

Thirdly, he gives him hope even in death (vv. 9-11). Now that he sees his whole being is safe in God's hands, he can be glad and rejoice with all his powers: *heart ... tongue ... body* (v. 9). Some think he was fatally ill at the time; others that he expected assassination. But however and whenever death came it would not be the end of him. Even his body would not rot away in Sheol (*the grave*), the place of darkness and desolation (v. 10). He was God's holy or faithful (NIV mg) one. Here is David the prophet again, glimpsing 'the Holy One of God', his Son, dying, but not remaining in the grave long enough to decay, but rising again (see Acts 2:31; 13:35).

Meanwhile he continues to walk the path of life which God has made known to him. The two most important features of this are: to live in God's presence now and to anticipate eternity, when, instead of God at his right hand, it will be him at God's right hand – another glimpse of Christ, this time exalted after his resurrection (Eph. 1:20; Heb. 1:3). Here and here alone is true *joy ... and ... pleasure*.

Questions:
(1) How can we turn our problems into blessings, as David did his? (See Phil. 4:4-7; James 1:2-5, 12.)

(2) What does true worship involve (v. 9)? (See Ps. 103:1; Luke 1:46-47; John 4:24; Rom. 12:1.)

(3) How much pleasure and enjoyment (v. 11) do you find in your Christian life? (See the three-fold occurrence of 'rejoice' in Rom. 5:1-10 and the frequent use of 'joy' and 'rejoice' in Philippians.)

Psalm 17

David Pleads With God Against His Enemies

This psalm comes from a time when David was surrounded by enemies (vv. 9, 11). Its similarity to 10 may point to Absalom's campaign of character assassination (2 Sam. 15:1-6), so that his enemies would be those of his own family and nation.

Verses 1-5: David seeks a hearing from God
The intensity and depth of David's prayer is brought out in two ways in verse 1: first, the threefold repetition of his call to God: *hear ... listen ... give ear*; second, the threefold description of his actual request: *my righteous plea ... my cry ... my prayer*. To call his plea righteous or, better his 'just cause' (ESV), is not self-righteousness and ignoring his sins, but refers to the accusations his enemies were making. He is innocent of those; his lips are not deceitful as were theirs.

This is clarified in verse 2: it is God who vindicates him, not himself, the God who sees what is right. His life is open to God's scrutiny; indeed David spends his sleepless hours examining himself before God (v. 3). He finds nothing that justifies the charges brought against him and resolves not to respond in kind. This applies not only to their words but their deeds (v. 4). Evidently they were resorting to violent ways, possibly coercing those who were loyal to David. David is resolved not to go down that road because it would be against 'the word of your lips' – God had forbidden it. David had made certain pledges on taking the throne and was not going to deviate from them (v. 5).

Verses 6-12: David seeks protection from God

Having gained the ear of God David turns to his actual request: for God's protection from those who were trying to destroy him. This is just as intensely prayed as his opening appeal, with the thrice repeated plea, *Hear ... listen to my cry ... give ear to my prayer* (v. 1). But a greater assurance has come in: *for you will answer me.* The grounds for this come out in verses 7-9. He is pleading, not his innocence, as in verses 3-5, but God's covenant love. This is the great love which he pledged to those who take refuge in him, that is, his own people who have entrusted themselves to him. His promise is to stretch out his right hand, that is, to deal powerfully with 'those who rise up against' (as *foes* is literally, v. 7) the children of his covenant. The covenant language is even clearer in verse 8 with its reference to *the apple of* (God's) *eye* (the pupil) and *the shadow of* (his) *wings*, expressions used in the Song of Moses at the end of their journey from Egypt (Deut. 32:10-11).

His plea gains strength as he speaks of those from whom he is seeking protection. They are not just personal enemies but the wicked (v. 9), and therefore God's enemies. Nor are they merely trying to annoy him, they are out to kill him; they are mortal (deadly) enemies, literally 'enemies against my life' (v. 9).

The extreme danger he is in when he speaks of their surrounding him is developed in verses 10-12 with graphic imagery. Their lack of any human feeling is evident in their arrogant speech. *Callous hearts* is literally 'their fat', depicting self-indulgent men whose only interest in others is in what they can get out of them. They do not care what methods they use so long as they get what they want. This is borne out in the warrior imagery of verse 11. A soldier aims to get his enemy off his horse or his feet and on to the ground where he is at his mercy. The change of imagery in verse 12 intensifies this: heartless, selfish men have become *lions ... hungry for prey.* Like lions these men are only awaiting the moment to strike.

Verses 13-15: David seeks punishment on the wicked

David seems to have reluctantly come to the conclusion that ultimately the only way he will escape his enemies is for God to destroy them. Thus he is in tune with God's mind, for he does not desire the death of the wicked (Ezek. 33:11) and only judges as a last resort. This partly explains David's extraordinary call on God to rise up, which does not mean he thought of God as sleeping, but simply recognises his reluctance to punish. As his prophet David is impelled to call for him to act and draw his sword. The words *rise up* may also be aimed at the wicked who did believe God ignored what they were doing (10:11). Their downfall would be David's rescue.

He backs up his appeal in verse 14 by pleading the radical difference between himself and his enemies. They are men of this world whose whole way of thinking and living is about obtaining a reward in this life. The next line of verse 14 is problematic and many alternatives have been suggested. To keep the train of thought consistent it is better to read it 'with your treasure you will fill their belly'. This leads on to the last two lines which show them as having amassed so much wealth they have plenty to leave for their children.

David's own view of life is the opposite (v. 15): his heart is set on righteousness not riches, for he knows that only the righteous see (his) face. Whatever earthly treasures are given or withheld this is the only way to be satisfied. What David himself understood by *when I awake* we cannot know: every morning? When I wake up from the present nightmare? Or awake from the sleep of death? With the hindsight of the gospel we can certainly see it in the last sense, for *the pure in heart ... shall see God* (Matt. 5:8).

Questions:

(1) **Verses 1-5**: When unjustly criticised, what is your first reaction? Indignation? Self-justification? Or Prayer? – not only for yourself but for your critics. (See Matt. 5:44-45; 1 Pet. 2:23.)

(2) **Verses 6-12**: What use do you make of our covenant relationship with God in your praying and thinking? (See Zech. 2:7-13.)

(3) **Verses 13-15**: What 'satisfies' you? Is it the pursuit of righteousness (Matt. 5:6)? How different are we from our worldly neighbours?

Psalm 18

David's Special Thanksgiving For the End of His Wars

David's wars with the surrounding nations ended with the subjugation of Ammon (2 Sam. 12:31) which was thus a turning-point both in David's reign and Israel's history. It is appropriate it should be celebrated with an extended psalm of thanksgiving. 2 Samuel 22 places it much later in David's reign, after Absalom's rebellion. However, there is no reason why it should not have been re-used at that time, following a further war with the Philistines recorded in chapter 21. In fact the latter may be placed out of chronological sequence, like the incident of the Gibeonites in the first part of chapter 21. The closing chapters of 2 Samuel appear to be a kind of appendix to the book.

The title of the psalm ties together his deliverance from the neighbouring nations and his deliverance from Saul, which points to the earlier part of David's reign. He had been fighting almost continuously since he had fled Saul's court. When Saul died and David became king he had to take over Saul's battles until his enemies were subdued. Now that they were, the nation could settle down. This lengthy psalm and the two which follow reflect a more leisurely life.

But this did not mean all his troubles were over. In a way they were to increase, for they would arise from within his own family and nation. However, at this point he knew nothing of what was to follow, and gave himself to unrestrained thanksgiving. The quality of the poetry is superlative and there is development of thought. This does not apply to the allusions, which were sometimes to his experiences with Saul and sometimes to the Philistines or other enemies.

Verses 1-3: David praises God for all he has learned of him
His experiences have taught him so much about God that his love for him has increased (v. 1). The word for love is unusual and implies emotion and tenderness. His sufferings have brought him closer to God because he has been his strength in weakness, his rock or fortress under attack: as when he sheltered in the cave of Adullam. *Rock* in line 2 is a different word from that used in line 1, used of 'the Crags of the Wild Goats' which formed a refuge in 1 Samuel 24:2. As well as places of shelter God was also like weapons of defence to him: his *shield* and *horn*. He has also found him to be, not a static God, but one who comes to his aid when he calls to him (v. 3).

Verses 4-6: He recalls instances of answers to prayer
His mind now flashes back to an occasion when the situation was so serious he could do nothing else but cry to God for help (v. 6). It is possible to translate the verbs in this passage as present tenses and see David re-living an occasion or occasions when death and destruction seemed so certain that it was as if he were inescapably enmeshed in their cords (vv. 4-5). An example of this was when he was betrayed by the Ziphites in the Desert of Maon (1 Sam. 23:24-29). God providentially intervened: when David was about to fall into Saul's hands, news came of a Philistine invasion. David attributes this to God hearing his prayer (v. 6).

Verses 7-15: He recounts the awesome manner of God's intervention
The God who heard him from his *temple* (v. 6) came out of it in awesome power. The poetry reaches sublime heights as he recalls how God appeared for him in ways reminiscent of his coming at the Red Sea and Sinai. He came like an earthquake

(v. 7), a fire-breathing dragon (v. 8), a great storm (vv. 9-13) and a warrior (v. 14). The devastating consequences are described in verse 15. This is of course metaphorical language for the great defeats inflicted upon those nations which came against him during the early part of his reign.

Verses 16-19: He describes the resulting deliverance

What was disaster for his enemies was salvation for him, so spectacular he can only describe it in language which recalls the Red Sea (vv. 16-18). Just as Israel had come out of that narrow place where they were trapped between sea and mountain, so he was rescued from tight corners and brought into a spacious place (v. 19). No longer did he have to hide round corners – he was free to roam the whole country. Later, when hemmed in by the surrounding nations, he threw them off and extended his borders.

Verses 20-24: David attributes all this to God's justice

At first sight this looks like self-righteousness, or, in the light of his fall in the Bathsheba incident, blatant hypocrisy. It may be that David is referring to his life prior to his fall, particularly to his experience of Saul. God vindicated David and exposed Saul's unjust and cruel treatment of him. More probably he is referring to the principles on which he was ruling the nation. The king's duty was to administer God's laws and decrees (v. 22, Deut. 17:18-20). To these he had committed himself on his coronation (Ps. 101), relying on God's promise that he will honour those who honour him. David has kept his vows, dealt wisely with his people and justly with his enemies, and God has rewarded him with peace.

Verses 25-29: He claims God deals similarly with all

Although as king he was special, David acknowledges that God deals similarly with all who seek to honour him, any who are *faithful ... blameless ... pure* (vv. 25-26). He himself is proof of this (vv. 20-24), which will encourage the people in their allegiance to God (vv. 25-26a).

What about those who do not behave thus: the crooked or perverse (v. 26b)? God himself does not act perversely, but he does deal with them in a way which corresponds to their own attitude and behaviour: he shows himself shrewd. Jacob provides an example of this: he acted craftily towards Esau, but met his match in Laban who tricked him more than once. Although God is not directly responsible for Laban's deceitfulness, he did providentially use it to open Jacob's eyes to himself and bring about a change in him.

In David's case, God had frustrated the plans both of Saul and David's later enemies. This he acknowledges in the beautiful words of verse 28. He gives two instances in verse 29: in line 1 his defeat of the Amalekites who sacked Ziklag, for the word *troop* is the word translated *raiding party* in 1 Samuel 30:8, 15; in line 2 he recalls the capture of Jerusalem by means of scaling a vertical water-shaft (2 Sam. 5:6-10).

Verses 30-36: David ascribes it all to God

Lest he should sound as if he were boasting (vv. 20-24, 28-29), he attributes all this to God: *his way*, which never errs, *his word* or promises, which never miscarry, and his personal protection (*shield*, v. 35). In these ways God is out on his own. This is the source, not only of David's personal integrity, but even his military success. Although brought up to be a shepherd, David turned out to be one of the greatest of all warriors. He had physical strength (v. 32) yet also agility to move over rough terrain (v. 33) without mishap (v. 36). He even attributes his skill with weapons to God, for he had known no human instructor and had no military training. God taught him to wield a sword (*my hands*, v. 34), a *bow*, even a heavy bronze one, and a *shield* (v. 35). God was not above stooping down to train soldiers for his battles (144:1).

Verses 37-42: David revels in his partnership with God

Here is the perfect balance of faith and works, which makes our service a matter of co-operation with God. David had to wield the weapons and engage the enemy – God did not do this for him (vv. 37-38). But God unseen was behind him and ensured the victory (vv. 39-40).

This passage obviously relates to the wars with his neighbouring nations, since he never actually engaged Saul in battle (God enabled him to avoid this), and Saul fell by the hands of the Philistines. Humanly, a small nation just getting on its feet could never have survived against more established ones. Israel had at least six frontiers to defend – impossible without supernatural help, as David here acknowledges. Verse 41 proves it: even when these nations cried to Israel's God, not just their own, no answer came, as it did for Israel, whose victories in this period were total.

Verses 43-45: David reviews the whole period

How different is the situation now from what it was when David first came to the throne! The tables have been turned. He has not only beaten back his enemies but subjected them to him (e.g. 2 Sam. 12:29-31). No longer do they boast and fight but cringe and come trembling to him. When God wins a victory he does it thoroughly. This anticipates Christ's overthrow of the powers of evil on the cross (Col. 2:15) and his ultimate triumph at the final battle (1 Cor. 15:25; Rev. 19:11-16; 20:7-10).

Verses 46-50: Praise to the living God!

This is a victory not merely for David and Israel over hostile nations, but for the One God over the many gods. What had they done for their devotees? Nothing, since they are dead, non-existent. But *the LORD lives!* (v. 46). He has demonstrated this and asserted his right to avenge his people on their enemies (v. 47). Their downfall is Israel's rise (v. 48). Verse 49 suggests they had to send representatives to Jerusalem, possibly with tribute or to receive instructions (vv. 43-44), for the nations must have been there to hear the people *sing praises to* (his) *name* (v. 49).

Paul takes verse 49 as prophesying the conversion of the Gentiles (Rom. 15:9). This prophetic note climaxes in verse 50 with David's conviction that he is God's anointed, whose descendants will enjoy God's favour for ever. David's kingdom would give way to Messiah's, who would be both *a light for revelation to the Gentiles and for glory to his people Israel* (Luke 2:32).

Questions:

(1) David's long struggles had led him to know God better and love him more (vv. 1-3). What have you learned about God from your tribulations?

(2) What prayers have you seen answered in your life, even if they are not as spectacular as David's (vv. 6-19)?

(3) Check through verses 20-29: how far does this passage reflect your life and experience of God's dealings?

(4) Look again at verse 26b and the comment. Has God ever had to deal with you as you have dealt with others, in order to open your eyes to yourself? (See Matt. 7:1-5.)

(5) How is your 'military training' (vv. 32-36) for the conflict with sin and Satan going? Are you learning to wield the weapons of Ephesians 6:10-18 more effectively?

(6) Comparing verses 37-42 with Christian service, in what ways is the latter also co-operation with God? (See 2 Cor. 6:1.)

Psalm 19

A Noontide Meditation

When David was working as a shepherd he had plenty of time and opportunity to contemplate God's creation. In Psalm 8 it was the moon and the stars; here it is the sun.

Verses 1-4a

The shepherd's life is an outdoor life and no-one is more conscious than he of what is going on in *the heavens ... and the skies*. But David's response is more than 'O what a beautiful morning! O what a beautiful day!' Those without God can only see what their eyes behold, but one who has the word of God hears as well as sees. The works of nature do not use speech or language, *no ... voice is heard* (v. 3 mg, cf. RV, RSV, NEB, ESV), but to those with a mind tuned in to God they 'pour forth speech ... and display knowledge' (v. 2). This is there for *all the earth*, even those at *the ends of the world* (v. 4), for all live under the same celestial canopy.

And the message they speak? *The glory of God ... the work of his hands* (v. 1). While it is good and right to admire and enjoy the natural creation for itself, it is better to see it as a window through which the being of God and his acts in time can be perceived. David is expressing poetically what Paul puts theologically in Romans 1:18-20: that the natural creation is there as a witness to God, even a proof of his existence, power and nature. This is what he preached to ignorant pagans in

Lystra (Acts 14:8-18) – that the works of nature should not be made objects of worship but seen as pointers to the God who made them. He took a similar line in preaching to educated pagans in Athens (Acts 17:24-30).

Verses 4b-6

At noon one thing stands out above all others – *the sun*. This too is not to be worshipped but seen as an agent of God who has *pitched* (his) *tent* for it (v. 4b), that is, given it a permanent place in the order of things, so that day by day it performs the function he has appointed for it: to *make its circuit ...* (from) *one end of the heavens ... to the other* (v. 6), so that it can give light and heat to all the earth. This is a cause for rejoicing which he expresses by two appropriate metaphors: of a bridegroom leaving home to claim his bride and a champion doing his lap of honour (v. 5). Everyone sees, or at least benefits from, the sun. Let all see the God who gave it and rejoice in him!

Verses 7-11

The voice of nature turns his thoughts to the voice of Scripture. He speaks of this in a different way from what we would, using terms like *law... statutes ... precepts ... commands ... ordinances*. He has in mind the books of Moses, the only Scriptures in writing available at that time. The stories of Joshua and the Judges may have circulated in oral form, but there were no histories, prophets or wisdom writings, and he himself had yet to write the first collection of psalms!

But limited as his canon of Scripture was, what he had was *perfect ... trustworthy ... right ... radiant ... pure ... enduring ... sure ... righteous*. Unlike the natural creation, which does not explain why it is there and how it came to be, the Scriptures give an explanation of all these things. Though the material at David's disposal was limited to the *the Law*, it was still the living word of God and could do what the sun and sky could not do: *revive the soul ... make wise the simple ... give joy to the heart ... light to the eyes*.

It may be that to us the law books of Scripture seem to be the least profitable part, but when they are all a person has they are more precious than gold. Evidently it was possible with only these few books to form a view of God complete enough to worship him and clear enough to find salvation. For they are the foundation of the remainder of God's revelation. The moral law shows a righteous God and defines sin; the political and social precepts show the way to an orderly society and good relationships; and the ceremonial details are all about atonement, and did duty for the way of forgiveness until he came who was to fulfill it all.

No wonder that to David they were sweeter than honey, for in them he found things to warn him from going down the road to disaster, and to encourage him to seek the reward of faith and obedience. Unbeknown to him, this deep appreciation of God's word was later to be the foundation of his throne, as he expressed in the psalm composed for his coronation (101).

Verses 12-14
It is the word of God rather than the works of nature that inspire prayer in him. Here we have, in Old Testament terms, the story of a conversion of heart: conviction of sin (v. 12a), a cry for forgiveness (v. 12b), a concern for holiness (v. 13) and for a clean mind and mouth (v. 14) – not so that he may be admired as a pious man, but that his God may be pleased.

Questions:
(1) What is the connection between the two aspects of God's character in verse 14 (my Rock and my Redeemer) and David's thoughts on nature, scripture and his personal life?

(2) Is there any way you can make your knowledge of God and his word bear upon your daily work?

Psalm 20

The King Goes Out to War

The early part of David's reign was one of almost continual warfare with the neighbouring nations. But he believed his wars were God's wars and that he could therefore invoke God's aid. He also recruited the people to call on God. No doubt there was a first occasion for this, for which this psalm was composed; but it was then placed in the collection of the Director of music (title) and used whenever necessary.

Verses 1-3: The people pray for their King
The people's prayer echoes what David himself was praying: *may the* LORD *'answer you'* (v. 1a), that is, answer the prayer you are putting up in your distress, which refers to the particular war he was going out to fight. But the cry for *the name of the God of Jacob* (to) *protect* (him) (v. 1b), came from the heart, since their fortunes as a nation depended very much on those of the king (2 Sam. 21:17; Lam. 4:20). These are not exaggerated statements, since it was through David and his successors that God governed and maintained his people. Remember too that the monarch prefigured the King Messiah.

This confidence is confirmed by two things. Firstly (v. 2), that the God they prayed to was present in *Zion* where David dwelt, and the glory of the Lord shone from his *sanctuary* where the ark resided. He was as really among them as when they had followed the ark across the desert. Secondly,

David had been following the right procedures for obtaining help from this God, for (v. 3) he had offered *sacrifices and ... burnt offerings* which expressed his unworthiness of victory and his dependence on God in going out to battle. It seems it was the done thing to offer sacrifice before going into battle (1 Sam. 13:8-10). The prayer is that these would be efficacious, not in themselves, but because God accepted them: 'remember' recalls the idea of sacrifices as 'memorials' to God (Lev. 2:8-10).

Verses 4-5: They anticipate his victory

After a brief musical interlude (*Selah*), the prayer bursts forth again in verse 4. The people were confident that David's desire for victory was God's will, and his plans for bringing it about were directed by God and would succeed. The prayer slides naturally into anticipating he would be victorious, and they imagine themselves shouting for joy and parading in their tribes with their banners unfurled (v. 5). This is not mere jingoism but for the glory of the name of God. When it happened it would be because the Lord had granted his and their requests.

Verses 6-8: The King responds

This united praying and the spirit of confidence it breathes inspires David to voice his own assurance of victory in this campaign. This does not mean he is putting his trust in the people. Verse 6 shows him looking to his calling as the Lord's *anointed*, the one the Lord has promised to preserve (save). Also he is trusting that the God who shines from the ark is the God who dwells in *his holy heaven* from where he rules all things. The *right hand*, that is the sovereign power, by which he exercises his universal rule will both strengthen Israel's army and crush the enemy.

This confidence is further expressed in verse 7, which is not saying that chariots and horses are unnecessary in war, but that they should not be relied on, for this would be inconsistent with trust in *the name of the LORD our God*. As Cromwell said, 'Trust in God and keep your powder dry.' With this assurance he can expect a crushing victory (v. 8), just as the people had done in verse 5. In fact, in changing from 'I' to 'we' he is clearly attributing success to the united effort of the whole nation: king, army and people.

Verse 9: The people assent

The psalm ends as it began with the people calling on God, except in slightly different language and with the order reversed. The first line is an abbreviation of verse 1b, perhaps the more effective for its brevity, as prayers often are. The second line says answer **us** whereas verse 1a has answer **you** (in each case emphasis mine). What a great blessing it is when leaders and people agree in what they ask! What expectation it creates in our hearts! It is the victory over the Canaanites again, as Deborah celebrated it: *When the princes in Israel take the lead, when the people willingly offer themselves – praise the* LORD! (Judg. 5:2).

Questions:
(1) In World War II George Orwell wrote: 'I can never work up any disgust over Bishops blessing the colours of regiments, etc'. In the light of this psalm do you agree?

(2) How much confidence and assurance is there in our church prayer meetings? If it is little, could it be enhanced by emulating this psalm in the light of Matthew 18:19-20?

(3) In what way(s) does this psalm throw light on our Lord's brief call to us to pray *your kingdom come* (Matt. 6:10)?

Psalm 21

The King Returns Victorious

As Psalm 20 was sung when the king led his army into battle, so this one was composed to be sung when they returned in triumph. Like Psalm 20, it was probably first composed for a particular battle, but was subsequently used whenever the King returned in triumph, and so was added to the director of music's collection.

Verses 1-7: Thanks for past victories

Although in the third person singular, these could be words David composed for the people to sing at the thanksgiving service following a military victory. The link with 20 is very clear. There the people had asked God for *help* (v. 2); here they are thanking God for giving it, thus bringing about the victory over which they were rejoicing (v. 1). In 20:4 they had prayed God would give him his 'heart's desire'; here they acknowledge God had granted him the desire of his heart (v. 2).

Now as David leads his triumphant forces up to Zion, God is seen as welcoming them with *rich blessings* (v. 3), as he enters, possibly wearing the crown he had taken from the head of the defeated king In 20:5 they had prayed God would *grant all* (his) *requests*. This is acknowledged here in verse 2 and specified in verse 4 as *life ... length of days*. It was common in the ancient Near East to wish the monarch 'long life' (e.g. Dan. 2:4) and the custom has not completely died out in modern western nations: 'Long live our noble queen!'

But David is seen here as God's representative on earth and the forerunner of the Messianic King, hence the way this is developed in verses 5-7. *Glory ... splendour and majesty* (v. 5) are all attributes which belong to God and are present in Christ on entering his kingdom (Heb. 1:8-9; Rev. 5:12-14). Verse 6 is far more applicable to Christ than to David, for it is he who has eternal blessings and dwells joyfully in the presence of God the Father. But verse 7 is true of his forerunner David, for this is covenant language. *The unfailing love of the Most High* is God's covenant love (Heb. CHESED) and the trust is the response of the covenant people led by their King. Since that trust can waver; therefore it is not their trust but God's unfailing love through which he shall not be shaken.

Verses 8-13: Anticipation of future victories

David sees this particular victory as a token that, should his enemies rise up again, his hand will lay hold of them (v. 8). These words are addressed at least as much to God as to David, and anticipate the Messiah even more strongly than verses 5-7. If David's appearance at Rabbah had clinched the victory over the Ammonites (2 Sam. 12:29-31), what would Christ's victory be like at his appearing (v. 9)? It is in such words that the last prophet of the Old Testament predicts Christ's coming (Mal. 3:1-2), words taken up by Christ himself when confronting the Jews who opposed him (Matt. 21:40-41) and ultimately by Paul describing Christ's final battle with his enemies (2 Thess. 1:7-9).

Verses 10-12 depict David going through the earth ridding it of Israel's and God's enemies, but the language verges on the apocalyptic, and looks on to Christ's kingdom and the ultimate overthrow of his enemies, as described in Revelation 19:1-21. Finally in verse 13 king and people unite in their desire that Israel's life, in peace or war, might demonstrate the strength and might of God.

Questions:

(1) What do you think of 'services of Thanksgiving' following modern wars (Falklands: 1982, Gulf War: 1990, Iraq: 2003)? Have they anything to do with this psalm?

(2) If not, what does it mean for us today? (See Micah 7:8.)

(3) Re-read the psalm, thinking of Christ instead of David: his entrance into glory, his present war against his enemies, and his final victory over them.

Psalm 22

David in the Darkness

The contrast between the first 21 verses and the last 10 reflect a 'darkness to light' experience, such as David frequently underwent during the days of his exile in the time of Saul. The title of the tune 'Doe (or Hind) of the Morning' suggests he saw himself as a hunted deer. A slight alteration of the Hebrew vowel points gives us 'Help' instead of 'Doe'. The full title then becomes 'Help at Day-break', perhaps indicating that David had spent the night in prayer and during it composed the psalm. It certainly reflects a darkness to light experience. David's life was taking on the pattern that Christ would follow, hence the quotations and allusions to the psalm in the New Testament.

VERSES 1-21: DAVID IN THE DARKNESS

These verses form the substance of David's all-night prayer, when everything seemed as black as the night around him. It is comparable to Jacob's all-night wrestling with God at the ford of Jabbok (Gen. 32:24-25). 'I' sections alternate with 'you' sections, showing David's fluctuating feelings.

Verses 1-2: Forsaken by God

In David's case this was not how things were but how they seemed. He means he is receiving no immediate, conscious, visible help from God and seems at the mercy of his enemy.

But he does not know God's mind because God is not revealing it – yet. In Christ's case the abandonment was total (Matt. 27:46). The Son knew the mind of the Father; he knew that sin separates the sinner from God (Isa. 59:2), and at the moment when he uttered these words the sin of the world was being laid on him (Isa. 53:6), bringing about the separation. This was not the case with David.

Verses 3-5: Recollecting God

The first 'I' section is followed by the first 'You' section. Here David recalls who is the God to whom he is crying – the Holy One, who does not forsake those to whom he has pledged himself. As such he is enthroned on the praises of Israel (NIV mg) – that is, God's dwelling is not a temple but his people; therefore his throne is not a seat in a palace but the praises of his people. This has been proved countless times by *our fathers*, who in their extremity *cried to you* because *they trusted* you, and their trust was *not disappointed*. Thus David recovers some hope that his experience would be similar.

Verses 6-8: Present reality

In the next 'I' passage David returns to the present. Whatever has happened or will happen, the present reality is that everyone has cast him off. He is trodden under foot like a worm, that is, he is *scorned ... despised ... mocked ... insulted*, even to the extent of having his expressions of confidence in God thrown back in his face. David may be alluding to someone in his own band who has lost trust in him as God's chosen. If so he was experiencing in advance what Christ would later endure when his enemies used the literal words of verse 8a (Matt. 27:43). In both cases it was not only the world which did not recognise them but their own who did not receive them (John 1:10-11).

Verses 9-11: Recollecting his own past

In the previous 'You' passage he took comfort from God's faithfulness to the fathers of long ago. Now he recalls God's care of him in his own past. He goes back to his earliest babyhood. It is not clear whether there was anything abnormal in this, or whether he is just referring to the fact that all childbirth was precarious then and many did not survive it. The fact that God had watched over him at birth gives him some re-assurance in his present circumstances, as it does in Psalm 139:13-16.

Verses 12-18: Fierce enmity

Coming back to the 'I' theme, his complaint now goes far beyond what he said in verses 6-8. These are not mere verbal attacks but a physical onslaught, or at least the threat of it. Since these things were not happening at that moment, it seems as if David's imagination was working overtime. He sees himself like a little creature thrown to the lions or the dogs to be torn to pieces. He sees his hide-out encircled by evil men, who in his nightmare turn into bulls. To be chased by one bull is hazardous; to be surrounded by many bulls is certain death. The terror of this reduces him to jelly (vv. 14-15), which is probably the most vivid description anywhere of a state of total panic.

But he is not getting any sympathy, only gloating stares (v. 17). The crowning humiliation is to strip off his clothing and gamble for it, since he has no further use for it. This and the piercing of the hands and feet (v. 16) are the nearest to a dress rehearsal for Jesus on the cross to which anyone came before that event. Verse 16 does not mean that David imagined himself being crucified. It probably follows the imagery of the dogs and lions, whose bites and scratches were tearing his flesh. Notice the alternative reading to 'pierced' in the NIV mg: 'like a lion.'

Verses 19-21: Desolate cry

This last of the 'You' passages is the most poignant. In such an extremity as that just described who wouldn't cry out *help ... deliver ... rescue*? But David's crying is to God, to the One who had forsaken him! Here is the triumph of faith over experience – to call on the God you have concluded is not there! The very ability to do so is the evidence that God never totally and finally forsakes his children. Perhaps the promise of Deuteronomy 31:6 sustained him, even if unconsciously, as it did a later persecuted people (Heb. 13:5). How could a God with a tender heart resist the pathetic reference to his precious life (v. 20), literally 'my only one', all I am left with, when even my clothes have gone, torn off by the dogs ... lions ... and oxen (bulls). His naked flesh is now open to them.

This is the turning point of this traumatic experience, for *save* (v. 21) is better translated 'you have heard' (NIV mg). How this assurance came is not stated, but there are three possibilities: a word from the prophet Nathan, who was there (2 Sam. 12:13-14); an 'oracle' from the ephod interpreted by Abiathar the priest who had been with David since joining him at Keilah (1 Sam. 23:6); or a direct word from the Spirit to David himself, since he had the gift of prophecy. Whatever the truth, this leads to a sudden key-change in the whole mood of the psalm (usually expressed by a musical key-change by choirs who chant the psalms).

VERSES 22-31: DAVID IN THE LIGHT
Verses 22-24: Rousing the people
First he shares the 'oracle' with his people and exhorts them to join him in praising the Lord. He gladly confesses he was wrong to accuse God of forsaking and hiding from him, of despising his sufferings and ignoring his cries. This he had not done (v. 24). Christ was to experience this sense of abandonment in effecting our salvation and in this way identifying himself, not just with David but with all he came to call 'my brothers,' hence the quotation of verse 22 in Hebrews 2:11.

Verses 25-26: Feasting with the people
David's imagination now fixes, not on his sufferings, but on the sacrificial feast of thanksgiving he will hold with his followers when all this over. This expectation he sees as a kind of vow which he will fulfill when his deliverance is complete.

Verses 27-31: Enlarging the vision
Here is the real significance of the whole experience. It is not just a personal trauma out of which God delivers, such as might happen to any one of us. David was the anointed king, whose task was to succeed where Saul had failed and establish God's reign through Israel over all those places promised to them in the time of Moses and Joshua (Exod. 23:31;

Josh. 21:43-44). This indeed David would accomplish and bequeath to Solomon (1 Kings 4:21). But as David typified the Messiah in his sufferings, so here he typifies him in the glory of his universal kingdom. This theme David would take up at his coronation (Ps. 2) and then that of his son and successor Solomon (Ps. 72).

Questions:

(1) Should we feel guilty when our prayer begins with 'Why?'? (See Hab. 1:3, 13 and Jer. 14:8-9.) Look up 'Why?' in a concordance and notice how often Jeremiah put this question to God.

(2) When God seems absent, how helpful is it to recall past times when God was present? (See Ps. 44; Heb. 11.)

(3) Do we relate our prayers for our personal needs to the universal purpose of God? In what order did Christ teach us to put these two concerns? (See Matt. 6:9-13.)

Psalm 23

David Shepherds his Sheep

This best-known and loved of all psalms is ascribed to David and reflects his early life as a shepherd. In these six verses he gives us a full picture of the shepherd's daily round: walking, resting, feeding, facing danger, celebrating and returning home. Uppermost in David's mind is the question, 'I do all this for my sheep, but who looks after me?' Answer: 'the Lord is my shepherd – all I do for my sheep he does for me.' We could call this psalm, 'The shepherd's Shepherd.'

All this came from an obscure youth engaged in the lowliest of occupations (1 Sam. 16:11), yet his relationship with God exceeded that of all his contemporaries – rather like the kitchen-hand Brother Lawrence, whose spirituality surpassed that of all the brothers in his community, and has come down to us in his 'Practice of the Presence of God'. What an encouragement to us to know that our closeness to God does not depend on our position in society!

Being such an important psalm, it is worthy of greater space than some many times its length.

In verse 1 David is affirming his confidence in the all-sufficient God. It is this that directs him to the shepherd analogy, for a shepherd provides total care for all time for those in his charge. A mother provides total care for her baby for a short time and a father and a mother partial care for a longer time. But from birth to death sheep are totally dependent on the shepherd, who does everything for them, as the remaining verses show. This is what God is to each believer, for the words are not 'our' shepherd but *my* shepherd, a phrase apparently used by only one other – Jacob (Gen. 48:15). To David God was the one who 'performs all things for me' (Ps. 57:2 KJV). Only this kind of relationship to God can give contentment for the present and confidence for the future, enabling one to say *I shall not be in want*.

The ministries performed by the all-sufficient God follow.

Verses 2-3a: Restoration
The resting in verse 2a and the refreshment in verse 2b are in order to revive the strength of the sheep who have spent several hours walking in search of pasture and then grazing when they have found it. The shepherd finds them a cool place to rest and a well or pool from which to drink, to refresh them before their return journey. This gives a picture of the godly life as a journey, which consists of searching for spiritual food, serving the Lord in the activities of daily life and battling against sin, the world and the devil. The Lord knows about this, gives his sheep peace of mind (Phil. 4:7) and refreshes them with the waters of his grace (John 4:13-14).

Verse 3b: Guidance
After grazing and resting, the sheep have to find their way home. But sheep have no sense of direction, do not recognize landmarks and have to be led. The shepherd performs this ministry also. God's people need guidance, not just in matters like careers and marriage, but in how to live day by day, which is what the paths of righteousness are, cf. Prov. 3:5f; Eph. 2:10. For believers, a righteous life is the way home (Matt. 7:13-14).

Verse 4: Protection
The road home may pass through difficult and dangerous places, such as the valley of the shadow of death, or 'deep darkness', probably a ravine near Bethlehem from which the light was almost completely shut out. It was rough and stony with cracks and crevices below, and rocks and caves on either side from which beasts or bandits could jump out

with no warning. But the sheep had no fear of evil, since their shepherd was with them. If they stuck in a crevice his crook (*rod*) could lift them out; if they were attacked his club (*staff*) would beat off the attacker. The God who saves us from our past sins does not leave us to face the troubles of life on our own. He does not miraculously enable us to avoid them (Acts 14:22), but each one of us can say *you are with me* in them (Isa. 43:2; Heb. 13:5).

Verse 5: Victory
Some think the shepherd metaphor has given way to that of a traveller entertained by a Bedouin, since sheep don't sit at a table or drink from a cup! The Bible however is not beyond mixing its metaphors! Perhaps the sheep are being treated like guests at a banquet. Be that as it may, this is a celebration meal after surviving the ordeal. They are almost gloating over their enemies who are looking on enviously but dare do nothing while the shepherd is with them with his club. The God who allows us to pass through trials (v. 4) assures us of victory over them (Rom. 8:35-39), so that we can live in a constant state of rejoicing (Phil. 4:4).

Verse 6: Assurance
Leupold (p. 210) argues that all the verbs apart from verse 5b should be rendered as futures. Nowhere is the future stronger than here, for it encompasses our whole future – the rest of our lives and our life hereafter. The sheep have now survived the hardest part of the journey home and it is all downhill from here. A believer's deliverance in a particularly hard time gives him the assurance he will triumph over whatever lies ahead, for his God has proved his faithfulness. Even death cannot take us away from him – in fact it is the door into our eternal home (John 14:2).

Question:
Look through Jesus's teaching on himself as *the good shepherd* (John 10:14-30) and see the points at which he fulfills all this and the points at which he even exceeds it.

Psalm 24

How to Worship the God
Who Dwells Among Us

The reference to 'the hill of the LORD (and) ... his holy place' indicate that what is in view here is the tabernacle with the ark of the covenant, which David brought in after he had established himself in Jerusalem (2 Sam. 6:17). David is teaching the people how to approach the God who dwelt there. The tabernacle and later the temple was the place where the priests would offer him sacrifices and the people would come to worship him. Although they had been in the land nearly three and a half centuries, the appointed place of worship had never been permanently established. The ark had moved from place to place and the worship of God had been neglected for long periods. Priests and people alike needed to know how to ascend the hill of the Lord. The fact that we live under a different covenant and with a long tradition of Christian worship does not mean we have nothing to learn from all this.

Verses 1-2: Know the God whom you worship
He is the One who made the earth and everything in it (v. 1), all the beauty we behold and the fruit we enjoy. There are not separate gods for seas, rivers, mountains, trees, etc. This is why Paul quoted this verse when he told the Corinthians they could eat 'food offered to idols' with a good conscience

(1 Cor. 10:25-26). To abstain would imply these idols had reality and power. He qualified this in verse 28 to allow for a Christian present at the meal who lacked this understanding and would offend his conscience if he ate. God caused the earth to rise from the waters (v. 2, Gen. 1:9-10), thus asserting his control over them too. There is no Poseidon to stir up floods or bring calm, no rain god to appease in time of drought. The God of the ark is the one universal God.

Verses 3-6: Know how to approach this God

The Israelite priest came up the hill to Zion, ascended the steps and stood in the holy place where the ark was. Christians who are all priests of God have a spiritual concept of a God who is Spirit and invisible, ubiquitous not local (John 4:24), but we must search ourselves to see if we are fit to approach such a God. Because we believe in 'public worship' and our services are open to all, this does not mean that all who take part are coming to God and finding acceptance with him. What was required of Israel is required of us: purity in thought, word and deed (v. 4a) and loyalty to the one God (v. 4b).

Verses 5-6 may seem to suggest that we qualify for this by our character and deeds. But even those under the old covenant knew their approach must be preceded by a blood sacrifice and they must look to the God who is our Saviour. We are clearer than they were that our acceptability is through Christ's blood, and our fit state of heart is the work of the Holy Spirit. The blessing of finding acceptance is from God's grace, and the vindication comes from Christ's righteousness imputed to us and our sin imputed to him (2 Cor. 5:21). Our contribution is to *seek him ... seek* (his) *face*, that is, behold him by faith and be accepted. We must be acceptable to God before our worship can be.

Verses 7-10: Know how to worship this God

With these words the ark entered the city. The *gates ... ancient doors* were those set up by the Jebusites who had built Jerusalem (or 'Salem' as it then was, Gen. 14:18). Thus God is seen as a conqueror taking possession of his enemy's capital and entering it in triumph. Paul saw Christ's enthronement in heaven as the fulfilment of this (Eph. 4:8 quoting Ps. 68:18). It complements verses 1-2: the God we worship is not only Lord of all created things below, but of all the powers above. In a fallen rebellious universe he still reigns; those who captured us he has captured in order to set us free (Col. 1:13-15). Worship offered only to a creating God is inadequate; it must centre around our redeemer and his redemption.

Questions:

(1) When you pray privately or worship publicly do you spend time considering the One to whom you are coming? Look again at the structure of the Lord's prayer (Matt. 6:9-13).

(2) Do you also take time to examine your own heart and life in order to come in a right frame of mind to such a God? (See 1 Cor. 11:28-32.)

(3) Do you always base your approach to God on the person of Christ and his saving work on the cross? (See Heb. 10:19-22.)

Psalm 25

David Seeks God's Wise Guidance

This psalm, like many others, comes from a time when David was under threat from his enemies (v. 2) These were not necessarily foreigners, for in the latter part of his reign his son Absalom turned against him and drew many people on to his side. David was always determined that, come what may, he would maintain his godliness. To do so in such circumstances required clear direction from God. So the emphasis of Psalm 25 is on the guidance of God, who alone can show him the best way to proceed.

This probably explains the structure of the composition, which is 'acrostic' or alphabetical, each verse beginning with a different Hebrew letter in alphabetical order. This is a device used in 'Wisdom' literature. The Epilogue to Proverbs (31:10-31) employs it, as do six other psalms: 34, 37, 111, 112, 119 and 145, plus 9 and 10 if considered as a single composition. It is a method that gives them a certain memorability, along with comprehensiveness: the A to Z of wisdom. Thus, while it arises from a certain occasion, the psalm has abiding relevance.

This one falls into three sections, marked by the change from second to third person singular in verse 8 and then back to second person in verse 16.

Verses 1-7: David brings his needs to God

In the opening section he is addressing God personally: *to you, O Lord, I lift up my soul* (v. 1). He begins by re-affirming his trust (v. 2a), which is based on his close relationship with him: *MY God* (emphasis mine). The covenant promise behind this expression comes again in verse 14.

What a good way to begin a string of requests, showing us how important is the way we open our times of prayer! He asks God for three things:

First, that he may prevail over his enemies. The negative *nor let my enemies triumph over me* implies the positive. His chief concern is of being put to shame, which is not to be seen as fear for his own reputation, but concern that the whole foundation of his reign and the nation's godly basis would be overthrown. For it had come to a contest between God and evil (exposed in the immorality in his own family) and between God and idols (see 16:3-4).

Having reasserted his resolution (in Ps. 16) and put his trust in God here, he can confidently expect an affirmative answer to his prayer (v. 3). Because his hope is in the Lord, he and those with him will not be put to shame. It is the treacherous without excuse – those who have turned against him and his God (and theirs) in full knowledge that he and God both hate false gods – who will be put to shame.

Second, that God will guide him in his (God's) *ways ... paths* (vv. 4-5). He is not expecting a miraculous victory, such as God had granted when foreign powers invaded. He knows he will have to take a hand in dealing with the situation. His problem is that he does not know how to do this and deperately needs some light. Most of all he wants to act according to God's will, in accordance with his truth. If this should not be forthcoming he has no Plan B. God is his Saviour and his hope is in him all the day long, that is, he has no other to turn to at any time.

Third, that God will forgive his own sins (vv. 6-7). He is aware that he who must discipline his sons and citizens for their misconduct is himself not free from the sins of youth and rebellious ways. Although God had truly forgiven him for the Bathsheba-Uriah episode, he had warned him that he would reap what he had sown (2 Sam. 12:10-12). Those verses show this is only the beginning of the harvest. So he has to ask now that God will moderate this with mercy and love. This he can ask with some confidence, since God covenanted his *love ... from of old*. He is only asking for what God has promised and what suits his character.

Verses 8-15: David is sure of God's guidance

Apart from verse 11 this passage is couched in the third person singular. It is not supplication but affirmation. We may therefore assume God has given David the assurance he needs of forgiveness, guidance and ultimate victory. He now turns this into a proclamation of the ways of the Lord in verses 8-10 (*way* features in each of these verses). These ways derive from God's character as good and upright. The word therefore shows that the things for which David has prayed must have been granted, since God acts consistently with what he is in his character. So he will give David the guidance he needs (v. 9), he will deliver his covenant child (v. 10), and he will forgive his sins (v. 11). For this last assertion David reverts to the prayer mode by using the second person singular, as if he dare not presume it, partly because he is humble (v. 9) before God, and partly because his *iniquity ... is great* (adultery and murder are not peccadilloes).

Having received this assurance, he can now offer it to others (vv. 12-15). Whoever is of his mind – the man who fears the Lord – can be sure he too will be instructed in the way chosen for him (v. 12), whatever it be. He can count on receiving the blessings of God and on passing them on to his descendants (v. 13). But there is more! He will be admitted to God's 'confidential counsel' (v. 14), which is at the heart of his covenant (v. 15). For, while there were those who only knew the Sinai covenant, which granted tenure of the land to those who kept its laws, there were also those who knew the covenant of grace, the intimate knowledge of him who was their God (Jer. 31:33-34). Paul draws this distinction in Romans 2:28-29 and 9:6. It is fulfilled in the disciples of Jesus when he calls us not his *servants* but his *friends* (John 15:15). This latter thought inspires him to even greater loyalty: my eyes are ever on the LORD (v. 15), which expresses both concentration and expectation. His present troubles are like a snare, causing both pain and immobility; but *he will release my feet* – but only he.

Verses 16-21: David prays more earnestly

He reverts to the second person singular and to prayer. This may sound as though he has lost the assurance of verses 8-15 and become disheartened. Not so. Assurance is not euphoria, though the two are often confused. Euphoria can be an irrational condition (as in the manic side of manic depression), but assurance looks the situation full in the face. David here is facing facts, not giving way to despair. He is lonely and afflicted (v. 16), having discovered that many in his family and nation do not share his godly aspirations. Since he takes this seriously, *the troubles of* (his) *heart* (are) *multiplied* (v. 17), and he is in *anguish ... affliction and ... distress* (v. 18). He accepts that he is partly to blame because of his sins. His enemies have increased and their hatred has become more fierce (v. 19).

But he is not lying down under all this; he is falling on his knees in prayer: *turn to me and be gracious to me ... free me ... look upon* (me) *... see*. To bring troubles to God is not to give way to despair, it is to exercise faith and hope. It shows not lack of assurance but expectation of great changes. Prayer is not the whingeing of a wimp but, as Tertullian put it, 'assaulting the throne of heaven like an army besieging a castle'.

So, having asked the Lord to take note of his affairs, he now petitions him, as he did at the beginning: 'Guard my life' from the assassin, 'rescue me' from the conspirators, *let me not be put to shame* by allowing ungodliness to triumph. That David's faith is as strong as when he wrote verses 8-15 is clear from what follows: *I take refuge in you* (v. 20). He is 'venturing on God', as Christians used to put it, casting aside all other props and trusting God alone. He is going to persevere in *integrity* and *uprightness*, believing God will protect him as he does so. The final line of verse 21 is characteristic of the spirit of the psalm: *my hope is in you*. If that is not an expression of assured faith, what is?

Verse 22
Verse 22 lies outside the acrostic pattern and was probably added when what was essentially a personal psalm was included in the corpus for public worship. What applied to the king applied equally to the people.

Questions:
(1) How can complete forgiveness of sin be consistent with the idea that it still has consequences? (See Gal. 6:7-8.)

(2) What principles of guidance do you deduce from this psalm?

(3) Do your prayers spring from assurance or desperation?

Psalm 26

David Examines Himself Before God

The theme of this psalm is strikingly similar to Psalm 1, for David is concerned about the company he keeps. Look at verses 4-5 and compare them with Psalm 1:1. However, the two psalms are by no means identical, as we shall see by looking in more detail.

Verses 1-5 show the struggle David is having to avoid ungodly company. The opening word Vindicate betrays a certain amount of tension in the matter. The atmosphere of freedom and joy which Psalm 1 breathes is noticeably lacking here. Evidently his resolution to avoid ungodly company (Ps. 1:1) is not going down well in his social circle. Perhaps people feel he is judging them, which if he was still a youth they consider precocious.

What should he do then? Loosen up and join the deceitful, the hypocrites, the evildoers and the wicked? He cannot do this. Nor, as a youth, is he in a position to have a stand-up debate with these people. So he turns the matter over to God – something that was to characterise his attitude to hostility throughout his tempestuous career. He tells God that as far as he knows he has lived blamelessly (v. 1), which does not mean sinlessly, but rather that he has not followed the example of the wicked. Nor has he done this of himself, but through trust in God.

However, recognising that we tend to be inaccurate in our self-image, he is prepared for the Lord to *test*, *try* and *examine* him (v. 2). Knowing he is an ever-loving God (v. 3), he has nothing to fear from this. He feels confident God will find he has been walking continually in his truth and resisting the temptation to renege on his resolution about the company he keeps (vv. 4-5).

Verses 6-8 take us on from what he has not been doing to what he is doing. He prefers to be praising God in his house to carousing in the assembly of evildoers. The references to God's altar (v. 6), his house (v. 8) and the great assembly (v. 12) may refer to a possible use of Bethlehem as a place of worship while the ark was residing at Shiloh. Or they may refer to some other place to which the people resorted for special festivals. This brings out another difference from Psalm 1 – David is not meditating quietly under a tree by a stream, but is back in his home town participating in worship.

Verses 9-10 show us that being back among the people makes him even more conscious of the ungodly state of many of his fellow-Israelites. For, notwithstanding the efforts of Samuel and his fellow-prophets, sin among the people of God was far from stamped out. The atmosphere of the period of the Judges still hung over the nation (Judg. 21:25). Saul did not support Samuel in his attempts at reforming the nation, nor encourage the Levites in their teaching and leading of worship. The Philistines were still a serious threat and the people were not uninfluenced by their Canaanite religion.

But David had not forgotten the thought that came to him while tending his flock and watching the chaff blowing around in a nearby farm (Ps. 1:6). He remains convinced that whatever kings, prophets and priests do or do not do, God will deal with those who murder (v. 9), conspire (v. 10a) or act corruptly (v. 10b). His concern is lest he himself, by consorting with them, is judged with them (v. 9).

Verses 11-12 show him even more resolute to preserve his integrity in view of the powerful influence of society and its imminent judgment by God. His resolution is not only about morality (v. 11) but also spirituality (v. 12). Even his feet are involved! The contrast between the rough ground he normally trod as a shepherd and the floor of the house of God he was or had been standing on have strengthened his determination to be true to God, no matter who is false to him.

Questions:
(1) How can we as Christians, living in the midst of ungodliness, keep a balance between spiritual pride and censoriousness on the one hand, and worldliness on the other? (Cf. 1 Cor. 5:9-11 with 2 Cor. 6:14–7:1.)

(2) Do you think the neglected practice of self-examination before or at public worship should be revived? (See 1 Cor. 11:28; 2 Cor. 13:5.)

Psalm 27

David Growing in Confidence

This is another psalm composed when David is seeking deliverance from his enemies (vv. 2-3). In this situation he focuses his thoughts on his relationship with God (v. 4). So the confidence with which he begins (v. 1), is greatly strengthened by verse 13.

Verses 1-3: David is confident in God
This is one of the greatest expressions of confidence in God in the whole Bible, perhaps only surpassed by Romans 8:28-39. David had been saved from an army of evil men who were advancing toward him like a pack of hunting animals (v. 2). But they had been stopped in their tracks. David sees the Lord's hand in this: it was light in the darkness, salvation from certain destruction (v. 1). After this he feels there is nothing he need fear, even an outbreak of war, even a siege (v. 3) Nothing could be more dangerous than the situation from which he had just escaped. If God could save him from that he could save him from anything.

Verses 4-6: David rededicates himself
This long period of David's weakness and vulnerability was serving a good purpose: it was strengthening his faith. Having no other to protect him he was cast totally on God. Now he is reaping the fruit of that trust in this remarkable providence.

Its effect is not to make him relax into complacency and worldliness, but the opposite – to give him a desire to live more completely with God. References to *the house of the* LORD *... his temple ... his dwelling ... his tabernacle* are not to be taken literally (who would want to LIVE there?). They are metaphors for living close to God. Psalm 23, written out in the fields with the sheep, ended with the desire to *dwell in the house of the* LORD *for ever*, which no one takes to mean David aspired to the office of priest everlastingly; everyone interprets it spiritually. So it is with these verses: he wanted to be near God in his spirit. This is what his experiences of danger had taught him.

Here David is really ahead of his time, virtually living under the new covenant, seeing him who is greater than the temple, through whom we dwell in God (John 14:20) and in whom the beauty of the Lord is revealed (John 1:14, 18).

Verses 7-12: David returns to prayer

David knows he is not out of the wood: his enemies will return and David would not be any stronger when he came back. Everything depended on God continuing his providential care. David cannot assume this will be automatically forthcoming; he must continue to ask for it.

He asks for this in several different ways, which all amount to the same thing, but show the depth of his need. First, (v. 7) he prays that God will simply *hear* ... and *answer*. Then, (vv. 8-9) that he won't hide (his) face, that is, he won't turn away from him. If the NIV margin is right on verse 8, David is quoting God's own words as his authority: HE has said, 'Seek my face' (emphasis mine), probably with Deuteronomy 4:29 in mind.

Next he asks God not to *reject* ... or *forsake* him (v. 9b), that he will not leave him on his own, as his parents have done (v. 10). This is not intended as a slur on them, since David himself had left them with the king of Moab (1 Sam. 22:3-4) and would not have wanted them exposed to the danger he was in. The idea is that, whereas he can no longer depend on his parents, he is always God's child, dependent on him. This is the assurance he expresses here: *the* LORD *will receive me*.

Further, he prays God will keep him in his way (v. 11). *Because of* (his) *oppressors* he is not only in physical but spiritual and moral danger of being knocked off God's straight path. David is aware that fear and despair are very wearing and can make a godly person careless about his whole life. His enemies wanted to see David discredited before the nation and the world. So, though they were called away, they were keeping up the pressure of the propaganda. Verse 12 shows how aware David was of this and how he prayed against it.

Verses 13-14: David encourages his people

Having got his own thinking straight, he is able to make a clear statement to his company. First, he expresses his own confidence (v. 13), for there is nothing the people of God need more in a leader than firm trust in God, which is of more value than any amount of skill or charisma. The Hebrew of verse 13 is an incomplete sentence: 'Unless I had believed ...' He is underlining the bottom line – his belief that through the goodness of the Lord he would remain in the land of the living. On this basis he encourages the people to join him in waiting for the Lord, that is, not acting rashly either by giving up altogether or by lashing out wildly. The latter might seem like strength but is the opposite. To be strong in heart comes from dependence on God.

Questions:
(1) Refer to verses 1-3 in which David reasons that if God can do the greater he can do the less; how are we Christians even better placed to use this argument? (See Rom. 8:31-32.)

(2) How do we react to a great deliverance in answer to prayer? Do we pray less or more? (See Luke 18:1; Rom. 12:12; 1 Thess. 5:17.)

(3) What quality do you look for most in your spiritual leaders? (See Heb. 11:1-2, 13:7.)

Psalm 28

David Sustains His Confidence

This psalm shows that David's troubles are continuing, even increasing; but so is the confidence he expressed in Psalm 27.

Verses 1-2: David continues in prayer

His triumph of faith over fear in 27 does not mean David could relax his praying. He is now in danger of death (v. 1). Even if he did not actually die (for he says *like*) God's silence would be tantamount to death, for he would be taking no more notice of him than of a dead man. In fact God's silence would indicate that he had rejected David, for the pit is not just the grave, but a deep hole where the disgraced would be put out of reach.

This explains the earnestness of his prayer: he needs both mercy and help and his hands are outstretched in the direction of the place where the ark of God was. *Most Holy Place* does not imply the temple was already built; the little room which came to bear that name was not Most Holy in itself, but only because it contained the ark where the Lord resided.

Verses 3-5: David appeals for God's justice

Mention of the *Most Holy Place* seems to bring to his mind the covenant which the ark symbolised, since it contained the *book of the covenant* (Exod. 25:21; Heb. 9:4). This was what marked the difference between David and his enemies: while he was keeping its terms they were breaking them. Since he dissociated himself from them in life, why should God *drag* (him) *away* with them in death (v. 3)? It would be injustice, out of keeping with God's character. They might appear outwardly friendly, but their hearts harboured malice. Let God show justice to David by saving him from these enemies, and to them by carrying out the curses of the covenant (v. 4). For they weren't just acting against David but against God himself (v. 5). Once again David speaks with the Spirit of prophecy as he declares God's curse on them (v. 5b).

Verses 6-7: David is sure God has heard
The Spirit of prophecy by whom he had cursed his enemies now becomes a Spirit of assurance by whom he praises God. In a sense he is still in prophetic mode: whereas he had predicted ruin for his enemies in verses 4-5, he predicts salvation for himself: *he has heard my cry for mercy ... I am helped ... I will give thanks to him*. With this assurance he pours out his thanks, affirms his trust and leaps for joy – all fruits of the same Spirit.

Verses 8-9: David speaks as King of God's people
Do we wonder why so much is made of one man's troubles? Surely there were others, even among David's contemporaries, who were victims of injustice? Yet it is mainly David the Bible concerns itself with, mainly his prayers and complaints that form the main body of the Book of Psalms. Here we see the reason: David was God's anointed one; the fortunes of Israel were tied to his fortunes. If the Lord were David's strength (*my Rock*, v. 1), he would be the strength of his people. So he ends by praying for them, for God to save ... and bless ... and carry them as their shepherd. Here, intentionally or otherwise, the psalm becomes Messianic, for *anointed one* is literally 'Messiah', the one whose office it was to *save ... and bless* those God gave him as his inheritance (John 17:2), the *good Shepherd* who would give his life for his sheep (John 10:11).

Questions:
(1) Do you find Christians today are failing to persevere in prayer? If so, why do you think this is? What can David teach us?

(2) If David's praying was moved by the Old Covenant, how can we find encouragement in the New Covenant?

(3) Why do not 'Christians' today have the unity that seemed to exist under the Old Covenant, which enabled believers to be spoken of collectively as 'his inheritance'?

Psalm 29

In a Storm

This psalm was written either during a thunderstorm or when one was still fresh in the mind. In Israel the chief rainy period occurred in the seventh month, Tisri (see 84:6). This month was also the highlight of the festal year. It was the first month of the civil year and was believed by Israel to be the month when creation occurred (see the reference to creation in v. 10). The tenth day of the month was the great Day of Atonement, followed on the fifteenth day by the Feast of Tabernacles. On the first day the Feast of Trumpets acted as a summons to prepare the people for what lay ahead. The opening verses of the psalm suggest a special gathering for worship led by the priests. Perhaps on this occasion the storm had actually coincided with the feast.

Verses 1-2: The God of glory
The call is going out to those conducting the service to *ascribe to the* LORD *... glory and strength*. The call may go even higher, for *mighty ones* or 'sons of God' can mean not only rulers (82:6) but angels (89:5-7). Human praises at their best are inadequate to give such a God as is in view here the glory due to his name, the glory he deserves. So we seek the assistance of angels, as in the well-known hymn:

Ye holy angels bright, who wait at God's right hand ...
Assist our song, or else the theme too high doth seem
For mortal tongue.

(Richard Baxter)

Even less are we equipped to worship a God of holiness, whose dazzling splendour silences rather than loosens our tongues.

Verses 3-9: The God of glory speaks

Whatever is happening inside the tabernacle, from outside there comes a loud crack of thunder which only adds to the thought of God's holiness. It begins out at sea, over the waters (v. 3), so it may be imaginary, since the sea was a long way from Jerusalem. Ever since God spoke on Sinai, thunder had been seen as the voice of the Lord (Exod. 19:16-19). The God whom the trumpets were calling the people to worship was speaking in awesome reality (v. 4).

And he was getting nearer and nearer. There is devastation on Lebanon and Hermon (Sirion) (vv. 5-6), which were near the sea. Next he can be seen in the flashes of lightning (v. 7). For the storm is travelling through the land right down to the desert of Kadesh (v. 8), where Israel had halted on their journey from Sinai to Canaan. We can almost feel the sand and dust of the desert stinging our faces as the Lord shakes it. By contrast, in the forests we witness mighty oaks being split in two or torn up by the roots as lightning strikes them (v. 9).

Terrifying? Then why the response inside the tabernacle with people crying, *Glory*? The answer is in –

Verses 10-11: The God of Glory blesses

The storm as the voice of God recalls not only Sinai but *the flood* (v. 10). This may refer to the great Flood of Genesis 6–9, over which God presided, but more likely it means the waters which covered the earth at Creation, where *the Lord* (sat) *enthroned as King* (Gen. 1:2). On that occasion he brought everything to order, creating this vast, varied and beautiful earth out of that chaos. So the God whose voice is heard in the thunder was coming not to strike fear into his people but to give them assurance. The strength released in the storm is the *strength* (he gives) *to his people*. Whatever fears they have, of elements or enemies, are calmed: he *blesses his people with peace*.

Questions:

(1) Many Christians are dumb-struck at a time of open worship or prayer, but is this ever due to a sense of awe in the presence of the holy God? (See Hab. 2:20.)

(2) What do we learn about God from the convulsions in nature: floods, storms, earthquakes, volcanoes? (See Heb. 4:12-13.)

(3) Does the voice of God speaking through his word give you assurance, strength and peace? (See Isa. 26:3-4.)

Psalm 30

David's Recovery

David is here giving thanks for his recovery from illness, but this does not appear to fit the title. However, shortly before the dedication of the temple David had conducted a census of his fighting men. This displeased God and he punished them with a plague (1 Chron. 21). Through David's intercession the plague ceased at Araunah's threshing floor, and this was chosen as the site for the temple (1 Chron. 22:1). When David dedicated it he recalled the suffering brought on by the plague. Possibly he himself had been afflicted by it, or he so identified with the people that he felt it for them.

Alternatively, 'temple' may be translated 'house', referring to David's palace (NIV mg). If David had been ill of the plague his house would have been shut up; and on his recovery he rededicated the house.

Verses 1-3: Answered Prayer

God had done for David the two things he had asked (v. 1): he brought him back from death's door, lifted him from the depths (like a bucket drawn up from the bottom of a well); and also silenced the glee of his enemies over his imminent demise. Although his recovery had seemed unlikely at the time, in retrospect it was all quite simple: David had prayed and God had answered (v. 2). But he could not forget what a 'close-run thing' it had been (v. 3): he was on the very edge of the pit of Sheol (the grave), that abode of darkness where the dead cannot praise God (v. 9; 6:5; 88:11). This reflects the limited knowledge of the after life which was revealed to people of Old Testament times. It was this God had spared him and from which he had *brought* (him) *up*.

Verses 4-5: Corporate praise
The call to the people generally to join him in the praise of God's holy name (v. 4), might seem to favour the connection with the plague of 1 Chronicles 21, but since David was king, his health was a matter of major importance to the nation, as the monarch's health still is with us in spite of the curtailment of royal power. His recovery therefore was a cause of general rejoicing.

Verse 5 reflects a beautiful attitude towards God: *his anger* is like an overnight visitor who remains for a night, whereas *his favour* is like a permanent resident. *Weeping* is something to which we soon say 'Goodbye', like the lodger; but rejoicing in his favour lasts a lifetime.

Verses 6-7: Complacency recalled
In any case there had been a reason for God's anger – David's false sense of security, possibly because of his census of the army. God has frequently warned us not to trust in our earthly prosperity but in him (e.g. Jer. 22:21). We should avoid letting prosperity breed carelessness, just as we should not let adversity breed carefulness, in the sense of anxiety. For David this lesson was learned very painfully, for *dismayed* is a word containing the idea of terror. David faced the gaping black hole of death for himself, plus the prospect of an evil regime taking over his people. God did not let it happen and David learned never to say *I shall never be shaken* (v. 6).

Verses 8-10: Mercy sought
Recalling the terror of his experience brought back to mind the prayer he had prayed in his extremity, and how it had been motivated by his concern for God's glory. What was there for God in his death? Who would there be to inspire others to

praise him and proclaim his faithfulness (v. 9)? But he was not
relying on his high motives, only on God's mercy (vv. 8, 10).

Verses 11-12: Joy restored
David proves how sincere was the motive he had professed
in verse 9. Now he was healed he would not be like the
nine lepers healed by Jesus (Luke 17:11-19), but would use
his restored powers to *sing* (and) *give thanks* to God. This he
would express in every way possible: silencing his *wailing*
and taking up *dancing*; casting off his mourning clothes and
putting on clothes fit for celebration. When he had done this
on a former occasion (2 Sam. 6:16) Michal had despised it as
mere animal spirits. But it had not been then, and it was not
now. *Heart* (v. 12), is literally 'glory', the glorious faculty God
has given humans to worship him by using our powers of
voice and limbs to express our joy in him and admiration for
his greatness. David's dancing did just this.

Questions:
(1) Do we have the simplicity of the faith that believes God's
promise to answer prayer (v. 2)? cf. Matthew 21:22?

(2) Compare verse 5 with 2 Corinthians 4:17. Consider how
much better equipped we are with our clearer view of death
and the hereafter.

(3) How can we avoid becoming complacent in prosperity
and anxious in adversity? (See Matt. 6:25-34; Phil. 4:12-13.)

Psalm 31

In the Shelter of His Presence

This psalm comes from another occasion when David appeared to be at the mercy of his enemies, possibly when he was being pursued by Saul. In verse 4 he speaks of being 'trapped', possibly in a town with 'gates and bars' such as Keilah (1 Sam. 23:7, cf. *a besieged city*, v. 21). From this he seeks to be led to a place of safety. The psalm reflects the tension of one who feels he has a responsibility to keep his people calm and confident but must first get himself into that frame of mind. Gradually the tension is relieved until in the closing verses he is able to resume his ministry of encouragement.

No doubt this is why the psalm has been so meaningful to others who have ministered to God's people. Jonah alluded to verse 6 in Jonah 2:8 and Jeremiah to verse 13 in Jeremiah 6:25; 20:3, 10; 46:5; 49:5 – how similar was his experience to David's at this time! The same psalm was probably in Paul's mind when he spoke of the treatment he received in places like Ephesus (2 Cor. 7:5). Our Lord quoted verse 5 with his dying breath (Luke 23:46), and Stephen followed his example in Acts 7:59. Henry Lyte wrote a hymn based on verse 15 which has been precious to Christian leaders. There is also a delightful hymn by Ellen Goreh based on verse 20: 'In the secret of his presence how my soul delights to hide', which seems to have dropped out of our modern collections.

Verses 1-8: David's peace comes under great tension

These verses set the scene: David asserts that his trust is not in a mountain fortress but in *you, O Lord*, as his *refuge ... rock ... fortress* (vv. 1-3). But he is struggling to rest in this faith: the cries of verses 1b, 2a, 3b and 4 reflect the tension in him. But peace seems to triumph in verse 5 – he is in the hands of the God of truth, who will not break his word. Strengthened by this he renounces all temptation to idolatry (v. 6). In those days superstition was rife and it was hard to hold to the bare promise of an unseen God. But having resolved on it, he enjoys its fruit: a note of joy enters in (v. 7a) as he remembers how God has been true to him in his previous straits. He feels glad now he is not shut up in a walled city like Keilah but is in a spacious place (v. 8).

However, it's one thing to attain peace of mind, another to sustain it when under strain, as we now see.

Verses 9-13: The tension breaks

It's no good – he cannot restrain himself. He has been bottling up his many woes and now the cork blows off the bottle under too great pressure. Under the calm exterior, which was perhaps put on lest the whole company fall apart, is a soul in distress (v. 9). He is not just a man who needs re-assurance, he is a weak creature who needs pity: *be merciful to me*.

He has in fact been full of fears within, like Paul in 2 Corinthians 7:5. His sorrow of heart was intense (vv. 9-10). He was like a sick man if he was not one literally: his *eyes ... body ... strength ... bones* were all feeling the strain. Groaning was putting years on him and he felt prematurely aged.

As well as the ' fears within' were the 'fightings without': the campaign conducted by his enemies was so vigorous that he was totally isolated. Former neighbours and friends now held him in contempt and even dread (v. 12). They did not want to know him (v. 11); he was as though dead (v. 12), as much use as an old broken pot. So successful had Saul's campaign of slander been that he was fighting on all fronts (v. 13); there was no end to the plotting and conspiring. Who would not break under such a strain? Yet he still held to the faith he had confessed at the beginning which now receives its reward.

Verses 14-18: David recovers his trust

The cork may have blown off but he has not lost his bottle! A great wave of assurance sweeps over him; like John Wesley he 'feels his heart strangely warmed', he feels 'I did trust God' (v. 14). *I say 'you are my God'* says it all. If the one supreme being, the Lord of all, the God in covenant with Israel, was his, everything else fell into place. Whatever the times – good times, bad times, any of those times listed by the Teacher in Ecclesiastes 3 – they were *in your hands*, the hands of the one to whom he committed himself in verse 5. If he himself was in God's hands, so were his times.

Now he can go on the offensive and take up the weapon of prayer again. He is not powerful enough to fight his enemies, but he can pray against them, which he does, interspersed with requests for continued deliverance from them. These prayers are similar to those in 52, 120, 86 and need no further comment.

Verses 19-22: David's spirit rises to adoration

He is like a man who has got a heavy load off his chest. The outbursts of the two previous passages were necessary – psychologically and spiritually. They have cleared the air. His thoughts and words are now like the rarefied air he is breathing in the mountains. His eyes are no longer looking downwards and inwards, but upwards, to the glories of the open skies. God is not only goodness in himself, but in his stores of it for those who trust him (v. 19). In the shelter of his presence there is safety from those intrigues and accusing tongues which he had bewailed in verse 13. What can he do but praise the Lord for his wonderful love (v. 21)? That love was shown when he was shut in a place such as Keilah, the besieged city, had he but known it. Now he is ashamed of having given way to fright (v. 22). Yet in a way it served his purpose, for it showed him that God hears, even when in weak fear all we can do is cry for mercy and help. Now he is fully recovered and ready to face his people.

Verses 23-24: David resumes his ministry

Now he can encourage his followers to *love the LORD ... hope in the LORD ... be strong and take hear'*, for he has the evidence that the Lord preserves the faithful and pays back the proud in full. No longer is he saying words that do not reflect his true feelings. This comes from 'a heart in every thought renewed and full of love divine' (Charles Wesley). Now he could see it was true that God did not give him into (Saul's) hands (1 Sam. 23:14).

Questions:
(1) Do you think that those who in any sense are 'encouragers' (whether parents, teachers, preachers or just friends) should hide their own inner feelings from those they encourage, or let them come out? Is it hypocritical to hide them? Would it discourage them to know that their 'betters' are just as weak as they? Or would it gain them more respect to reveal they are human too? Is the answer for the leader to keep his problems to himself until he has recovered, and then use them to show how God brings us out of the depths?

(2) If this psalm has helped so many others in positions of responsibility, even Christ himself, can you see in it the way to recover from deep depression?

Psalm 32

David Rejoices in God's Forgiveness

If Psalm 51 was David's confession of his sin, this is his joy over God's forgiveness. When David's eyes were opened to his sin by Nathan, he confessed 'I have sinned against the Lord' (2 Sam. 12:13). Psalm 51 may be seen as the full expression of that confession. As a result God forgave him: *Nathan replied, 'The LORD has taken away your sin. You are not going to die.'* God punished his adultery, chiefly through Absalom (2 Sam. 12:11-12) but not with death. Neither did he pay for the murder of Uriah with his life. However, to David forgiveness meant more than being spared punishment; it meant chiefly restoration to fellowship with God – the joy of salvation (Ps. 51:12). In the next verse he spoke of 'teaching transgressors ... turning sinners back'. This is what he is doing in Psalm 32: sharing his experience of conviction, confession and forgiveness with others who may be in a similar position. This is why it is called a *Maskil*, which probably means 'instruction'. There is nothing in which we more need instructing than repentance and forgiveness.

Verses 1-2: Forgiveness leads to God's blessing

Here David describes it in three ways: removing the threatened punishment ('forgive' is literally 'lifted'); covering the shame of one who has 'fallen short' (as 'sins' here means); and not counting against him the damage he has done to his nature and character (*sin* here has the sense of 'distortion'). What greater blessedness could there be for one who had been in David's position? But the confession, repentance and desire for forgiveness had to come from within his spirit and be utterly sincere, with no deceit. This is such a complete statement of the subject that Paul quotes it in his discussion of justification by faith in Romans 4:7-8.

Verses 3-5: Forgiveness changes one's entire nature
David vividly recalls what he had felt when he was repressing his sin and failing to face it in God's sight. Covering up his adultery by removing Uriah and taking Bathsheba to wife did not make him happy. The pleasure of their first union had gone. So great was the burden of guilt that it even affected him physically; he felt constantly exhausted.

Then came the change, perhaps emphasised by a pause, change of key or tune (*Selah*). The same three terms used in verses 1-2 appear here, showing David actually did this at the time as well as reflecting on it afterwards. He had God's own assurance through his prophet for saying *you forgave the guilt of my sin*. See 2 Samuel 12:13.

Verses 6-11: Forgiveness enlarges ministry
The first five verses should be enough to show those who were or will be in a similar state to himself the way back to God. But what of others? Prevention is better than cure. The godly can be *caught in a sin* (Gal. 6:1) unawares. For David himself this episode was against the whole tenor of his life (1 Kings 15:5). So it is the godly he addresses here: pray not to be overtaken by sin; *pray to* (God) *while* (he) *may be found*, before *the mighty waters rise* and 'the enemy (comes) in like a flood' (Isa. 59:19). He knows that when this happens, prayer and all thoughts of God go.

Nor is he asking others to do what he is not (v. 7). Now that he is restored he is continually coming to God for protection from trouble, especially when he senses the uprising of sin in his mind. When he makes God his hiding place from temptations, God surrounds him with *songs of deliverance*, he praises him for saving him from the temptation. He himself will do all he can to keep the godly *in the way* (they) *should go* (v. 8). He pledges himself to be available for counsel and care. But they must play their part (v. 9). They must be willing to hear and obey. He cannot force them in the way the horse or the mule can be controlled.

Then (v. 10) he confirms it all with a warning and a promise. Sin tastes sweet for the moment, but is bitter afterwards: it creates many woes. But trusting God and walking in his way is the road to the blessedness of which he spoke in verses 1-2. What happier experience can there be than to have the Lord's unfailing love surrounding you? So what is there to be worried or depressed about? Live in that simple way and you will rejoice ... be glad and sing all the days of your life.

Questions:

(1) Is there any evidence that unconfessed sin has mental and physical effects and that forgiveness restores health? (See vv. 3-5; Matt. 9:2.)

(2) Are you taking sufficiently seriously the exhortation of verse 6 (cf. Isa. 55:6) and the promise of 1 Corinthians 10:12?

(3) Make Wesley's hymn 'Jesus, lover of my soul' a prayer for yourself and others against the power of temptation.

Psalm 33

How to Praise God

This anonymous psalm appears to be occasioned by a military victory (vv. 16-17). This is attributed, not to the king, the generals or the army, but to the Lord's direct action out of love for his people (vv. 18-19). The occasion is used for general rejoicing in God as Creator and upholder.

Verses 1-3: The people are encouraged to praise God
Here, either the people are encouraging each other or being exhorted by the priest leading the worship. The three elements that make for a fitting act of praise to God all come together: fervency – *sing joyfully ... shout for joy*; skill in e.g. the choice and use of the most appropriate musical instruments available (v. 2); and freshness – *a new song*, since a fresh experience of God's sovereignty calls for a fresh song.

Verses 4-11: God's glory has been revealed
Verse 4 shows this is not irrational emotionalism, mere euphoria. They were not rejoicing because they had won but because God had proved himself true to his promises (v. 4) and to his righteous and loving character (v. 5). This he has shown in his general supervision of the earth, which is *full of his unfailing love*. Indeed, the God whose word of 2 Samuel 5:19 had brought about this victory was the God whose word had brought creation into being (v. 6; Gen. 1:3, etc); the God who

also keeps nature under control as easily as a man keeps water in a bottle or a tank (v. 7; Job 38:8-11). There may be an allusion to his promise after the Flood to keep the waters above and below from covering the land (Isa. 54:9).

Since he is sole creator and upholder of the earth, *all the people of the world* (should) *revere him* (v. 8). For his word has authority, not only to create and establish (v. 9) but to destroy (v. 10). Everything depends on his *plans* and *purposes*, not on the plots and schemes of men (v. 11).

Verses 12-19: God takes special care of his people

If the psalm opened with a call from the priest, this may mark the point at which the people respond to the call. All they have heard makes them glad that they have a special place in his plans and purposes, since they are *his inheritance* (v. 12). They are glad too that he is not a remote God but one very conscious of what is going on (vv. 13-14) – not only outwardly but inwardly, for he who made the heart knows its thoughts.

So he is aware of what their enemies are up to – trusting their large army, its weaponry, and especially its horses, which gave an army superiority from that time until the invention of the automatic gun (vv. 16-17). At the same time he is conscious of those who trust him (vv. 18-19), as they proved when David led them to enquire of God before either attempting to resist or surrender to the Philistines (2 Sam. 5:17-25). This faith was effective: they have been delivered from death and saved from the famine which would have resulted had they been shut up in one of their fortresses.

Verses 20-22: They renew their joyful praise

The fervent praise for which the leader called in verses 1-3 is now forthcoming. Nor is it mindless noise but based on hope and trust in the *unfailing love* which God has demonstrated.

Questions:
(1) Does the worship of the average evangelical church have the characteristics of verses 1-3, 20-22? If not, why not and what can be done about it? (See John 4:23-24; Eph. 5:18-19.)

(2) Consider the place in worship of the word of God and our knowledge of him (vv. 6-11).

(3) What can we learn from verses 12-19 about facing our 'enemies': the devil, sin and unbelief? (See 2 Cor. 10:4-5.)

Psalm 34

In Philistine Territory

First Samuel 21:10-15 recounts the background to this psalm, as the title indicates. The cynic might say David was already mad to put himself into the hands of the enemy, especially as he was the one who had inflicted heavy defeats on them and killed their champion. But David must have expected he would pass unrecognised, as he came out of uniform or armour and with a small band of unarmed servants. There is also an implied reproach to Saul in his action – that Saul was now a more dangerous adversary than Israel's national enemies. David was recognised however, and the only way of escaping imprisonment or even execution seemed to be to pretend to be insane. This would remove any fear of danger from Achish's mind and dispose him to get rid of David quickly, which is what happened. The name Abimelech in the title is probably the official or dynastic name of the Philistine kings (Gen. 26:1).

This incident may not appear to show David in the best light, but he himself saw the Lord's hand in it and learned much from it, as this psalm shows. It is one of a number of 'acrostic' psalms: the 22 verses begin with the 22 letters of the Hebrew alphabet, with the exception of the letter WAW (which is only used for the conjunction 'and' plus about three other words!).This is replaced by repeating the letter PE in verse 22. David thus took great trouble over this psalm, to aid his own memory and to make it easier to teach to others. It has indeed become one of the most popular psalms.

Verses 1-10: David worships God

David saw this episode as God's providential deliverance – from the fire as well as the frying pan (vv. 4, 6-7) and it moved him to great praise, so much that he wanted others to join him and swell the song. The extremity of his adversity and the weaknesses in himself it brought out only enhanced his praise and inspired him to commit himself to a whole life of praise (v. 1). If he could praise God at this time he could do so at all times. Boasting is not usually found on the lips of the afflicted (v. 2) or poor (v. 6), but this is in the Lord who has intervened for them (cf. Gal. 6:14). David wants his servants to share in this (v. 3) – indeed all *the afflicted* (v. 2).

Verses 4-7 go into the details of this deliverance by alternating present experience with general principles. He himself found deliverance from his *fears* through bringing them to the Lord (v. 4), as will anyone else who does so (v. 5). It will even show in their faces – *shame* will become shining ('radiant'). To emphasise this he returns to his own experience (v. 6) as a *poor man* who ventured on the Lord and was heard and spared. This attitude of *fear* (humble trust) will bring to the aid of those who need him that Being (v. 7) who came to the aid of the patriarchs, as God promised (Exod. 23:20-23; cf. Ps. 35:5-6).

On this basis he encourages his little band of followers to discover this for themselves (vv. 8-10) so that they may learn that *the LORD is good*, that those who come to him in their afflictions will be *blessed* (v. 8) and those who adopt a consistently right attitude of fear will never *lack*, even when famine strikes those creatures who through their strength and ferocity are last to go hungry ('the young lions', v. 10).

Verses 11-22: David teaches the people

He now develops what he began in verses 8-10 by adopting the mantle of the man of wisdom who gathers his pupils around him (v. 11), rather in the style of Solomon in 'Proverbs' (Prov. 1:8, etc.). Since the enjoyment of these promises depends on the attitude of fear towards God, he must instruct them in how to cultivate it.

In true didactic style he begins with a question (v. 12 – NIV is on its own among English versions in rendering this in the indicative). This is to provoke thought and encourage attention, since everyone loves life enough to *desire ... good days*. Previously he has advocated right attitude (fear the Lord, v. 9), but this must lead to action in terms of honest speech (v. 13), separation from evil, good works and good relationships (v. 14).

Instruction is accompanied by the encouragement (vv. 15-16) that those who live in this way are owned by God as the righteous and assured of his personal attention. At the same time they are spared the kind of attention God gives their opposites, the wicked. Peter quotes these verses to Christians suffering persecution (1 Pet. 3:10-12).

David takes this further in verses 17-18. For in spite of what he says in verse 15 the righteous may suffer grievously and not see many good days in human terms. Nevertheless verse 15 is still true, for the Lord compensates for their material loss by blessing them spiritually: they have greater assurance that they are still in his mind and he will hear them. They may even reach rock-bottom and be broken-hearted and crushed in spirit, yet he will still be close to them and save them (as David himself could testify).

All this he now sums up in sure promises strongly asserted. First, concerning God's dealings with the righteous: they must not expect to be exempt from troubles; but they can expect to be saved from them (v. 19). Verse 20 does not mean the righteous never suffer fractures! It becomes more meaningful in the light of John 19:36: Jesus in his extremity did not suffer the usual indignity of the crucified – breaking their legs to expedite death. So he will preserve his afflicted ones from becoming utterly contemptible, looking as if they were forsaken. The Messianic note is enhanced by the use of the words *redeemed* and *no one ... condemned*, recalling gospel language.

Second, concerning his dealings with the wicked who do not fear the Lord. The evil they perpetrate will rebound on them in this life, and thereafter they will be *condemned* (vv. 21-22) at his judgment. This means that the righteous not only escape the hands of the wicked but are also spared the judgment under which the latter fall.

Questions:
(1) How necessary is humility to effective prayer (vv. 6, 18 cf. Isa. 66:2b; Luke 18:13-17)?

(2) Do verses 4-7 teach that the balanced spiritual life is a combination of experience and principle?

(3) Is it still true under the gospel that believers have many troubles (vv. 17, 19)? (See Acts 14:22.) How are Christians to view them? (See Col. 1:24 and Peter's quotation of vv. 15-16 in 1 Pet. 3:10-12 in relation to the increased persecution of Christians.)

Psalm 35

David Prays Under Threat

This psalm is attributed to David (title) and clearly comes from a time when he had enemies who were plotting to take his life (v. 4). We know Saul had hurled a spear or javelin at him (1 Sam. 18:10-11) and this psalm may reflect that or a similar experience. In verse 3 he asks God to brandish *spear and javelin* against those who were threatening him.

Verses 1-8
Three things stand out here:

(1) David is aware he has enemies conspiring against him. He speaks of *those who contend with me ... fight against me* (v. 1), *those who pursue me* (v. 3), *those who seek my life ... plot my ruin* (v. 4). But they are not obvious enemies who come out into the open, like the Philistines, but secret ones who make plots from which they can distance themselves: *they hid their net for me ... dug a pit for me* (v. 7). He is beginning to see that Saul had not sent him to the front line to gain glory but to expose him to the danger of death. To obtain the required marriage dowry involved a high-risk enterprise (1 Sam. 18:25). What a pity David did not remember this later when he dealt with Uriah, husband of Bathsheba, in the same way (2 Sam. 11:14-15)!

(2) David brings the situation to God for him to deal with (v. 1): contend O LORD, uses law-court language, meaning 'be my advocate, give me justice'; *fight*, uses military language,

meaning 'if the dispute cannot be settled by argument and comes to blows, you fight for me, Lord.' This is developed in verses 2-3 where he asks God to take up both defensive (v. 2) and offensive (v. 3) weapons. In figurative language he is asking God to make their plots ineffective. Until then he looks for assurance that God is on his side; he wants to hear his voice within him saying *I am your salvation* (v. 3).

(3) In verses 4-8 he goes further, asking God to do to his enemies the kind of thing they are trying to do to him – bring *disgrace ... shame ... dismay* (v. 4), be driven away as *chaff before the wind at the hands of the destroying angel of the* LORD (v. 5), be driven along a *dark and slippery* path on which they are likely to stumble in their haste (v. 6), and ultimately be overtaken by ruin (v. 8), such as they had prepared for him.

Here we have another example of an 'imprecatory' or cursing psalm, such as was found in Psalm 5:9-10. Such passages afford one of the Psalms' chief problems, since they seem to exhibit a vindictive spirit which should be far from a godly person (Matt. 5:43-48; Rom. 12:14, 17-21). Apart from the fact that David lived long before those words of Jesus and Paul were uttered and under a different covenant, we have to take them in the context of David's whole life. He was the anointed king, whereas Saul was now rejected. David did not take this to mean he had the right to usurp Saul, but neither did it give Saul the right to kill him. Perhaps the fact that Saul plotted against him secretly and did not publicly execute him indicates he realised David was God's chosen man. This meant that in plotting against David Saul was plotting against God (79:12). In praying against, denouncing and even cursing the plotters, therefore, David was simply speaking in God's name. David spoke by the Spirit of God and what he said was what God said. He was a successor to Abraham to whom God said *whoever curses you I will curse* (Gen. 12:3). This is the language of the covenant, which contains cursing (Lev. 26; Deut. 27-28). These therefore are not simply David's curses but God's. The New Testament itself does this: Paul told the Corinthians Christians to *hand over to Satan* a grossly immoral member (1 Cor. 5:5) and he uses cursing language in 1 Corinthians 16:22 and Galatians 1:8-9. In fact the last book of the Bible almost ends with a curse (Rev. 22:18-19). For further information see the Introduction, page 9.

Verses 9-10
These verses bear this out for they anticipate the fulfilment of the curse, upon which David will give the credit to God. This will glorify him as the unique One: *who is like you, O LORD?* which are words uttered on the greatest deliverance in Israel's history, the crossing of the Red Sea (Exod. 15:11); reflected in the words Isaiah uses to describe the God of creation (Isa. 40:25-26) and Micah the God of salvation (Mic. 7:18). That God destroys those who oppose him is part of his uniqueness. It shows him as the God who will have the last word against evil, as the later chapters of the Book of the Revelation bring out.

Verses 11-16
Here David enforces his case by pointing out that his enemies had no evidence against him (v. 11). As with Jesus later, they trumped up charges and produced false witnesses. Also they put questions to him about things in which he was not involved. In fact the opposite was the truth: he had only done them good (v. 12), perhaps referring to the hours he spent calming Saul with his music or to his delivering of the nation from Goliath or to his campaigns to drive the Philistines out of the land. He had every right to feel forlorn at this worse-than ungrateful treatment.

Not only that, but he prayed and fasted for their recovery from illness (v. 13), which shows how concerned he was for Saul's condition, so that he added to his periods of music-making long hours of prayer and fasting. Nor was this a mere formality; he was really cut up when his prayers returned unanswered, as much as he would have been with a close relative (vv. 13b-14). Yet if the boot was on the other foot and he was in trouble, they gloated over it and used it to justify their accusations (vv. 15-16).

Verses 17-18

These verses show he is saying all this to God. This is why the frustration and desperation of verse 17 quickly give way to thanksgiving in verse 18. The man of faith can endure anything because he knows he will eventually be vindicated (cf. Job 19:25-27).

Verses 19-20

The note of confidence sounded in verse 18 has calmed David and he confines himself to praying for God simply to restrain his enemies, on the grounds that their hostility had no cause or reason, but was merely malicious (v. 19). Moreover this attitude was spreading and disturbing the peace and order of society, threatening to divide the whole nation (v. 20).

Verses 21-25

Over against his enemies' false witness about what *with our own eyes we have seen* (v. 21) is God's true witness, for he has seen not only David's righteous behaviour but his enemies' treachery (v. 22). He can therefore with a clear conscience appeal to God to take his side (vv. 23-24), which is how the psalm began (v. 1). But it comes more forcibly after all he has written about his enemies. It would be utterly wrong for them to be able to say 'we have won', which is what verse 25 amounts to.

Verses 26-27

These verses are not just a further outburst of cursing like verses 4-8, but show this was more than a personal dispute; two parties were beginning to appear: Saul's servants (v. 26) and David's supporters (v. 27). The issue was whether the nation was to be governed by righteousness or wickedness.

Verse 28

Assuming justice is going to prevail, the outcome would be a victory for God and his righteousness rather than for David's integrity, for the result will be that God will receive great and continual praise.

David's prayer was not in vain. For one thing, because Michal loved him she protected him from Saul's men (1 Sam. 19:11-17) and for another, David's further victories over the Philistines (1 Sam. 18:27) increased his standing with the people, making it harder for Saul to get rid of him.

Questions:
(1) How does this psalm encourage us to use the full scope of prayer, on the lines of John 15:7 and Philippians 4:6?

(2) Although we Christians are not in the business of cursing our enemies (Rom. 12:14), what positive help can we derive from verses 4-10?

Psalm 36

David the Prophet

The plotting of the previous psalm is still going on (v. 4), but the positive note on which 35 ended is taken up and developed here in an outburst of great confidence in God (vv. 5-9).

Verses 1-4: The truth about the wicked
David is reflecting on what lies behind his troubles with Saul and his court. What he comes up with is not just a view of the present situation, but of the cause of all human sinfulness. For this is an oracle, a revelation from God such as he gave the prophets (e.g. Isa. 13:1; Hab. 1:1). In this sense David was a prophet; in 110:1 he reveals what the Father (*the Lord*) said to the Son (*my Lord*). What God reveals to him here is that the reason people commit wickedness is that they are ignorant of God and unaware of him: they have no fear (v. 1, cf. 14:1). As Isaiah put it (53:6) the nature of *iniquity* is that *each of us turns to* (our) *own way*; and its cause is that *like sheep (we) have gone astray* (from the Shepherd).

He is then given to understand the consequences of this, as he himself was experiencing them at that time:

- Sinners congratulate themselves that they will get away with it, since God is as unaware of them as they of God (vv. 1-2).

- They can say what they like for they are accountable to no one for their words, so that it does not matter if their words prove unreliable (v. 3a).
- They live like fools, because wisdom and righteousness are companions – wisdom is a moral fact, as folly is (v. 3b).
- Their whole life is spent plotting evil (v. 4); being evil themselves, they cannot think on any other lines. If a wrong course of action is required to achieve their aims they do not reject it. They are not restrained by moral law.

These thoughts are therefore not just about Saul's plot but about human thinking, speaking and behaviour as a whole. They form a universal statement on the heart of man under 'the god of this world' (cf. Jer. 17:9; Eph. 2:1-3).

Verses 5-9: The contrasting truth about God

He is all that the wicked are not: loving and faithful (v. 5), righteous and just (v. 6). While these terms may be used of righteous humans, in God's case they are infinite – they reach *to the heavens* (v. 5), unreachable, like the mighty mountains, and unfathomable, like a great deep (v. 6). Human virtues are relative, divine are absolute. This does not mean they are irrelevant to our lives, in fact they are essential: they give protection (*refuge*), as a bird does for its young (v. 7); and they make abundant provision of food and drink (v. 8). What Israel's worshippers enjoyed when they came to God's house (the temple) for fellowship offerings (65:4; Lev. 7:12-15), people in all the world can enjoy from his hands (145:15-16). So to call his *unfailing love 'priceless'* is no exaggeration.

Verse 9 goes beyond material protection and provision to refer to spiritual salvation; the life of which God is fountain is eternal life, his life (John 4:14). This too he has revealed, not only to David but to all believers (*in your light we see light*). We who hear this word see him who is the light and are saved (cf.27; 1 John 8:12).

Verses 10-12: The appropriate prayer

Now that he is clear both about his enemies and his God, he can pray with intelligence and confidence about his situation.

Because God is love he can ask for his protection to continue; and because he is righteous he can ask him to restrain his enemies. This gives him such confidence that he feels the prayer is as good as answered already (v. 12).

Like many of its predecessors this psalm was later issued for use in public worship, and so was put into the hands of the director of music (title). But David adds to his name as author something significant: *the servant of the Lord*. He writes in his official capacity as one called by God to speak on his behalf to the people, to pronounce an oracle. This confirms that we have here universal truths about man and God. Perhaps there is also a hint of that coming servant of the Lord, the Messiah, who would suffer at the hands of sinners even worse things, but gain the victory (Isa. 52:13–53:12).

Questions:
(1) What enemies are plotting against us who live in gospel times? (See Eph. 6:11-12; 2 Cor. 11:13-15; 1 John 2:22.)

(2) What does this psalm teach us about the essential preliminaries before we come to the petitionary part of prayer? Cf. Acts 4:24-30.

Psalm 37

David the Aged Gives Advice

David is speaking as one now old (v. 25), giving his successor the benefit of his experience. In his old age David had two main interests: to build the temple and to instruct the rising generation, especially his son and heir, Solomon. In this psalm he seems to be doing the latter, basing his counsel on two main things: firstly, the covenant between God and Israel, by which he gave them all a share in his land and undertook to bless it with prosperity. At the same time he required trust and obedience from each of them. Then secondly, he bases it on his own experience of God's faithfulness and care. David had found throughout his life that evil men in the holy nation were hindering the full enjoyment of the blessings of God's covenant and provoking him to implement its curses. David had struggled with this from the beginning through to old age, and had learned how to handle this problem. These are the threads we find running through this long and repetitive psalm.

As regards its form: firstly, it is 'acrostic' like several others, that is, it follows the twenty-two letters of the Hebrew alphabet in order, but in this psalm there are two verses to each letter. The reason there are only 40 verses and not 44 is that the letter 'AYIN is omitted, and the pairing breaks down in one or two places. Secondly, it is proverbial. There is no logical framework to the psalm, which is rather like the Book of Proverbs. This explains the frequent repetitions. However, the attempt is made here to try to trace some development of thought.

Verses 1-9: Exhortations negative and positive
How does a believer face the problem that God seems to be blessing evil men with wealth but depriving the righteous?

(1) **Verses 1-2**. He does not *fret*, literally 'burn' with anger, over the apparent unfairness, for this would be judging God. Also, behind this anger lies envy, which would be totally wrong because it is like saying 'I would rather be wicked and wealthy than righteous and poor'. Nor is there any reason to be angry and envious, for this situation is very short-lived. Scripture writers frequently use grass and green plants as illustrations of human frailty (103:15; Isa. 40:6-8). In the land of the Bible dryness and the heat of the sun meant that grass did not stay green very long.

(2) **Verses 3-4**. What he does do is trust in the Lord, for his covenant promise still holds. In the Old Testament this was to give the people the land to dwell in, and safe pasture, free from foreign interference. If there were evil-doers among his people, that still did not annul the promise. Instead of thinking of what others had that they did not, let them think of what they had – the Lord himself. Be content with him, delight in him and you will find he satisfies the desires of your heart, for your desires will be not for wealth but the knowledge of God.

(3). **Verses 5-6**. When you are having a hard time materially and do not feel you are enjoying his blessing, but rather are under his judgment, then *commit your way to the LORD*, literally 'roll it on him', hand the burden over to him (cf. Prov. 16:3; 1 Pet. 5:7). Then you will find that in some way he will vindicate you, so that your righteousness, the justice of your cause, becomes clear, This will be like sunrise (*the dawn*) and even more glorious (like *the noonday sun*, cf. Prov. 4:18).

(4) **Verse 7**. Be patient before the Lord when he does not do immediately what verse 6 promises, when the wicked seem not only to devise wicked schemes but succeed in carrying

them out. God has his times and seasons, which do not always correspond to ours. We are in such a hurry and get so restless. We need to know how to be still.

(5) **Verses 8-9**. To sum up, we must control our anger against evil men, and our sulkiness (*fret*) towards God. We must believe his word when he says he will deal with evil men and cut them off from his covenant promise, but that he will confirm you in your inheritance in the land. There is a suggestion here that what was happening was that the unscrupulous were grabbing land belonging to the faithful (as Ahab seized Naboth's vineyard, 1 Kings 21) and enslaving the faithful by making them tenants or peasants. God puts this right.

Verses 10-16: Confirmation of the promise

This part of the psalm is mainly stressing what is said in verse 9a. God knows what is going on and his sympathies are with the victims of the wicked. So he undertakes to remove them soon: a little while and the wicked will be no more (v. 10). This is emphasised by graphic descriptions of how the wicked behave and how God reacts (vv. 12-13). They plot against the righteous and threaten them fiercely, but the Lord is not intimidated. To him they appear only ridiculous because they do not know what they are heading for: the day (of destruction) is coming (cf. Ps. 2:1-5).

In verses 14-15 they are carrying out their threats: their swords are drawn and their bows bent; but God will step in at the last moment, break their bows and turn their swords against them. Their land-grabbing ambitions will be thwarted, so that the meek will resume their ownership of the land and be able to cultivate it in peace (v. 11).

But it is not just a matter of land; behind this is their covenant with God who gave this part of the world to Israel and instructed Joshua in how to divided it up between the tribes (Josh. 14–19). The tribes then portioned it out to the families to hold in perpetuity. To interfere with this arrangement was to infringe God's covenant, for which the penalty was to be *cut off* from it, which is the significance of that expression in verse 9. This explains why our Lord quoted this verse in his 'beatitude'

(Matt. 5:5). Disciples of Christ can expect to be victimised by the ungodly and must bear it patiently, knowing that *theirs is the kingdom of heaven*. For to them is given, not a portion of land to till but 'the earth', the whole sphere over which Christ their Master reigns; all that is his is theirs. This is the new covenant, sealed in his blood (Luke 22:20).

Verses 16-20: The blessings of the righteous

To talk of 'the end' is all well and good, but how do we cope until then? How *little* is *a little while* (v. 10)? If the last question cannot be answered the first can. We have to get our values right and see the moral and spiritual as better than the material (*wealth*, v. 16; cf. Prov. 15:16; 16:8).

We also have the Lord on our side to uphold us (v. 17), whereas his power goes out against the wicked to destroy them. Moreover, *disaster* and *famine* affect the wealthy as well as the righteous poor (v. 19). But whereas God has his ways of looking after his own at such times, so that they will not wither but enjoy plenty, the wicked enjoy no such favour and will perish. Those who flourished like the beauty of the fields ... (will) vanish like smoke (v. 20). The reason again lies in God's covenant with the righteous. Because they faithfully keep their side of the covenant, they remain in the Lord's love, they are *known to*, that is, loved by the Lord (v. 18), and because his love is everlasting their inheritance will endure for ever.

Verses 21-26: Righteous and wicked compared

The wealthy wicked never have enough money and borrow more. The righteous, even though poor, always have something to give (v. 21, cf. Luke 21:1-3). The rich live on credit, the poor on generosity. This is because the latter have behind them the Lord (who) blesses and makes rich (v. 22, Prov. 10:22), even when they are poor (2 Cor. 6:10). Under the old covenant terms like 'blessing' and 'rich' were mainly material whereas under the new covenant they tend to be more spiritual. Because there are always poor does not mean God is unfaithful. The riches of the ungodly are not acknowledged as given by God, nor used as he wills, and so are under his curse (James 5:1-6).

Ultimately the blessing is inclusion in the covenant (inherit the land) and the curse is being cut off from it.

This is emphasised by the promise of security to the righteous (vv. 23-24). The rich seek it in their money, the righteous poor in communion with the Lord. This does not mean they do not have their crises and shortages – they stumble, but do not fall into permanent poverty.

Not only is this God's promise, it is true to experience (v. 25). David himself spent long years living from hand to mouth with his band of followers. They were often on the bread line but never fell below it, were never given up to it. God saw they had enough for themselves, for others and for their children (v. 26).

Verses 27-33: Exhortation to the righteous

He balances this stress on the promise and performance of God with the responsibility of those whom he blesses (v. 27). The covenant includes the obligation to obey God – negatively by turning from evil and positively by doing good. The promise to dwell in the land is conditional on this. Nor is it arbitrary: it is a response to his love and faithfulness (v. 28a). So, to encourage them, he repeats the covenant promise to the righteous and his warning to the wicked (vv. 28b-29).

Verses 30-31 beautifully describe the wholeness of the righteous man: he treasures the word in his heart, because of which he utters what is wise and just with his tongue; and walks in the ways of God with his feet. Contrast this with the behaviour of the wicked (vv. 32-33). They spend their lives preying on others, exploiting their weakness and vulnerability. But they have the Lord to reckon with. Though temporarily they may seem to have their way, it will not last, they will fail in the end.

Verses 34-40: Final encouragements

The hints that God's promise of deliverance from the wicked may be delayed (e.g. v. 33) mean that the righteous will need patience. But remember that the One for whom you are waiting is the Lord, the all-powerful One, who is faithful to his promise, but is not subject to time and in no hurry. But he knows the right time to act and will do so then: you will see it (v. 34).

Again the voice of experience comes in to confirm the promise (vv. 35-36). The ascendancy of the wicked may seem long, but with patient waiting on the Lord it soon comes to an end, like the flourishing of a green tree (cf. v. 2). Best of all, it is final: once God acts there is no recovery.

What a contrast are the blameless (v. 37)! Their future is the best thing about them, unlike that of all sinners (and) the wicked, as he says in verse 38 yet again. And, in case he has not said it enough times already, the Lord is on the side of the righteous and is everything to them: a Saviour, a stronghold, a deliverer and a refuge (vv. 39-40). If this does not take away the fretting (v. 1) what will? So he ends with a hint of our responsibility: we must take refuge in him, that is, trust him and not give way to despair and unbelief.

Questions:

(1) What message has this psalm for Christians in our current consumer society?

(2) 'Trust and obey, for there's no other way to be happy in Jesus, but to trust and obey.' What is the relationship between these two duties?

(3) Does your experience of life confirm the promise of God's faithfulness or is there some contradiction?

(4) What hope does the New Testament give to Christians struggling with the oppression of the wicked? (See 2 Pet. 3.)

Psalm 38

David's Grievous Sickness

A severe illness here is aggravated by a sense of God's displeasure and an unsympathetic attitude from those around him. There is no way of precisely locating the occasion of this experience. It may have been the illness referred to in 41:4-9, when he was encamped at Mahanaim and the local chiefs brought him supplies and men. He was reminded of a time when he was ill and his enemies were spreading rumours of his imminent death. This would have given support to Absalom's attempt on his father's throne. Psalm 38 may have been composed at the same time.

Alternatively it may describe wounds suffered in a battle that is not recorded in Scripture. This would certainly help explain the references to *wounds* in the psalm. Perhaps it is even more likely that it belongs to David's old age, when we know he suffered illnesses (1 Kings 1:1). This psalm may have been one written then. It shows how the guilt of his sin still clung to him and that he still had rivals who were waiting to take his throne, even among his own family.

Verses 1-4: Burdened with guilt
David's uppermost thought here is that his sin has brought this affliction on him. God's wrath and anger were against him; God was rebuking him. His pains were God's arrows piercing

him or his hand punishing him. He is not complaining that this is unjust, but admitting it is because of *my sin ... guilt*. This was the burden he found too heavy to bear. Is he referring to the Bathsheba/Uriah incident? God had forgiven him for this and spared him from the punishment of death which was appropriate for adulterers and murderers (2 Sam. 12:13), but there was still a harvest to be reaped in what he would suffer at the hands of his family (2 Sam. 12:10). This could well be what was on his mind. If it were for some other grievous sin committed subsequently we are not told of it. The title of the psalm ('a petition', NIV), is literally 'to bring to remembrance'. This may indicate that he saw his affliction as a reminder of his sin.

Verses 5-12: Tortured with pain

What the illness was is not stated. Perhaps even the doctors did not know! It may have been battle wounds, though it is unlikely David fought any more wars after the Absalom episode. Whatever it was it was certainly severe. His wounds were discharging and giving off a loathsome smell (v. 5). He could not stand upright (v. 6) because of the pain in his back (v. 7), making his whole body feel ill: *feeble and utterly crushed* (v. 8). He is suffering palpitations of heart and partial blindness (v. 10).

All joy in living has gone and he can only mourn (v. 6), groan (v. 8), and sigh, longing for healing (v. 9). The situation is worsened by its effects on his friends and companions, who are avoiding him, either because they cannot bear the sight and smell of his wounds (v. 11), or because they see him as under the judgment of God, like a leper to be ostracised as part of the punishment; or both. On his enemies the effect is worse (v. 12). They are taking advantage of his indisposition to spread rumours of his impending demise under God's judgment, and taking the opportunity to plot against him (cf. 41:7-9).

The one hope to which he clings is that God knows the condition of his body and the state of his mind (v. 9). It is *open before you, O Lord*. This gives an alternative explanation of the title and perhaps a better one: that the psalm is to bring before God a situation with which only he can deal. Some even connect it with the *memorial offering* of Numbers 5:26.

Verses 13-22: Waiting on God

Such is David's sense of his own responsibility for his sickness (e.g. *because of my sinful folly*, v. 5), that he has no reply to friends who forsake him and enemies who accuse him. He accepts their verdict as just. In fact their attitude is almost passing him by unnoticed. He is more concerned about what God thinks: *I wait for you, O Lord*. If there is a case to answer against anyone else, God will see to that.

However, although he looks for nothing for himself personally, he has not lost sight of the moral implications for society. It is not God's way to let people gloat over others' misfortunes; this is not in keeping with the spirit of unity and love which should prevail among his people. So he prays against it (v. 16).

Verses 17-20 enlarge on this. His sins are against God, to whom he has confessed them (v. 18), and God is severely punishing him (v. 17). But there is no reason for this ostracism and enmity from others, against whom he has done nothing (v. 19). In fact he has sought to serve them, only to receive hatred and slander for his pains (v. 20).

So he turns to God to vindicate him by coming to him again with his help, and that quickly, for he is nearly gone. His only plea is the name and office of God: *O Lord my Saviour* (vv. 21-22).

Questions:

(1) Ought our assurance of forgiveness in Christ negate any thought that a period of suffering is God's punishment? If guilt feelings are inappropriate, what are the right feelings? Does Hebrew 12:7-13 help?

(2) Do verses 11-12 give warrant for regarding AIDS sufferers as like lepers of old – guilty and punished by God and to be avoided by us? (See Matt. 8:2-4.)

(3) What can you learn about Christ on the cross from David's experiences and his reactions to them here?

Psalm 39

David in Shock

This psalm comes from a man who has had a severe shock. He is finding it difficult to prevent himself from bursting into a tirade against God (v. 1) and is, if not suicidal, under a death-wish (v. 4). There were many occasions in David's life when he suffered shocks: when pursued by Saul, when serving with the Philistines, when facing enemies among his own subjects and when driven out by Absalom. This psalm would fit any of these and so was committed to Jeduthun, one of David's directors of music (title, 1 Chron. 16:41) for use in public worship. At this point the musical direction *Selah* (vv. 5, 11) was introduced. However, the intense emotion in which it was composed is in no way blunted.

Verses 1-3: David controls his feelings
David is suffering from shock and the anger in his heart burned like a raging furnace (v. 3). But he vows not to express it and muzzles himself (v. 1). He imposes a vow of silence on himself to such an extent that he will not even say anything good (v. 2) lest his words should turn into anger.

The reason for the sealed lips is that his anger was not just against men but God himself, whom he seems to blame for the situation (vv. 9-11). Since anger is so often sin (v. 1, Prov. 29:11; Eph. 4:26; James 1:20), anger against God is doubly sinful. But David is restrained by another consideration: the honour of God. Evidently unbelievers were present (v. 1), and bitter words against God would 'cause them to blaspheme' (Rom. 2:24).

However, this self-restraint served only to increase his anguish (v. 2). Some say verse 2 should read 'it did no good, my anguish increased'. So eventually he gave way and spoke, though it seems he took care to do it privately to the Lord alone, for the rest of the psalm is in the form of a prayer.

Verses 4-6: David speaks his mind

There are two ways of looking at this passage. One is to see David asking God to teach him a lesson about life from this mishap: how short it is (vv. 4-5) and how devoid of purpose and meaning (v. 6). But would it be sin to utter this before the ungodly? Surely it is what they need to hear! So another way of looking at it is as a prayer for a swift end to his short and meaningless life. David may still have been a young man, but he feels his life has been wasted. He could have been doing properly the job Saul was mishandling, instead of being chased from the land, fighting for foreigners and ending up losing his wives and letting down his followers. How long was this to go on? He is in the mood Job was in (Job 14) and later Elijah (1 Kings 19:4).

This is sinful despair, complete distrust in God, something David would feel ashamed to say before others. This way of looking at it also leads more logically to the next passage, which shows him making progress in his thinking.

Verses 7-11: David begins to repent

As David reflects on what he has been feeling and saying, he realises he has gone too far. He has only considered the tragedy and not seen that, but for God's providential intervention, the tragedy might have become a catastrophe. So he begins to consider whether anything can be salvaged: *But now, Lord, what do I look for?* (v. 7). Since his question is addressed to God, he feels there is still hope. He is beginning to see God is in this.

But first he must get himself right and so begins by confessing his transgressions (v. 8). His anger and despair had gone too far – it was sinful. Honest confession of this gives him the right to make a request (Prov. 28:13). His first concern, however, even before the recovery of the families, is how this looks in the eyes of the ungodly, the fools. Their scorn of him would reflect on the God he trusted and served. This was why he had held his peace in their company (v. 9). Had he said openly, 'God is punishing me', they would not have understood. The God of Israel would appear no better than their own capricious deities. So he first asks God to save him from this.

Now in private with God he could indeed speak of this experience as God's scourge and the blow of his hand (v. 10). It was God's *rebuke and discipline for ... sin* (v. 11). Perhaps he is coming to see that his faith in God's promise and power had begun to lapse. Whatever the chastisement was for, it was having its due effect: he had lost everything, his wealth had been consumed *like a moth* (as a moth consumes fabric); and he had been forced to see the brevity and emptiness of his life and the life of each man. He was turning from himself to God and was in a position to make his main request.

Verses 12-13: David prays again

What David's specific prayer is we are not told. What is important here is the argument he uses to persuade God to act. But first we see how earnest and sincere was his plea: *hear ... listen ... be not deaf ... weeping* (v. 12). This is not self-pity any more, but genuine concern for those who were as devastated as he. Then comes the ground of his prayer: *I dwell with you as an alien, a stranger.* For he really dwells not on earth at all, but with God, and anywhere else is foreign. Nor is he the first to realise this – his fathers as far back as Abraham were the same, as Hebrews 11 brings out (vv. 9-10, 13-16). If God did not look after him, who would? He sees the truth of his own words: *My hope is in you* (v. 7).

So finally he asks that God will graciously disregard his anger and self-pity (v. 13): *look away from me,* 'do not take any notice of the stupid things I've been saying.' Then he will feel differently and rejoice again. For in this brief uncertain life there is not much time *before I depart and am no more*.

Thus does David surmount this great crisis; but he has learned much from it.

Questions:

(1) How do David's anger, bitterness, self-despair and death-wish encourage you on the one hand and warn you on the other? (1 Cor. 10:11-13.)

(2) Has our greater security, health and prosperity dulled our sense of the brevity of life? Has this in turn made us complacent and self-righteous? If so, what should we do about it? (See James 4:13-17.)

(3) Have the things mentioned in question 2 made us more worldly and taken away our sense of alienation from the world? (See 1 Pet. 2:11-12.)

Psalm 40

David in Recovery

If this psalm follows Psalm 39 chronologically it shows how well David had now recovered from the shock he had suffered. His waiting on the Lord in prayer had borne fruit.

Verses 1-5: David praises God for a great deliverance
These verses show the recovery was not as clear-cut as the account may suggest. The language of verse 1 reveals an inner tension (literally 'Waiting I waited'), expressing some suspense, that in spite of the promise the situation remained critical and David had to *cry*. It seems victory was snatched out of the jaws of defeat, since verse 2 describes a near-death experience. The pit of slime, mud and mire is probably metaphorical for virtual disaster. But God turned the tables (v. 2b) and the cry turns to praise, the defeatism to encouragement (v. 3).

It had been a victory for faith in God (v. 4) and for refusing to resort either to relying on superior numbers (*the proud*) or to idolatry. This does not mean that David, as the one whose faith had held, attributes the victory to himself – it was one of God's miracles (v. 5) to add to the list of those experienced by him and his predecessors.

Verses 6-10: David's resolve to serve God is strengthened
The incident from which he has recovered may have been a battle which was almost lost, for sacrifice and offering usually

preceded a battle (v. 6, cf. 1 Sam. 13:7-10). Either David did not perform this or he was not trusting in it. This does not mean he rejected sacrifice altogether; no doubt if it had been possible he would have performed it. But there was something more important, in fact indispensible – obedience to God. Hebrew often makes absolute statements in order to emphasize what matters most. First Samuel 15:22 states it more precisely. David is saying that the victory was won through believing what his ears had heard from God (v. 6b) – his command and promise – and then going out to *do (his) will* (v. 8). This may refer to the word of a prophet or priest or to the instructions for kings written in the scroll, that is, Moses' law (Deut. 17:14-20). His obedience was truly heartfelt (v. 8).

Although David is not being intentionally prophetic in verses 6-8, the passage is applied to Christ in Hebrews 10:5-7. His obedience resulted in the sacrifice to end all sacrifices. The alteration from *my ears you have pierced* to *a body you prepared for me* is due the apostles' use of the Septuagint, since they had no access to the Hebrew scrolls. The difference is not as great as may appear: if you listen to God with your ear you will submit to him your whole *body*. The author of 'Hebrews' saw this as fulfilled in the incarnation of the Son of God.

What was *within* (his) *heart* during this dangerous operation he now proclaims out loud (v. 9). But he is not advertising himself as a model of godliness – it is God's *righteousness ... faithfulness ... and salvation* he proclaims – the Lord's love and truth. It was the Lord who had commissioned the battle and the Lord who had won it against all odds. Let the people know this and let it inspire them to trusting obedience towards God. It deserves to be reported to the whole nation, the great assembly. Ultimately it was reported, if not at the time, for it was committed to the director of music for use in public worship.

Verses 11-17: David prays for God to continue his mercy
Great as was the victory it has not altered David's present situation. It might even have worsened it. So he still needs God's *mercy ... love ... and truth* to protect him – not only from the troubles without number that surround him (v. 11), but

from the consequences of his sins (v. 12). He is still very conscious of his mistakes, and no doubt his lies and failure to trust God were also on his conscience. He is so overwhelmed with the thought of all this that he cannot see through it to a settled peaceful time. In spite of the victory he is still in low spirits and has to cry out to God.

His chief prayer is for his own speedy deliverance (v. 13). The best way of deliverance would be if God dealt powerfully with his enemies (vv. 14-15). The curses of previous psalms are much toned down here: he simply asks that they be struck with shame for desiring his ruin. The worst thing was that they enjoyed seeing him suffer: 'Aha!' is an expression of malicious joy (35:21, 25-26).

This does not mean he thinks he is the only one remaining faithful to God; he prays that *all who seek you (may) rejoice and be glad in you* (v. 16). He is thankful that he has at least some to share his sufferings, and also for all throughout the land whom he did not know but was sure were of his mind.

He still feels however that he is the chief victim and that the future of the godly in the land hangs very much on what happens to him, so his closing prayer is for himself (v. 17). Basically he is still as he was before Keilah (1 Sam. 23:3) – *poor and needy* (cf. 86:1). But his recovery has encouraged his assurance that the Lord thinks of him and is his *help and ... deliverer*. But the matter is urgent, things cannot go on like this: *O my God, do not delay.*

Questions:
(1) Compare the 'new song' of verse 3 with Revelation 5:9. Can you see your own conversion in verses 1-3?

(2) Consider the use of the OT in the NT: verses 6-8 in Hebrews 10:5-10. What justification is there for giving a passage a somewhat different meaning? Does John 15:26 help?

(3) How does the train of thought in verses 11-17 help save a victimised person from paranoia?

Psalm 41

David in Weakness and Sickness

This psalm comes from a time when David, to whom it is attributed in the title, was in a state of great weakness (v. 1) and sickness (vv. 3, 8), and someone had come to his aid. This may have occurred during the long time when he was an outlaw because of Saul. Alternatively, it may have been during his flight from Absalom, since verse 9 seems to refer to the treachery of Ahithophel who went over to Absalom's side (2 Sam. 15:31). When David arrived at Mahanaim he was met by three local chiefs who brought food for David and his men (2 Sam. 17:27-29)

Verses 1-3: David responds to this kindly aid
This is how the godly man says 'Thank you' to one who has helped him in his need: he promises to pray for his benefactor and assures him that God will deal favourably with those who minister to the needy, so that when their turn comes God will send someone to deal similarly with them (v. 1). God himself favours the weak and poor (Prov. 23:10-11) and therefore rewards those who do likewise (Matt. 10:42). He protects, preserves, prospers and delivers (v. 2). When they are ill he sustains and even restores them (v. 3).

Verses 4-9: David recalls his own affliction

Mention of sickness in verse 3 reminds David of a time when he had been grievously ill and no one had come to aid or comfort him. The history books do not document this but the description here fits the time when Absalom's rebellion was getting under way and Ahithophel deserted him (v. 9). He admits that this was no more he deserved because of his sins against God (v. 4) and he was therefore primarily seeking God's mercy rather than human sympathy.

Nevertheless he felt it keenly and pours it all out here. His only visitors were his enemies who could not wait for him to die and only came to see him to find out how near death he was so that they could publicise it. To their mind this would prove David was forsaken by God, leaving the throne clear – for whom but Absalom?

Worst of all, his closest friend and counsellor, presumably Ahithophel (v. 9), had turned against him. The treachery of this is shown in the fact that this was the verse Jesus quoted when he announced to the twelve assembled in the upper room that one of them was about to betray him to the authorities (John 13:18). The perversity of the actions of both men is seen in David's metaphor of a horse or donkey who kicks back at its master who has come to feed it.

David describes all this to confirm the sincerity of his prayer in verses 4-6. He who knows what it is like to be deprived of those who have regard for the weak would not wish his experience of desolation in sickness on anyone. His attitude is the opposite of 'Well, I had to put up with it, so why shouldn't you?'

Verses 10-12: David recites his assurance of God's mercy

The experience had its beneficial side, however, for David learned from it that God does not deal as man does. *But you, O Lord* is emphatic – *you* contrasting with them, his enemies. God did have mercy on him, when he raised him from his sickness; and he is now showing him mercy, for in his exhausted and weary state, far from home, he has sent him help and comfort. This to David was proof that God had forgiven his sin; this was the mercy he sought and found; the healing and the aid were simply tokens of it.

This has given him the assurance that his enemy will not triumph over him (v. 11). He did not die of his illness, nor will he be killed in battle. In all this he maintained his integrity through the upholding grace of God. He expects now to be restored to his place and be *set in your presence for ever* (v. 12).

Verse 13
This was probably added by the director of music when the psalms were arranged into five books, each of which closes with a doxology. Psalm 41 was chosen to close Book I.

Questions:
(1) Does this psalm, especially verses 1-3, show you that there is a better way for a Christian to show gratitude than a mere 'Thank you'?

(2) How does David here show the spirit of the Sermon on the Mount, especially Matthew 7:12?

(3) When may we see a connection between sin and sickness and when may we not? (Cf. Luke 5:17-20 with John 9:1-3.)

Psalms 42–43

Away from the House of God

One only has to read through these two psalms to conclude that they belong together. The theme is the same and the refrain of 42:5, 11 is repeated in 43:5. Most of all, 43 resolves the problems raised by 42, which is incomplete without it. Neither one on its own would justify the name *Maskil* (see comment on Ps. 32). This would also explain why 43 lacks a title.

Psalm 42 is attributed to the sons of Korah (title). They were a family descended from Levi, whose ancestor perished as a result of a rebellion against Moses (Num. 16). However, God did not punish the children for the sins of the father and gave them a valued place in Israel's worship, for they became a guild of singers (2 Chron. 20:19).

The writer speaks as one accustomed to lead the procession to the house of God (42:4) but he is now far away, on the north near the source of the Jordan (vv. 6-7). He could have been accompanying David on his flight from Absalom and this could have been the Sabbath day when he would have experienced his absence from Zion most acutely. It is certainly full of passion and longing. The pair of psalms falls naturally into three sections punctuated by the refrain of 42:5, 11 and 43:5.

42:1-5: Missing God

Away in desert places the psalmist's thoughts are on what he would normally be doing at that time: leading the procession to the house of God (v. 4). He would be in godly company and together they would be singing with *shouts of joy and thanksgiving*. How different it was here! Instead of the festive throng there were just these bedraggled refugees for company; instead of sharing the thanksgiving people were taunting them with *where is your God?* (v. 3); instead of shouts of joy there were floods of tears (v. 3), which had to serve for food in place of the portions of the sacrifices.

In this situation he could only pant *for you, O God* and *pour out* (his) *soul* (v. 4). For it was not just the happy crowd and the trappings of worship he missed but God himself: *my soul thirsts for ... the living God*, an unusual phrase, occurring again only in 84:2, in a psalm which has other similarities with this psalm. In fact in the very next line *meet* before *God* is also in 84:7. A better translation would be 'see the face of God', the 'shekinah' glory by which God revealed his presence and which was the highlight of attending a tabernacle or temple service. Here he could only long for this, as the deer do when cut off from streams of water (v. 1), for unlike camels, deer cannot survive drought.

But the very fact that he has these thoughts and is expressing them shows he is not so far from God after all. He seems to realise his inconsistency in verse 5 with his two Whys? This God whom he worshipped but missed was the God of hope, his Saviour. There was no way he was going to leave his faithful worshipper in such a condition. So he is able to pull himself together a little.

42:6-11: Fluctuating feelings

The author's feelings reflect the sights and sounds that met his eyes up there by the cataracts at the foot of Hermon where the melting snow rushes down with great power. First he is overwhelmed by these events – he is *downcast (in) soul* (v. 6). But he bobs up like a cork in a swirling river as he remembers God, the God who sings his song of love by day and night

(v. 8), which he turns into a prayer to *the God of my life*. He is still desperately *thirsting for the living God* (v. 2).

Indeed God is his only security when all around has collapsed: *my Rock*. But down goes the cork again: *I will remember you* (v. 6), but you have *forgotten me* (v. 9). It is as if God were dead and the writer was in mourning for him. Yet he never needed him more than now. Not only is he suffering physically (v. 10, perhaps as a result of the long difficult march made in great haste), but also mentally from the taunts of his foes, to whom it is so obvious that God has rejected him: *where is your God?* Where indeed? For if he was accompanying David, there was no evidence that God was with David at all.

But he again makes a supreme effort to rally his spirits, to lift his soul from its *downcast ... disturbed* state and hope in God that, whatever the present situation, the time would again come when, instead of complaining, he would praise him. This he is able to do through one thing: the covenant, by which he has authority to call him MY Saviour and MY God (emphasis mine).

43:1-5: Praying in faith and hope

Up to now he had complained, wept and reminisced before God, but he had not prayed to him, at least he had not asked specific favours of him. This he now puts right. First, he appeals for justice from God (v. 1). It was not merely that he was suffering from his deposition, but that God's righteous will was being violated by ungodly, deceitful and wicked men. Let God show he was on his side by rescuing him from them! He enforces his plea with the arguments of verse 2. If God was what he said he was to him (*his stronghold*), then God must explain why he is allowing his enemy to oppress him. Let God prove his justice!

Next, becoming bolder, he prays for restoration to *the place where you dwell* and from which he had been banished by ungodly men (v. 3). His declared motive (v. 4) is not to restore his own reputation, authority or comfort, but to resume his life of praise which was what he was chiefly missing (42:4). He is on firm ground here and therefore refers again to the covenant by which he calls God MY God (emphasis mine).

So in a better spirit he can repeat the refrain (v. 5). Having challenged God to give a reason for his treatment (v. 2), he now challenges himself: after all he has said, what reason can he have not to hope in God that he will be restored to his sanctuary?

Questions:
(1) In what way can Christian believers, who do not locate God in a particular place, speak of being away from God, 'forgotten, rejected' and 'mourning' as if God were dead?

(2) To what extent are we responsible for the state of our own spiritual life and able to encourage ourselves (42:5,11; 43:5)?

(3) Are things ever so bad that we cannot make specific requests of God? (See James 4:2.)

Psalm 44

Recalling Past Glories

This psalm appears to have come from the Babylonian captivity (vv. 11-12). In Psalm 137 the people are very conscious of being humbled before their captors. This psalm goes deeper and expresses their feelings of rejection by God himself. Yet there is no acknowledgement of their own responsibility for the situation; rather they protest their loyalty to his covenant (vv. 17-18) and are perplexed at what is happening to them. This perplexity is reflected in a constant switching between first person plural and first person singular.

The probable explanation is that the psalmist represents the faithful remnant who had gone into captivity with the rest. That there was such a remnant is clear from Isaiah's prophecies, e.g. Isaiah 8:16-18; 11:10-11. Alternatively, if the psalm comes from later in the captivity, it may be assuming the repentance that Daniel expresses in his prayer of Daniel 9, and wondering why God has not duly forgiven and restored them as yet. When placed in the corpus of psalms for the director of music it was termed a *Maskil* (see comment of Ps. 32), drawing attention to the lasting importance of the points it makes.

Verses 1-8: Recalling the past
It was the responsibility of each generation of Israel to pass on to the next one the great acts God had performed for them

(see Ps. 78). Even in captivity this was continued (v. 1); this generation was not ignorant of the conquest of Canaan when *with your hand you drove out the nations and planted our fathers* (v. 2). This had clearly been of God since as virtual refugees they had no trained or equipped army (v. 3). In this way God proved he loved them.

He was still the same God, still King of Israel and God of Jacob, who decreed victories for his people (v. 4). So the writer imagines similar things happening in his time: he sees them as bulls who *push back our enemies* and *trample our foes* (v. 5). Although better equipped now, they still could not *trust in* (their) *bow* or *sword* to bring victory (v. 6). It is still only God who can bring victory (v. 7), so that their boast is not in any army or general or weapon but in God, who would still therefore receive the praise (v. 8).

This seemed to be the great lesson to be learned from the past and a pause (*Selah*) is observed while it sinks in, and also to mark a contrast with what follows.

Verses 9-16: Facing the present

The pattern he had traced in verses 1-8 has unravelled with the Babylonian invasion and captivity. They had been defeated and deported. Why? Because God had *rejected ... and humbled* them. This was the logical deduction from the preceding. If victory was due to God fighting for them, defeat was caused by his rejecting them and not going out *with our armies* (v. 9). So the sad events of recent times are all attributable to him: YOU *made us retreat*, leaving us to be plundered by our adversaries (v. 10); YOU *gave us to be devoured like sheep*; YOU *have scattered us among the nations* (v. 11, for it was not only to Babylon that the people were taken, but to other parts of the empire too, just as the northern kingdom had been spread through the Assyrian empire, 2 Kings 17:6). God had sold them into slavery and returned them to the state in which he originally found them, yet gained nothing from the sale (v. 12). (N.B. Each emphasis in quotations from the text here is mine.)

Nor was it only defeat they had suffered; perhaps worse was their utter demoralisation. Their present state was such a contrast to what they had been: a free, proud, prosperous, law-abiding people, the envy of the surrounding nations.

Now they were *a reproach ... the scorn and derision of those around us* (v. 13), *a byword among the nations*, a kind of proverbial warning, so that when their name was mentioned, people just shook their heads (v. 14).

Speaking in the first person singular for greater poignancy, he complains of perpetual *disgrace* and *shame* (v. 15), of *the taunts ... of the enemy*, who see the plight of the people as a just revenge for driving them from their lands earlier (v. 16). Perhaps there is a hint of the sufferings of Christ in these last two verses which may help to explain the change to the first person singular. The words are very similar to those in 69 (especially vv. 7, 19-20) usually taken as previewing Christ's sufferings on the cross (e.g. Matt. 27:39-44).

Verses 17-26: Hoping for the future

The note of hope may not appear very strong in this passage, but this is because they are struggling to reach it. It is born out of their professed loyalty to their covenant with God (vv. 17-19). As said in the introduction, we are to see this, not as a blind claim from an apostate nation, but the conviction of the faithful remnant, perhaps joined by those whom these sufferings had brought to repentance. If this was late in the captivity, a new generation would have grown up which would be looking at things differently, not with that proud stubbornness of their fathers, especially after the ministry of Ezekiel and the example of Daniel.

Yet God still seemed to be against them, he had crushed them, removed the light of their happiness, and covered them with *deep darkness*, a place inhabited by *jackals* (v. 19). So hope has to wrestle against experience, and experience is perplexing. God knows the secrets of the heart, so, if their claim to loyalty was false, he *would ... have discovered it* (v. 21). He would know if they had *forgotten the name of (their) God* and *joined in the worship of a foreign god* (v. 20). The thoughts, words and feelings expressed in Psalms 123 and 137 showed this was not so. If therefore they are not being chastised for their sins, they must be being persecuted for righteousness and be facing *death all day* for God's sake, like sacrificial sheep (v. 22).

God will not allow such a state of affairs to continue for ever; it is only a matter of time before he will come into action.

It is as if he were asleep and needed them to rouse him by prayer (v. 23). Remembering Elijah's taunts against the priests of Baal (1 Kings 18:27), we have to be careful here. Elijah meant them to take it literally, but the psalm is speaking figuratively; it is as if God was asleep because he is not acting for them. He is hiding his face from them and seems to 'forget (their) misery and oppression' (v. 24). God can no more forget than he can sleep; the writer is using human language (a device called 'anthropomorphism') to express God's inactivity.

But God is brought into action by prayer, which may be what he is waiting for and which the psalm does as it closes. Once more they describe their condition, which is near death, for death is returning to the dust and being laid in the ground (Gen. 3:19; Eccles. 3:20; 12:7). Only the immortal God can raise the dead, so the cry goes up to him to *rise up and help us* (v. 26). He must rise before we can; he will redeem us from the grave by the payment of a price (Hos. 13:14). There is good hope that he will do so because of his unfailing love, which even sin and death cannot quench. Maybe Ezekiel's vision of a resurrected nation, which was given during this period (Ezek. 37), is the answer to the psalmist's cry.

Questions:
(1) Are Christians and churches faithfully passing on the story of God's great acts, not only in the Bible, but in the subsequent history of the church? Have you heard about the persecutions and the martyrs, the reformations and revivals? Are you passing them on to the rising generation?

(2) Are you, are the churches, trusting in what corresponds to the 'bow and sword' in the Old Testament? What does correspond to them today? (See Zech. 4:6; 2 Cor. 10:4-5.)

(3) How realistic are we in the churches about our present state? Does this have any connection with our lack of urgency in prayer?

Psalm 45

A Royal Wedding

There are many views about the occasion and meaning of this psalm. It could have been composed for Solomon's wedding to the Pharaoh's daughter (1 Kings 3:1), following his pledges of Psalm 127 and the responses to them in 128. The title calls it 'A Wedding Song', literally 'a song of loves', and, as such, it has similarities with Solomon's 'Song of Songs'. It came from the sons of Korah, the music school set up by David, composed for public use under the director of music.

But it is also a *Maskil* – didactic, instructive (see Ps. 32). It has something to teach us about the ideal king to whom Old Testament writers aspired and who would eventually appear in the person of the Messiah. Hence verses 6-7 are quoted in Hebrews 1:8-9. Parts of it are best understood as fulfilled in Christ and his present reign. Along with this goes the idea that the royal bride in verses 10-15 anticipates his union with his church.

Verse 1: The Author's inspiration
It is customary for the Poet Laureate to be commissioned to write a poem for a special royal or national occasion. If that was so here, this author is not having to strive for inspiration; in fact, he can hardly contain himself. F. D. Kidner calls it 'a theme clamouring to be heard'. This supports the idea that

there is more in this than the king of Israel taking a bride. The writer may not have been able to spell out what he sensed, but we can.

Verse 2: The Man
First comes the eulogy to the King as a man. But this is far from the flattery that characterised other courts. What makes him the most excellent man is that God has blessed him, particularly with the gift of wisdom, enabling him to speak as one whose lips have been anointed with grace. This reminds us of how Solomon came to enjoy this special gift, recorded in 1 Kings 3:4-15. Along with it came the ability to put his wise thoughts into powerful words, as his Book of Proverbs shows.

Verses 3-5: The Warrior
The king was the protector of his people under God and therefore the commander-in-chief of the army. Here he is extolled and encouraged to fulfill this office. Since however Solomon reigned in times of peace, as God said he would (1 Chron. 22:6-10), there are grounds for regarding this passage metaphorically. Verse 4 supports this idea: he is depicted as going out, not to conquer territory, but to fight on behalf of *truth, humility and righteousness*. The '*sharp arrows* [which] *pierce the hearts of the king's enemies*' are the words of truth which bring shame and remorse on the hearers; and *the nations falling beneath your feet* are their surrendering to God and forsaking their idols.

To some extent this happened in Solomon's reign: as trade developed and diplomatic relations with many nations became established, so Solomon's ideas and writings became widely known and had great influence (1 Kings 4:34; 10:1-9). Here too we have a glimpse of the coming Messiah, whose 'kingdom (was) not of this world', who both in his earthly ministry and his present reign through the gospel changes people in all nations by the force of his truth.

Verses 6-7: God
Here the vision of the King-Messiah reaches its height. The King is seen as the representative of God on his throne. Solomon's reign will end, but God's will last for ever and ever.

Also, it will be a reign of perfect justice, a perfection to which neither Solomon nor any other king would attain. This moral ideal is said to distinguish his rule from every other, to *set* [him] *above his companions* (v. 7). This verse applies even more clearly to Christ, for he is addressed not just as God (v. 6), but as one who has a God – your God (v. 7). When the writer to the Hebrews is looking for Biblical authority for placing Christ above all other beings, natural and supernatural, it is to these verses he turns: Hebrews 1:8-9.

Few psalms build up such a complete model of the coming Messiah-King as this one. *Anointed with grace* in verse 2, he is anointed with joy; going out to fight for *righteousness* in verse 4, he has conquered and is administering his kingdom with the sceptre of justice.

Verses 8-9: The Bridegroom
Here we come to the wedding itself. The bridegroom is decked out for the occasion, emerging from his ivory palace in robes fragrant with the finest perfumes, accompanied by the sweet music of the strings (v. 8), to mark the glad occasion. As he is marrying a foreign princess, her bridesmaids are also daughters of kings (v. 9). Outshining them all is the royal bride herself, glittering in garments of the gold of Ophir.

Having been led to think of Christ, we cannot help seeing a preview of his marriage union with the church, entered into on his coronation as King of the universe, and finally consummated on his return to claim her (Rev. 19:9; 21:1-8.)

Verses 10-15: The Bride
Attention now turns to the one to be given in marriage to the king. First, she is instructed in how to view this occasion (v. 10). The original institution of marriage required the husband or wife to *leave father and mother* [Gen. 2:24]. If this were the king of Egypt's daughter, she would indeed have had to make an effort to *forget* (her) *people and* (leave her) *father's house*, to go and live in a distant land with a foreign husband. Ruth did this willingly (Ruth 1:15-16) and this bride is encouraged to emulate her by the thought of the king's admiration for her beauty, which she should reciprocate by giving him the

honour due to him as her lord (v. 11). But she will not be the loser, for her wedding presents will be brought to her by men of wealth (v. 12), even by the daughter of the king of Tyre, the richest of the nations of the Near East at that time.

Thus made willing to contract the marriage, she is dressed within her chamber as a princess in a glorious gown interwoven with gold (v. 13). Then comes the bridal procession: in embroidered garments she is led to the king, accompanied by her bridesmaids, *her virgin companions* (v. 14). Everything is joy and gladness as they enter the palace of the king for the marriage ceremony (v. 15).

Verses 16-17: The Heirs
The king is now addressed again, as in verses 2-9, and in verse 14 (*brought to you*). The song ends by looking ahead to the sons he would raise. Here he is told these will occupy positions formerly held by the older men (*your fathers*), when these retired or died. Thus his sons would become princes throughout the land. How far this happened in Solomon's reign we are not told. The list of officials in 1 Kings 4 does not contain any of his sons, but of course at that time none of them would have reached maturity. In any case, we are told nothing whatever about Solomon's family, even in Chronicles. His son and heir Rehoboam is not mentioned until he actually succeeds his father on his death (1 Kings 11:43)!

The final verse too seems an exaggeration, if we think only in terms of Solomon. It is to some extent true that his name was perpetuated, especially as it became attached to the Temple he built, but though he received praise from the nations in his lifetime, it is unlikely that this continued for ever and ever. Indeed, the final verdict on him was quite shameful (1 Kings 11:11, 13).

Again we have to look to the One 'greater than Solomon', who through taking a people to himself 'brought many sons to glory' and became honoured throughout the nations of the world.

Questions:
(1) How does verse 2 anticipate Christ in his earthly ministry? (See Matt. 7:28-29, 13:54, 22:33; Luke 4:22; John 7:46.)

(2) What do verses 2-4 teach us about the use of military language in the New Testament? (See 2 Cor. 10:3-5.)

(3) Apply verses 10-17 to the story of the church of Christ from her birth in Acts 2 to her final union with Christ. (See Rev. 19:9, 21:1-8.)

Psalm 46

Singing on the Battlefield

This is one of a number of victory songs sung by the people of Israel when God had turned what looked like certain defeat into a spectacular victory. It may have been sung before the army left the field of battle, which would give meaning to verses 8-9, which sound like someone surveying the desolations a battle leaves behind. It confirms the words of the prophet: *The battle is not yours, but God's* (2 Chron. 20:15). **Alamoth** means 'girls', indicating that it was led by the sopranos, whose high voices were best suited to the note of triumphant joy sounded here.

Verses 1-3: Freedom from all fear

Verse 1 celebrates what this victory has taught them about God and what he is to his people: *our refuge*, the one who defends us when under attack, and *our strength*, the one whose power overcomes when we move into action. The people experienced both in wars with neighbouring nations. But this was not a one-off, for he is *an ever-present help in trouble*, always ready to step in, whenever the need arises. This knowledge takes away all fear (v. 2), even when things are very much worse.

The psalmist imagines the worst-case scenario, the total collapse of earth's fabric. The work of creation is put into reverse as the earth and the mountains which emerged from the water (Gen. 1:2; Ps. 104:5-9) are plunged back into it. But this is far worse than the primeval state, for the waters which were originally still now roar and foam and make the submerged mountains quake with their surging (v. 3). This puts local wars into perspective and leads to the confidence of the next section, after a pause for thought (*Selah*) or key change.

Verses 4-7: The peace of God

The river and its streams may not be literal, since no actual water flowed through the temple courts. Ezekiel later saw a river *coming out from under the threshhold of the temple* (Ezek. 47:1) in his vision of the new temple, as did John in his apocalyptic vision in Revelation 22:1. The point lies in the contrast with the surging seas of verse 3. However great the convulsions in nations or nature, peace like a river characterises the place where God meets with his people. The psalm is careful to point out that this is not due to anything special about the city or the holy place, but to the presence of *God ... within her* (v. 5). As verse 1 said, his presence is not a passive one; he is there to help, so that *she will not fall*. The night may be stormy, but it will pass and all will be well at break of day.

In verse 6 he envisages something even worse than what they had just been through: convulsions among the nations with kingdoms falling in a general conflict. But the God who has brought them through a recent trouble, the God who will take away fear when creation falls apart, has but to speak and they melt away. Nations with their armies may clash, but peace reigns among the people of God, because *the Lord almighty is with us* and if we are threatened, *the God of Jacob is our fortress* (v. 7).

Verses 8-11: God exalted

To prove this they only had to look around at the desolations which had once been their enemy's army. The battlefield is littered with broken bows, shattered spears and burnt shields, not to speak of the abandoned chariots, dead horses and soldiers' corpses. These are the works of the Lord. Let all peoples come and see them and be warned. Men start wars but God *makes wars cease*, not just in Israel's land but *to the ends of the earth* (v. 9). So the call goes out to acknowledge this and *Be still*, stop fighting before it is too late and *know that I am God'* (v. 10), who has power to destroy arms and nations, yes, the whole earth and cosmos. Give him his rightful place – *exalted among the nations (and) in the earth*. In view of all this, his own people have nothing to fear from men or God, for the Lord Almighty is with us.

Questions:

(1) How is this psalm (especially vv. 1-3) an example of the principle that the answer to most of our problems is in the nature of God?

(2) How can we face the dissolution of all things, or even the lesser preliminary ones most of us pass through? See the quotation of 102:25-28 in Hebrews 1:10-12. Of whom is the psalmist speaking?

(3) Do verses 8-11 help you to know how to pray in time of war?

Psalm 47

God Enthroned as King

This psalm celebrates God ascending his throne in Zion. As the ark of the covenant was regarded as symbolising God in his sovereignty, this psalm may have been composed to celebrate the entrance of the ark into the temple after its long absence from there (2 Sam. 6:17-19).

Verses 1-4: They give the ark a royal welcome
When the kings of Israel were crowned the people would clap and shout 'Long live the King' (2 Kings 11:12). Similar behaviour on this occasion shows this was like a celebration of God's coronation: he who dwelt between the cherubim carved on the ark's cover was about to ascend his throne.

Notice that the exuberance of verse 1 is balanced by the awe of verse 2. They did not forget what had happened when they mishandled the ark (2 Sam. 6:6-7). Also they were realising that the ark merely symbolised God; he himself was infinitely greater – 'awesome...the Most High' (a term used by the Canaanites for their god) ... 'a great King' (used by the Assyrians of their king, 2 Kings 18:19). The difference is what is meant by these titles: the Lord is no mere national God, but King over the whole earth. This he had proved from the time of Moses and Joshua when he had 'subdued nations under us, peoples under our feet'. He had done it recently by destroying the Philistine confederacy, confirming that the land was their rightful inheritance which he had chosen for Jacob whom he loved. While it was their own chief pride and glory, they recognised he was its real ruler. This they were doing by bringing his ark into the heart of the citadel.

Verses 5-6: The ark arrives in its appointed place

These verses correspond to the account in 2 Samuel 6:15 where the event was marked with shouts and the sound of trumpets. This was followed by singing psalm after psalm, for praises (v. 6) is literally 'psalms'. These would be (no doubt among others) 96, 68, 24, 15 and this one. The threefold repetition of 'sing praises' shows the celebrations went on and on, with shouting, clapping, singing and dancing to the accompaniment of all the instruments that could be mustered by the sons of Korah (see 1 Chron. 15:28). Whether or not we think our church services should be similar, we cannot escape the impact of their real sense of God's presence. How can anyone but be exuberant when God is clearly there?

Verses 7-9: God is acclaimed the universal King

It was this performance that Michal, David's wife, thought excessive, as she saw the procession pass her house (2 Sam. 6:16) and for which she reproached David on his return (2 Sam. 6:20-23). She seems to have thought that it was mindless fanaticism. In fact the word used for 'psalm' in verse 7 is 'Maskil' (as in the title to Ps. 32 and others), a word whose basic meaning is 'wisdom' or 'skill' (see 32). This is why the KJV translates it 'Sing praises with understanding'. So it was not just a frenzied noise; they were doing what Paul tells Christians to do: 'Sing with the understanding' (1 Cor. 14:15).

What it was they 'understood' and what we are to understand by this event is that it was a demonstration of God's universal sovereignty. The cherubim on the ark's cover formed a throne from the midst of which shone the Shekinah light signifying the glory and holiness of God. But this light was not only to reach Israel but all nations (v. 8). Apparently ambassadors ('nobles') were present at the Lord's enthronement ceremony (v. 9). The psalmist sees this as highly significant: the covenant promises to Abraham were beginning to be fulfilled – that 'all peoples of the earth will be blessed through you' (Gen. 12:3). God was staking his claim that the kings of the earth belong to God. This was indeed something to sing, shout, clap and dance over. How much more is there for us to celebrate now that the covenant promise is being fulfilled not symbolically but in reality by the preaching of Christ all over the world!

Questions:
(1) Is the suspicion many have of exuberant worship, with clapping, dancing and a number of instruments due to a loss of the sense of God's presence, or is it because of his presence?

(2) How can we ensure that exuberance does not degenerate into frenzy but maintains an awe at the greatness, majesty and holiness of God?

(3) Does the present poor interest of Christians in missions arise from a low view of the extent of Christ's Kingly authority in the world?

Psalm 48

Within the Walls of Jerusalem

The God whose enthronement was celebrated in the previous psalm is here seen to be established in his sanctuary on Mount Zion. The effect of this is not only to draw out the praises of his people but to terrify any strangers who approach with evil intent.

Verses 1-3: The greatness of the God who dwells on Zion.
Through the Lord's enthronement in the temple, Jerusalem has now become the city of our God (v. 1), built on his holy mountain. Their first duty therefore is to worship the Lord who is *great (and) most worthy of praise*. His greatness is reflected in the very situation and architecture of the city. It is built on Mount Zion (v. 2), elevated above the surrounding countryside with its suburbs and villages. So it is *beautiful in its loftiness*, symbolising its spiritual status as the place God has chosen to be *the city of the great King*.

Verse 2b has two possible translations (see NIV mg.), since Zaphon can mean 'north', referring to the fact that Zion, where the temple was built, was on the north side of the city. Since that is of no particular significance, most understand it as Zaphon, a much higher mountain than Zion and in which the rival god Baal was believed to dwell. Though Zaphon was higher than Zion, there was no comparison between Baal and the Lord, who was no mere local or national god, but *the joy of the whole earth*. So it is not the situation or the architecture that makes Zion great but the *God* (who) *is in her citadels* (and) *has shown himself to be her fortress* (v. 3). So the people continue to come to offer their praises.

Verses 4-8: The great power that emanates from his throne

Verse 3 was proved true when Jerusalem came under attack from a coalition of kings who joined forces and advanced together (v. 4). To their surprise what met their eyes and ears was not an army shouting and firing arrows from the walls, but a people celebrating the praises of their God. *Trembling seized them* and they were struck with pain *like that of a woman in labour* (v. 6). *They were astounded (and) fled in terror* (v. 5). But it was too late: the Lord destroyed them as suddenly and swiftly as the Tarshish fleet was shattered by an east wind (v. 7). They had heard that such things would happen, probably from the prophet of the day, and now saw it come to pass (v. 8). God had prevented their enemies from even approaching the city where he dwelt. Because of this they could be sure he would continue to preserve her (and) make her *secure for ever*. A pause (*Selah*) is needed to take this in.

Verses 9-11: The great love their God has shown

The past has been triumphant and the future is secure, all through God's *unfailing love* (v. 9), so they begin their service with a time to meditate on this, possibly under the leadership of a priest or prophet. This fuels a great spirit of praise to the God whose name is known and whose praise *reaches to the ends of the earth* (v. 10). Moreover, he has shown himself the One who governs the earth with his *right hand*, not whimsically like the pagan gods, but *with righteousness*. So it is not only Mount Zion, the capital, which rejoices, but the little places, *the villages*, are glad because of (his) judgments on their enemies (v. 11). For those enemies would simply have trampled them down on their way to take Jerusalem, the seat of Judah's God.

Verses 12-14: The great hope which lies before them

Now, exhorted by their leader, they leave the temple and process round the mount (v. 12), glorying in her *towers ... ramparts ... and citadels* (v. 13). This is not just pride in architecture, for it has a message for the next generation. The God who has come to dwell on Zion, from where he not only fights for his people but rules the whole earth, is the God of succeeding generations *for ever and ever* (v. 14). They have their human guides, but they are men who come and go, whereas God 'will be our guide even unto death'.

Questions:

(1) What are the advantages and disadvantages of church architecture? (Compare vv. 2-3 and 12-13 with Jer. 7:1-15; Matt. 16:18 and Eph. 2:19-22.)

(2) Do you personally and your church together meditate quietly on who God is before you open your mouth in his praises? (See Hab. 2:20; John 4:24.)

(3) What are the ingredients of the great spirit of assurance which is the climax of this psalm – verse 14? Compare with Romans 8:31-39.

Psalm 49

A Redemption Song

With its reference to redemption, this psalm echoes the Passover when the *ransom* was paid in Egypt's first-born sons (vv. 7-9). It also describes a dramatic overthrow of the rich and powerful (vv. 12-15), recalling the spoiling of the Egyptians followed by the destruction of Pharaoh and his army in the Red Sea.

Verses 1-4: Calling on all to attend

The psalm, like the Passover, has a message which all need to hear (v. 1). It is not just for 'the people' (of God) but for the *peoples ... who live in this world*, literally 'this age', the here and now. Verse 2 emphasises this by cutting across all distinctions: class: *low and high* (literally 'sons of Adam and sons of Ish', which NEB translates 'all mankind and every man'); and estate: *rich and poor*. Its message is beyond human wisdom and understanding; it is *a proverb ... a riddle*, a mystery not known except God reveal it, for it concerns the mystery of life and death itself.

Verses 5-9: The Heart of the Message

To bring out its universality the psalmist puts himself in the place of the poor surrounded by the rich (v. 5), despised and oppressed by those who *trust in their wealth* (v. 6), as were the

Hebrews in Egypt. The message is that whatever riches can do they are futile in the face of death. They may, if necessary, be able to pay huge ransoms to kidnappers or foreign powers, but no payment is ever enough to pay off death (vv. 7-8). None can do it for himself or for the life of another. Eternal life cannot be bought (v. 9). Human life is forfeit and only a substitute life can redeem it, for human life is more valuable than all the rest of creation (Mark 8:36-37). This is the meaning of the Passover, when Israel was 'redeemed' from Egyptian slavery by the death of the first-born sons (Exod. 13:1-16). This is a foreshadowing of the redemption of 'Christ our passover sacrificed for us' (1 Cor. 5:7).

Verses 10-15: The Message confirmed by Experience
The truth of this is something all can see and it applies not merely to the rich but to the wise, who are not clever enough to outsmart death. For the rich must *leave their wealth* behind for others to enjoy (v. 10). Those who have owned vast estates end up with only a few feet of earth for their houses. They vainly try to prolong their lives with expensive tombs, long-lasting dynasties and lands bearing their name (v. 11).

They themselves do not endure however and they end up no different from animals (v. 12). *The grave and death will feed on them* like sheep (v. 14). This is not because they have been rich, but because they have let their riches make them self-sufficient (v. 13). The same applies to their followers who approve their sayings, share their materialistic outlook, even though they might not share their riches. People who are not well-off can be as materialistic as those who are.

There is but one way to escape death and it is not in our hands but God's (v. 15). The believer in him may die but he will be redeemed from the grave so that God may *take* (him) *to himself.* The word *take* is that used of Enoch (Gen. 5:24) and Elijah (2 Kings 2:5) being taken up to glory. This foreshadows the redemption of believers in Christ: see the 'but God' in Ephesians 2:4, which is foreshadowed at the Red Sea when Israel saw their rich oppressors destroyed in a watery grave from which they themselves had been 'redeemed', so that God could take them as his people.

Verses 16-20: Encouragement of the Message to Believers

Even though the Egyptian situation may in some ways be repeated and believers find themselves at the wrong end of the social scale, they should not be *overawed* by the rich, (v. 16). However much the splendour of his house increases, the rich man *will take nothing with him when he dies* (v. 17). His riches may make him famous and popular (v. 18), but he will go into obscurity like his fathers and *never see the light of life* (v. 19). For all his opulence he ends up no better than *beasts that perish* (v. 20) – not because of his riches but because of his lack of understanding. Passover exposes the folly of the materialistic outlook and should make us thank God there is a way to redeem our lives from death – his way.

Questions:

(1) By comparing verses 1-4 with Ephesians 3:2-6 think how the events of Passover night and the annual celebration were relevant to all the world.

(2) How do the Passover night and the Red Sea help us better understand our redemption in Christ? Compare verses 7-9, 15 with 1 Peter 1:18-21.

(3) What have verses 10-14, 16-20 to say to our generation? Cf. Mark 8:36-37.

Psalm 50

God the Judge of His People

Here the theme of universality appears again (v. 1), but at the same time Sinai, the covenant and the law become more prominent (vv. 5, 16-20). The God who appeared at Sinai is present at all his people's gatherings for worship, and warns them of the danger of abusing the services of worship.

Verses 1-6: God as Judge of his people
Whereas in many psalms the people are gathered in a spirit of joy, praise and expectancy, the atmosphere here is more solemn. It begins with this array of divine titles: EL ELOHIM YAHWEH which indicate that he is the mighty God, the universal supreme being and the Lord, the God of his covenant people (v. 1). He speaks and summons all the inhabitants of the earth from east to west. They are to behold his glory shining forth from his house on Zion in all the perfect beauty of his holiness (v. 2).

But as well as beauty there is awesome power, for when he breaks silence it is like a storm bursting forth (v. 3). For he comes to judge his people and calls the whole creation as witnesses (v. 4). He came in similar fashion at Sinai, when he first entered into covenant with his *consecrated ones* (v. 5). As they made sacrifices on that occasion, so are they doing now. But God is not the God of ritual but of righteousness,

who is appearing among them as judge of their faithfulness
to his covenant (v. 6). The *Selah* pause must have turned into
a stunned silence!

Verses 7-15: God's Charges
(1) *On the count of motive and spirit*

God has two charges to bring against his people, which he
calls on them to hear (v. 7). The first relates to the spirit in
which they offered their sacrifices. He does not have a word to
say against their regularity and efficiency in performing their
services (v. 8). What he criticises is their attitude to them: they
seem to think God has set up the sacrificial system to meet his
needs (v. 9)! How can they be giving anything to God when
he made the creatures they offer him and they still belong to
him (vv. 9-11)? They had poor views of God, who they were
implying was one like themselves, who became hungry and
had to go and beg or buy food (v. 12), so that he could eat or
drink like them (v. 13).

Let them get two things straight:

(1) It was not God who should be grateful to them for
bringing animals to him, but they to him (v. 14). They should
therefore bring them as thank offerings to him, as they had
promised in their vows when they entered into covenant with
him.

(2) It was not God who needed them but they him (v. 15).
It was they, not he, who experienced days of trouble, when
they had nothing to bring him and could only call upon him.
This rebuke of the spirit in which their rituals were conducted
is very much the theme of the prophets, for example, in
Isaiah 1:10-20.

Verses 16-21: God's Charges
(2) *On the count of behaviour*

The second charge is against those whose lives were
inconsistent with their worship. They are *wicked* (v. 16), and
hate instruction: they will not hear his words of rebuke or
heed his acts of discipline (v. 17). Yet they *take* (his) *covenant
on* (their) *lips*; they repeat its terms and laws. But then they

go and break them: the eighth and seventh commandments (v. 18), the ninth (v. 19), and the fifth (v. 20). Worse, they think that, because God does not speak or act the moment they sin, it means he acquiesces in their behaviour (v. 21). There may even be a reminder of the covenant God in this verse, if the alternative translation in the NIV margin is correct: 'you thought the I AM was'. So, again, they reveal their low views of God; they are judging him by their own standards. They will soon learn how wrong they are when they come face to face with him as their Judge.

Verses 22-23: A word of exhortation

Here is the Judge giving them time to take all this to heart and act upon it. He sums up the two counts in reverse order:

(1) Consider this, that is, consider the grievousness of going through the motions of religion while in your life forgetting God (v. 22). Go on like this and God will act and there will be no hope.

(2) Put your heart into your worship: make it a real thank-offering, a *sacrifice of praise* (Heb. 13:15). Then you will have nothing to fear from him, for you have found 'the way (of) salvation' (v. 23).

Questions:

(1) Does the Bible teach that God judges his people more meticulously than he does others? If so, why? (See Amos 3:2; Luke 12:48; 1 Pet. 4:17.)

(2) How do we regard our personal devotions, public services and gifts? Are they duties for which we expect God to be grateful, or expressions of our gratitude to him? (See Luke 17:10.)

(3) Have we forgotten that God will judge us all and that his present silence is not acquiescence but space for repentance? (See Rom. 2:4-11; 2 Pet. 3:9-11)

Psalm 51

David Sins and Repents

The story of David's adultery with Bathsheba and his murder of her husband Uriah is well known, as are the two psalms connected with it (51 and 32). It is recorded in 2 Samuel 11 and 12, immediately following the defeat of the Arameans by the army of which David took command. But the Arameans had been recruited by the Ammonites who had originally started the war. When the Ammonites were defeated, the Arameans continued the war with extra forces, but were decisively beaten by David (2 Sam. 10:17-19). At the end of the winter David again sent out his army against Ammon. Why he did this is not made clear; perhaps he had received intelligence that the Ammonites were planning another attack and he felt that the best answer was to pre-empt it. This is what David did, except that he placed Joab in command and remained at home, not feeling his presence was required or that it was too dangerous.

A near neighbour of David's was the family of Eliam, father of Bathsheba. Uriah, Bathsheba's husband went to the war, leaving Bathsheba unprotected. By right such people were under the protection of the king. This greatly aggravates David's sin, in that instead of protecting he abused her, placing himself among the lowest of the low, corresponding in our society to children's workers or child minders who abuse their charges. This plus the attempted cover-up of having Uriah killed explains why God was so *displeased* (2 Sam. 11:27) with David. This was more than adultery (which was common enough in that nation), for the law-breaker was the law-maker himself, King David. It took a prophet from God and a clever, inspired approach to bring David to repentance. That repentance is poured out in Psalm 51 (see title).

Verses 1-5: David's total repentance

Through Nathan's words the enormity of his crimes has dawned on David and conviction of sin has struck every part of his being.

(1) His emotions (v. 1a). Here is a man stripped of all but God's *mercy ... love ... and compassion*. He is coming to God 'without one plea but' his reputation for sparing those who confess their utter demerit and rely on God's mercy. From this he moves up a rung to his unfailing or *covenant* love, pledged to him as one of that nation to whom God had covenanted himself (Gen. 17:7). Then up another rung to his compassion, for God's love is not merely one of promise and oath but of a heart which yearns to be reconciled to those who have turned from him.

(2) His mind (vv. 1b-2). He sees that neither his feelings of sorrow, nor even God's feelings of compassion to him are enough. There is an offence standing in the way, which he calls *transgression* (for he has broken God's holy laws) and *iniquity* (for he has acted unjustly and unfairly both to the woman and her husband). The three imperative verbs ask for the total removal of this: that God should *blot* (it) *out* of his record, *wash (it) away* from David so that it would leave no stain on his character, and he can be declared *clean*, the word used by the priest of the leper whose infection has disappeared (Lev. 13:6, 34).

(3) His conscience (vv. 3-4). Verse 3 describes a man in torment (described even more vividly in 32:3-4). He says *I know* because God has opened his mind through Nathan, and having seen his sin he cannot take his eyes off it, it is *always before me*, as it were 'driving me mad'! The absolute sincerity of this, the proof that it is more than mere remorse, is in verse 4. He is not denying he has sinned against the woman and her

husband, but recognising that they cannot punish him as he deserves – only God can do that. Whatever God's verdict on him turns out to be, it will be *right ... justified*. David is preparing himself to lose his throne, perhaps even his life. In the end it was only the child he lost, he himself was spared.

(4) His will. Verse 5 is not David making excuses and blaming his parents or God for a faulty gene. In fact he is doing the reverse: accepting full responsibility; the sins are his own and come from his own nature.

Verses 6-12: David's gradual recovery

First he realises that a sinful nature (v. 5) was not what God desired for man, whom he made with truth in the inner parts, a wholly integrated personality. In that case surely God will *teach* (him) *wisdom in the inmost place*?

This encourages him to expect God to *cleanse ... wash* him, for these may be statements rather than prayers: you will cleanse ... wash me. God will thus fulfill his own will (v. 6) and answer David's prayer of verse 2. The imagery of the first line of verse 7 is again from the leper (Lev. 14:4), who was seen as a social and spiritual outcast until cured. The imagery of the second line is from the laundry: 'keep treading me in the trough till I am whiter than snow'.

With this assurance he can anticipate the full restoration enjoyed by the cleansed leper (v. 8). He will be restored to society and hear the joy and gladness of the worshippers. Moreover, he himself will participate, for his strength has returned; he is like one whose crushed bones have been repaired and who can now leap and dance (cf. Acts 3:6-10).

Above all he can be reconciled to the God who had been 'displeased' with him (v. 9). He can now boldly ask that the God who had hidden his face from him because of his sins will now hide it from his sins, and thus look favourably on him. As he put it in verse 1, 'blot out all my iniquity from your record, erase it from your mind'.

He has now become assured of God's forgiveness for his crimes against him. But how can he ensure it will not happen again? How can he live this life of integrity? Forgiveness must be accompanied by renewal.

In keeping with his conviction that his sin has come from his inner nature, which God had originally made pure, he seeks a change within (v. 10). This God can do, but only he, for the word *create* is the one for 'primary creation', which always has God for its subject and is the word used in Genesis 1. Not that David is looking for creation to happen all over again; rather he is asking for the renewing of what had fallen and died.

To bring this about requires God's personal presence and action, the work of his Holy Spirit (v. 11). It was the Spirit who had originally equipped David for the kingship (1 Sam. 16:13) and whom he feared losing along with his throne, as Saul had (1 Sam. 15:28, 16:14). The renewal of our inward nature is a work only God can do, a work of the Spirit (John 3:3, 5).

Forgiveness without renewal leads only to a grim enforced obedience. David wants to enjoy God's salvation, to worship and obey him with a willing spirit (v. 12). This calls for more than confession, repentance and forgiveness. It requires a new nature which gives birth to those virtues Paul calls *the fruit of the Spirit* (Gal. 5:22-23).

Verses 13-19: The Blessings to follow

The fall of a leader has a much greater effect than that of a common person. This would not be the last time a king's sin would threaten a whole nation. Likewise, his restoration would renew the blessing of God on the people.

Others would be brought to repentance (v. 12). David was not the only sinner in Israel! But how could he rebuke them and urge them to *turn back to you* when he was guilty of the same sins? Now he had repented and received pardon, he could even use his lapse as an incentive to *teach transgressors your ways*.

David realises that during this episode his *tongue ... lips ... and mouth* had been silent to God. This too would damage the ardour of the other worshippers. 'Why is the king absent from the festival today?' Or 'Why does he sit there so silent and grim-faced?' The *bloodguilt* on his conscience ill-disposed him for singing 'your praise'. But if it were forgiven he would have an extra motive for worship, do so even more fervently and thus help revive the praises of God's people (vv. 14-15).

Moreover, all this has given David a deeper understanding of worship (vv. 16-17). He could have continued going through the motions and bringing his daily sacrifice and burnt-offerings. But of what avail would this be from the hands of an impenitent sinner? But when God's rebuke breaks the heart, that broken heart can be offered to him. This gives him more delight than all the animal sacrifices in the world. The best comment on this is Isaiah 1:10-20.

This does not mean that David was abolishing the sacrificial system, or belittling it. But his sin seems to have disrupted the spiritual life of the nation and its organised worship. It was as if the recently built walls of Jerusalem had been broken down. Their restoration would open the way for the resumption of regular worship (vv. 18-19). This would be all the more fervent following its absence, and above all would *delight you*. Some believe the two final verses were added by the director of music at a later date, possibly after the exile. David's repentance was thought to be a good model for the people's return to God after their sin had sent them into captivity, again disrupting the regular worship.

Questions:
(1) What is the difference between repentance and remorse? (See 2 Cor. 7:8-11.) Ask yourself how much you know of real repentance, even though your sins are doubtless not as grievous as David's.

(2) Distinguish between the various words for sin and forgiveness in verses 1-5 in order to bring out the enormity of the one and the richness of the other.

(3) What more do we Christians know about how to overcome a guilty conscience than David did, enabling us to come to him without fear? (See Heb. 10:22.)

Psalm 52

David at Rock Bottom

The story behind this psalm is told in 1 Samuel 21:1-9. David's childlike trust (expressed, for example in 131) was to be greatly needed – and sorely tried. It might seem that things could get no worse: he was an outlaw with a few attendants whom he left outside when entering the house or shrine where Ahimelech was (1 Sam. 21:1-2); desperately hungry (1 Sam. 21:3); weaponless (1 Sam. 21:8); and with no idea what to do next until he received supernatural guidance (1 Sam. 22:10, 15). This must be rock bottom.

One of Saul's servants, however, Doeg the Edomite, was also in the holy place, witnessed all that happened, overheard all that was said, and reported it to Saul, as the psalm's title states. David feared the likely outcome of this and sought to forestall it (or at least prepare himself for it) with a powerful denunciation of Saul and a re-assertion of his confidence in God.

Verse 1: David challenges Saul
The mighty man David challenges could not have been Doeg who was only Saul's *head shepherd* (1 Sam. 21:7). A mighty man (Heb. GIBBOR) was a specially chosen warrior often used as a bodyguard (1 Sam. 10:26; 14:52). Saul as king was commander of the army and therefore the chief GIBBOR – indeed it was for this he had been chosen king (1 Sam. 8:19-20; 10:23). It

was this physical strength and military power, of which Saul boasted, which he was abusing to harm David and which David was challenging. David had good grounds for his challenge, for Saul's words and deeds showed contempt for God's covenant. The NIV translation of the last clause is based on the Septuagint and is difficult to justify here. It is better rendered either 'God's covenant love continues' (in contrast to Saul's unfaithfulness to his promises to David and God); or Why do you boast all day long 'against God's loyal servant'? This is what David, with his new-found confidence (Ps. 131) was challenging with his *Why?*

Verses 2-4: David accuses Saul

David takes his challenge further as he dons his prophet's cloak again and denounces Saul in the name of God. Saul's words are deadlier than his sword. His sword was sharp but his tongue was a sharpened razor, which he was using for David's destruction by concocting lies. David knew Saul would take advantage of the compromising position in which Doeg had found him. It might be pointed out that David did not exactly tell the truth to Ahimelech (1 Sam. 21:2, 8), but this was the type of lie uttered on the spur of the moment to escape a tricky situation. Saul's lying was preconceived and endemic; it came from an evil heart – he loved it (vv. 3-4).

Verses 5-7: David pronounces judgment on Saul

The Spirit who had moved David to challenge and accuse Saul now works more powerfully to predict his overthrow (v. 5). This is strong language: *bring* (or 'break') *down from his high office*; *everlasting ruin*, from which he would never recover; *snatch up* (or 'away') from his tent (possibly predicting Saul's death on the battlefield); *uproot ... from the land of the living*, like a tree torn up by a storm, strong one moment and lying dead the next. This 'curse' fits very closely with the way Saul eventually met his end.

It is further solemnized by the expected reaction to the report of his death (v. 6): *see and fear* is a play on the words which are very similar in Hebrew. *Fear* indicates that the awesome power of God was made very real. This in turn exposed the ridiculousness of even a mighty king pitting himself against God – the laugh is one of scorn. This combined awe and scorn bring home the lesson (v. 7): Saul will become an example of what happens to one who constructs his power base on oppression, relies on it and therefore has no need of God. This was the story of Saul's life and explains his sticky end.

Verses 8-9: David voices his elation

All these are the words of a man at rock bottom, one who compared himself to a *dead dog* and *a flea* (1 Sam. 24:14) alongside Saul! Yet it was this man who had the greater security. Saul might have been like a mighty cedar, but David was like an olive tree, which survives for centuries whatever the weather throws at it, and which was basic to Israel's economy, giving the oil essential for both culinary and medical purposes. Whereas Saul was bent on destruction, David was devoted to serving. The ground for such an assertion was his trust in God's unfailing love. He was the one who in verse 1 referred to himself as 'God's loyal servant', who trusted in and was faithful to God's covenant of love.

So the Spirit who had moved him to prophecy now moves him to praise. To David God's name is good and gave him the hope which Saul, with all his other advantages, lacked. The final line referring to *your saints* may have been added when the psalm was edited for the director of music (title). This may also apply to *in the house of God* (v. 8), although the phrase can simply mean that the presence of God was with him wherever he was.

Questions:

(1) Do you have 'a sharp tongue' (v. 2)? What, according to David here, is its cause (vv. 3-4, cf. Matt. 12:34; 15:18)?

(2) Do verses 6-7 tell us anything of how people should react to the great disasters which still occur today (cf. Luke 13:1-5)?

(3) In these days of obsession with 'security' (national, domestic, personal), where does true security lie (vv. 8-9, cf. Prov. 18:10)?

Psalm 53

A Sick Society

This is almost a verbatim re-issue of 14, although the few alterations are interesting. It is not absolutely clear why David repeated it. Maybe what David had suspected was going on in people's hearts and against which he had uttered his warnings in 14 was now evident in reality. Although not saying 'I told you so' he is drawing attention to the truth of his warnings. The clue may be in the title of the tune: **mahalath**, which is close to the word for 'sickness'. The moral and spiritual condition to which he had earlier drawn attention had infected the whole of society.

Verses 1-4: The state of the people's hearts

Verse 1 uncovers the real cause of what was happening: departure from God himself. They were *corrupt ... vile* and did no good, for God was not in (their) heart, even though he may have been on their lips or in their actions. When he wrote the words of verse 2 in Psalm 142, this state of heart was known only to God. Now it is obvious to all. What may have begun in a few has become, as God foresaw and David foretold, universal and without exception (v. 3).

There may be significance in the change from 'the Lord' to *God* in verses 2 and 4. 'The Lord' (YAHWEH) is the covenant name by which God owned the people as his, and they owned him as theirs. God (ELOHIM) is the name by which he was known by which he was designated simply as divine. It is the name that can be applied to rulers (Ps. 82:1, 6) and even the heathen gods (Jer. 1:16; 2:11). They were in breach of their covenant with God, proved by the way they oppressed his people (v. 4) – the subject of the two previous psalms. What else could be expected since they had abandoned the practice of praying to him? They did not call upon God, and certainly they could not use the name 'the LORD' to him.

Verse 4 may indicate that there were still those who qualified to be called *my people*, but they were so ineffective that corruption could justifiably be said to be universal.

Verses 5-6: The overthrow of the rebels

It is in these verses that we find the chief differences from Psalm 14. The first line of each is identical. In both psalms David is speaking prophetically of a time when the terrorists would themselves be terrorised. When he wrote 53 this had not come about – indeed things were even worse. But it did not alter the fact that it would come true. To strengthen this David speaks less about God's protection of *the righteous* and of his being 'a refuge for the oppressed' (14:5b, 6b) and more about God's judgment on the oppressors. Before anything even started to happen they would suffer a panic attack (v. 5b). Then the oppressed would experience a great deliverance, for the words of verse 5c are addressed to those called *my people* in verse 4. They would turn the tables on them, put them to shame and see their corpses scattered on the field of battle unburied.

This gives the prayer of verse 6 even greater poignancy. The situation is dire, salvation must come out of Zion soon or all will be lost. David knows it will come, for in his prophetic vision he sees Israel rejoicing over its restored fortunes. When and how his words were fulfilled is not clear; perhaps not until after Absalom's rebellion had been crushed and the throne transferred to Solomon. Ultimately of course his words are looking on to the coming of the Messiah, who alone could deal with the corruption of the human heart, which is why Paul quotes these words in Romans 3:10-12 in the course of his account of the gospel of Christ. When David called it a *Maskil* he was saying more than he realised.

Questions:

(1) What is the value of repetition in the ministry of the word of God? (Phil. 3:1; 2 Pet. 1:12-15.)

(2) How do Psalms 14 and 53 show that the value of prophecy is to give certainty, not to answer curiosity? (John 13:18-19.)

(3) Compare verses 5, 6b (the prophecy) with verse 6a (the prayer). If prophecy makes something certain, what place has prayer? (Ezek. 36:37.)

Psalm 54

Betrayed

The occasion is specified in the title and the story is found in 1 Samuel 23:19-26a. The Ziphites were doing what the people of Keilah did, even though both were members of David's own tribe of Judah. Here we see how effective Saul's propaganda campaign had been. He had convinced them he was the victim of a usurper who was conducting a guerilla war against him and waiting for the moment to strike a *coup d'etat*. So in turning David in they were doing the Lord's will and would merit his blessing (1 Sam. 23:21). David is forced to move from place to place in the area (1 Sam. 23:24-26a), and this short, disjointed, rather breathless composition reflects the emergency during which it was composed.

This has to some extent been smoothed out by its editing for the director of music, for whom it was turned into a *maskil*. The word may describe a psalm with a specially important message, or perhaps one entrusted to particularly skilful Levites. See 2 Chronicles 30:22, where *service* has the sense of 'worship'. It was set to a stringed accompaniment, with an interval or key-change after verse 3: *Selah*.

Verses 1-3: David's emergency prayer
This is short but to the point: he simply appeals to God's character (*name*) as the God of justice: *vindicate me*. This is

followed by a simple request to be heard (v. 2), a statement at the grounds on which he can rightly appeal to God's justice (v. 3): that is, that those opposing him are behaving not like Israelites but foreigners (*strangers*) – men without regard for God, heathen, for they are opposing one of their own, in fact their anointed king. Moreover, they are not just opposing but trying to murder him, which was totally against God's express will. How can a just God refrain from protecting him from such men?

Verse 4: David re-affirms his confidence

In spite of this emergency, he has not fallen away from the confidence he reached in 62. Having brought the situation before God's eyes he now brings God before his own eyes: 'Behold!' (rather than *surely*) he says to himself and the people, *God is my help*. In adding *the Lord is the one who sustains me*, he is not overlooking the fact that he is not alone in the struggle but has hundreds with him, for it literally reads 'the Lord is with (or among) those who help me'.

Verse 5: David prays against his enemies

With this assurance he can again pronounce the curse of God on his enemies. Only one sure of his own standing with God can do that. Again it is God's character that he pleads – this time his faithfulness, that is to the covenant promises to keep those true to him from the wicked. This is not contrary to the New Testament attitude towards enemies: *Do not take revenge ... but leave room for God's wrath, for it is written, 'It is mine to avenge; I will repay', says the Lord'*(Rom. 12:19). It just does not go as far as the New Testament does – see the next two verses of Romans 12.

Verses 6-7: David anticipates deliverance

If this was composed during his flight and before Saul was called away (1 Sam. 23:26b-29), then David is expressing confidence that God will not merely help but save him. The future reference in verse 6 seems to indicate the deliverance was still future. This does not mean his promise of a sacrifice was a bargaining counter; it simply expresses his heartfelt thanks. He is looking forward to that time when he can give God all the glory for his great salvation.

Questions:
(1) How does praying protect us from panic in an emergency situation? (See Ps. 56:3.)

(2) What place does God's justice have in our praying? (Gen. 18:23-33.)

(3) How far can we be sure of the outcome of our prayers? How do you understand Mark 11:24? Is it qualified by John 14:12-14 and 1 John 5:14-15?

Psalm 55

Betrayed Again!

David's experience with the Ziphites in 54 was not the last time he was to experience human treachery. The supreme occasion was when his friend and counsellor Ahithophel defected to Absalom (2 Sam. 15:31). The words of verses 13-14 could very well refer to this and be the occasion of the psalm's composition. This explains why he specified stringed instruments, for these would give a plaintive tone to the singing, in keeping with David's feelings. However, the fact that he called it a *maskil* shows he was speaking to a wider audience, to teach us all how to react to betrayal.

Verses 1-8: David's distraught condition
David begins by opening his heart to God and showing how deeply he felt the attacks made on him (vv. 1-3). Whatever others say or do God must not ignore him. He fears there is worse to come: perhaps death in battle or at the hands of assassins (v. 4). He wishes with all his heart he could escape to a place of safety. He even envies the birds who, although vulnerable, can fly off to quiet spots and safe havens (vv. 6-8).

Verses 9-15: David's prayer against the treacherous
But he pulls himself together and clarifies his request. The writer of 2 Samuel reports that on hearing of Ahithophel's treachery David prayed: *O Lord, turn Ahithophel's counsel into*

foolishness (2 Sam. 15:31). This psalm may be the full version of that prayer. But it is motivated now, not so much by his fears for himself as for the city and nation. Jerusalem was no longer a city of peace (as its name means) but had become a place of violence and strife (v. 9). Its walls no longer offered protection but were the resort of rebels and terrorists (v. 10a). In the city centre people were turning against each other (v. 10b) and it was no longer safe to trade (v. 11). The only answer seemed to be that God should do again what he had done at Babel – confuse the confusers (v. 9) and divide the divisive so that their revolution would collapse. This is in fact what happened when Hushai and Ahithophel gave conflicting advice to Absalom (2 Sam. 16:15-23).

Meanwhile he continues with his prayer, bringing out the enormity of the sin against him. He was not a foreigner and an enemy, from whom David expected no better and for whom he would be prepared (v. 12). He was his closest advisor, *a man like myself*, literally 'a man of my own rank', one with whom he had virtually shared the government of the country (v. 13a). In fact he was more than a professional colleague, he was a personal and close friend (v. 13b). Even more he was a spiritual partner with whom he went to worship God in his house (v. 14). Two people could not have been closer than David and Ahithophel.

Now that he had joined this band of rebels who were so far gone in wickedness, it could be said that *evil finds lodging among them* (v. 15). This was not just a temporary lapse, it was a chronic condition. So, David felt there is only one thing to do with such – kill them! David has in mind a sudden drastic disaster falling on them, such as overtook Korah and his company when they rebelled against Moses and Aaron (Num. 16:30).

Verses 16-23: David obtains relief through prayer
Having made his request to God he continues to call to him (v. 16). He is in a crisis situation which calls for special prayer. Once a day is not enough – it must be as regular as his daily food: *evening, morning and* (at) *noon* (v. 17) – a Hebrew way of putting what we would call 'morning, noon and night', based

on Genesis 1 where evening is put before morning. There is a battle waged against him (v. 18), many oppose him, causing him to *cry out in distress*. As Jesus said of the demon-possessed boy, *this kind can only come out by prayer* (Mark 9:29).

But the prayer was availing, his faith that *the LORD saves* (v. 16) was vindicated. He receives assurance that *he hears my voice* (v. 17). He will not die in the conflict for *he ransoms me unharmed from the battle* (v. 18). For it is not a numbers game won by the majority but a matter of whom God favours. He decides who prevails, for he it is who rules *enthroned for ever* (v. 19). It is he to whom prayer is addressed who has power to afflict. At this point there is a sudden very dramatic pause or musical interlude in mid-sentence: *Selah*, perhaps to draw attention to the contrast between the God who is unchanging in his sovereign holiness and men who never change their ways and have no fear of God, who have not temporarily fallen but are hardened sinners.

Nor is he exaggerating his estimate of them; if anything he has understated their wickedness. For his betrayers were God's covenant people (v. 20), bound together by a sacred oath sealed with sacrificial blood. Yet they were attacking those they were bound to in that covenant, something that even the nomadic tribes who knew not God never did to each other. Of course they covered this up with smooth speech and soothing words (v. 21). Absalom won people over to him by flattering them and now Ahithophel had joined him in making promises to do what they accused David of neglecting. All the time they were set on war. No, he was not exaggerating; they deserved all that was coming to them.

The battle that David fights is that of wrestling prayer. So he has already won a victory in his own heart by entering into peace. Whether verse 22 is addressed to his own soul or to the people does not matter; it is the key to the problem. He came to God a burdened man, but he has *cast* (his) *cares on the LORD* and found that the Lord sustains him, that is, he does not so much carry the burdens as the one who bears them: he will sustain YOU (emphasis mine). So he ends on a note of sweet agreement with God over who does what. But YOU O God, your job is to do what I cannot and deal with these traitors and rebels in the way they deserve (v. 23). But as for me, my job is to trust in you, to do what you want me to do, believing that in this way I shall have peace and ultimate victory.

Questions:
(1) How do you cope with being let down by those you have been close to in Christ, and have loved and trusted? (See John 13:18-19, 30-31; 2 Tim. 2:17-19; 4:16-18.)

(2) Do you think the state of the churches and society today calls for 'special prayer?' (See vv. 16-18; Mark 9:29.)

(3) Study carefully the context of the encouragement to *cast your cares on the* LORD in this psalm and in 1 Peter 5:6. What light does it throw on our use of this exhortation?

Psalm 56

Struggling to Overcome Fear

According to the title this psalm was composed by David when the Philistines had seized him in Gath. The story is found in 1 Samuel 27:8–28:4 and chapter 29. For over a year David was loyal to Achish, king of the Philistines. From Ziklag he would go out against the remnants of those ancient tribes who annoyed both the Israelites and the Philistines (1 Sam. 27:8). David, however, had his own agenda: to prove to Achish that he had turned his back on his own people (1 Sam. 27:12) while at the same time not actually fighting them. To do this he had to resort to ambiguity and deceit with phrases such as *the Negev of Judah* (1 Sam. 27:10), which was not part of Judah but sounded as if it was.

Matters came to a head, however, when the Philistine commanders gathered all their forces together for a combined attack on Israel (1 Sam. 28:1). This was based on the area around Mount Gilboa in the north of Israel (1 Sam. 28:4). There would be no way David could avoid fighting hand-to-hand against the people over whom God had made him king. But again providence intervened. The army commanders did not share Achish's confidence in David's loyalty and voiced their suspicions to the king (1 Sam. 29:1-5). Although both Achish and David protested, David was seized by the Philistines (title) and forced to return to Ziklag. How he had intended to avoid fighting against his own people or justify it if it came to that we do not know, but Psalm 56 reflects the tension of this time and the way his confidence in God triumphs.

David recalled this when later he submitted the psalm to the director of music and called the tune *A Dove on Distant Oaks*, describing the innocent one forced to flee his native habitat for foreign parts. Although written in a time of tension and fear, the psalm has real shape and progression of thought as David wrestles with these enemies of the soul.

Verses 1-6: David struggles with fear

He begins in verses 1-2 with a desperate cry to God to come to his aid and take his part against those who oppress him. Verse 1 shows them almost succeeding; they are on his heels. The word for *hotly pursue* is literally 'panted', as if he can feel their very breath on him. He had indeed been very near to capture by Saul and had fled to the Philistines. Now they have turned against him and he is like Paul *pressed on every side* (2 Cor. 4:8). Although he has so far escaped, they have not given up (v. 2); they continue to pursue him or 'pant' after him. For they are very confident both of their right and their power to do so – they attack him *in their pride*.

David, however, is feeling far from confident, in fact he is afraid (v. 3). But he is not giving in to it. He had come there convinced that God was directing him (Ps. 11) and although far from Israel's shrines, he felt God was with him. His very fear and self-doubt only confirm this: *I will trust in you ... In God I trust.* Nor is this a mere mystical feeling – he has solid grounds for it (v. 4): God's word, the promise of him who cannot lie or be frustrated by man. The threats of mortal man, however fiercely he utters them, are insignificant.

However, these threats are still real (vv. 5-6) and his enemies were at work all day long to 'upset my plans' (rather than *twist my words*). Whatever course he took for his safety they were plotting how they could frustrate it. Verse 6 is very graphic: he sees them with their heads together, hiding in secret rooms, spying on him, waiting for the moment to strike. This could apply to Saul or the Philistines or both. He sounds like a KGB victim! How he needed that trust in God!

Verses 7-13: David triumphs over fear

Like the first half of the psalm, this part balances his awareness of the wickedness and ferocity of his enemies with his own personal feelings. Thus verse 7 shows him conscious of the size of the opposition – it was not just a few individuals but whole nations: it was Israel and Philistia as a whole who seemed out to destroy him. Such a situation demanded God's intervention in anger, to 'bring (them) down' and *on no account let them escape.*

Then in verse 8 he speaks of the depressing effect of all this on him, reducing him to tears. But in the light of verses 3-4 he can see it all in relation to God. For God knows and remembers: *record* (or 'you have recorded') 'my wanderings'. The word translated *lament* is NOD ('wandering'), familiar to us from Cain (Gen. 4:14, 16). 'My wanderings' are *in your record.* David feels homeless and friendless, a man of sorrows, whose comfort is that it is all known to God . There is a certain play on words here: 'wineskin' (NIV mg) is NO'D, very similar to NOD ('wandering'). Just as his journeys were in God's book, so his tears were on his scrolls – known to God and precious to him.

Recollecting all this he climbs above his fear and depression (vv. 9-11). He has but to *call for help* to this God who treasures his sufferings and his enemies will turn back. Then, if there is still any doubt, *by this I will know that God is for me.* In which case, what can man do to me? But as yet this has not happened, nothing has changed. Yet it has, for God has promised it, and when his word is trusted he is trusted, and the job is as good as done. But David goes beyond trusting the word – he praises it, that is, he is feeling, speaking, singing and acting as if it were already accomplished. True faith in God does not just say 'He will do it', but 'He has done it' and praises God for it.

This is confirmed in verses 12-13 where he is planning the thank offerings for which he has just put himself under vows. So he follows the logic of his faith and says *you have delivered me from death.* But even that is not the end of the matter. He is not delivered in order to live a quiet easy life, but to be able to walk before God in the light of life, openly obey and serve him without being hounded to death by the ungodly.

Questions:

(1) Consider prayer as a means of overcoming negative feelings (Phil. 4:6-7).

(2) Is it ever right for a Christian to pray for judgment on the wicked as verse 7 does? (See Rom. 12:19.)

(3) Consider Paul's allusion to verse 9b in Romans 8:31. To what adversaries and adversities does Paul apply this principle?

Psalm 57

The Triumph of Hope

The cave referred to in the title is probably the one David was hiding in when Saul arrived and went to sleep there (1 Sam. 24). This relates how David used the occasion not to kill Saul, as his men wanted, but to prove his innocence. His restraint was vindicated, since following his protest Saul admitted he had been unjust and conceded that David would become King, something he had really known for a long time (1 Sam. 13:14), which probably explains his long-standing jealous rage against David.

When David called this psalm also *Miktam* (title) he was probably drawing attention to its importance. He saw it as an example of the providence of God (v. 2), the basis of John Flavel's classic. '*The Mystery of Providence*'. The tune 'Do not destroy' he had already used with reference to himself on escaping from his house earlier (59) and was to use twice more (58, 75). Here it may have a different significance – that with Saul at his mercy God had said to him 'Do not destroy!' Saul was not to die at David's hands; God had a way which would leave David's ascent to the throne clear of blood.

Verses 1-3: David's true refuge
When David entered the cave at En Gedi he was hoping Saul would not discover him. But he did not know this for certain.

Only God knew and ultimately only God could protect him. So it was in God he was trusting: *in you my soul takes refuge*. For God, unlike the rocky cave, was a living protector, like the mighty bird which shelters its young *in the shadow of* (its) *wings* when the storm comes on, for *disaster* here means 'storms of destruction', referring to Saul and his men hotly *pursuing me* (v. 3).

So we find David here appealing to God: *I cry out*. He appeals to his *mercy* or 'grace', for he is not a God who likes to see his servants threatened. He appeals to his power as *God Most High*, a name used by Abraham after his defeat of the armies of the east (Gen. 14:22). He appeals to his providence, as the God who (literally) performs or 'accomplishes for me' (v. 2). God has called him to rule Israel and he will see him through.

This is why this section ends on a note of assurance: that this God will send help *from heaven* and rebuke his pursuers. Clearly no one is going to do that for him – they are all too afraid of Saul, nor has he himself the resources. But where others have let him down, God continues to show *his love and his faithfulness*.

Verses 4-6: David's trust vindicated

This is the turning point of the psalm. There is nothing new in what David says of his enemies in verse 4. He has likened them to *ravenous beasts* many times, not only for their bite but even their bark. When they cannot get near enough to strike him, their words or *tongues are sharp swords*. The fresh feature here is that he has to lie down to sleep encircled by them!

But he remembers the call and promise of God whose glory is very much linked to David's own fate (v. 5). So in seeking his own release David is seeking the restoration of the reign and honour of God which were being disgraced by Saul's regime. This God whose honour so deeply concerns him is the God who *fulfills his purpose* for him (v. 2). His providence has already intervened in that area when Saul was called away to fight the Philistines (1 Sam. 23:26-28). Now it does so again in a remarkable way when the man who had *spread a net for* (his) *feet* and *dug a pit (in his) path* has *fallen into it* himself. For Saul lay at David's mercy in that very cave in which he (David) seemed trapped.

Verses 7-11: David's hope triumphs

We need to understand the spirit of exhilaration which breathes through these verses in the light of verse 5. The fear, anxiety and weakness out of which he cried to God in verses 1-2 were not just for his own skin, but for the honour of God in Israel. His rescue would restore God's glory. So when that dangerous moment in the cave turned to David's advantage, it also became the means by which God would again be acknowledged as King of his people. This is what made his heart *steadfast* – not just free from anxiety but resolved on praising rather than crying. He wants to employ all his powers for this: his soul, his poetical and musical gifts (*harp and lyre*) and his time and energy, rising to begin this before *dawn*. So the key word is *awake*, that is, let those feelings and their expression which have been dormant be roused again.

Nor is this great witness to God to be confined to Israel. As God's praise resounds again from his people, so it will be heard among *the nations* (and) *the peoples* (v. 9). It is significant that this verse is quoted by Paul in Romans 15:9, where Paul is appealing for unity between Jewish and Gentile Christians on the grounds that 'Christ has become a servant to the Jews on behalf of God's truth so that the Gentiles might glorify God for his mercy'. So here God's love is so great and his faithfulness so high it cannot be confined to one tiny nation.

So once again David's life takes on the pattern of Christ's: this time not in terms of his sufferings but of his glorious reign (cf. 22:23-31). This serves to fortify his cry made in the midst of trouble (v. 5) expressed in verse 9 with greater conviction.

Questions:

(1) How much would it improve our prayers if we brought the providence of God more into them? (v. 2, Rom. 8:28.)

(2) Do you find your feelings of depression or elation fluctuate in step with the state of God's work on earth rather than your personal health or affairs? (See Amos 6:6.)

(3) When you feel physically jaded or spiritually low, do you ever tell yourself to 'Wake up!' or do you just lie and wallow in it? (See Ps. 42:5; 2 Tim. 1:6.)

Psalm 58

Corruption in Government

It is not clear whether David is denouncing the 'rulers' of Israel (Saul and his government) who were unjustly oppressing him and misgoverning the nation, or whether he is referring to foreign 'rulers', which would place him among prophets such as Amos and Isaiah, who condemned the leaders of other nations. A third possibility is that he was writing at a time when his own counsellors had become corrupt, causing them to forsake him for Absalom. Much depends on whether the last words of verse 2 should read *on the earth* or 'in the land'. Whichever it is, the psalm is a powerful condemnation of evil in high places, a phenomenon not unknown today.

The subtitle *Miktam* and the tune *do not destroy* are the same as for 57. This does not mean they relate to the same circumstances. These words were probably added when the psalm was given to *the director of music* for public use. But the words do show that both situations were times of great danger and that the psalms which marked them should be remembered. (See 16 for the meaning of *Miktam*.)

Verses 1-2: David's charge against the governors
He first of all calls in question the way these *rulers* were governing. Verse 1 reads literally 'do you indeed pronounce justice by keeping silent?' This is similar to Asaph's accusation

in Psalm 82: the judges were allowing these evil-doers to bring charges against *the weak and fatherless ... the poor and oppressed* and doing nothing to defend them.

In verse 2 he answers his own question: *No*, they did not *judge uprightly*, they were doing the opposite: *you devise injustice*; they gave the verdict against those who could not defend themselves. So they were to blame for the 'violence' that was beginning to take hold *on the earth* or 'in the land'.

Verses 3-5: David's diagnosis of the ultimate cause of this behaviour

David puts their corruption down to their inborn sinfulness (v. 3). Although they are *rulers* and *judges* ('gods' in Ps. 82), they are indeed 'like mere men' (82:7): *astray* from righteousness, *wayward* as regards the truth, so that they *speak lies* in administering the law. These *lies* are deadly (v. 4a), like a *snake's venom*. Deceitfulness on the part of governments tends to foment discontent. Worse, they are incorrigible (vv. 4b-5): keeping the snake simile David says they are deaf to the charms of music; however pitiful the plea of the innocent or persuasive their protestations of innocence, they shut their ears to them.

To attribute this to what Augustine called 'original sin' is not to excuse it. While none can change his basic nature any more than 'can the Ethiopian change his skin or the leopard his spots' (Jer. 13:23), power is usually available to restrain its worst effects, just as we can mitigate the symptoms of our illnesses when we cannot cure them. Moreover God has given his Law to assist this process (Gal. 3:23). But these men who not only knew the Law but were called to administer it, failed to apply it to themselves. The effect of this was so to harden their hearts that they would not even listen to the cries of their fellow human beings or their brothers in Israel.

Verses 6-9: David's declaration of the curse of God on them

As so often in his psalms David dons the prophet's mantle and speaks the very words of God himself. God who appointed them to office will swiftly remove them from it (cf. 75). That David is not saying that God will literally 'kick their teeth in'

(v. 6a) is clear from the metaphorical language of verse 6b – they are not *lions*, they just behave like them. The meaning is that God will deprive them of the power to do harm.

The effect of this is most graphically depicted in what follows. They will become as feeble as trickling *water* (7a); as ineffective as *blunt arrows* (7b); as harmless as a *slug's* slime trail (8a); as abortive as a miscarriage (8b); and as useless as *thorns* blown away by the wind before the fire can get through (9). What an indictment! What a judgment!

Verses 10-11: David's joy in the happy outcome

The removal of these so-called governors and judges will restore the equilibrium of society, to the general good of all. Although verse 10 sounds vindictive and as cruel as these men were, it is again prophetic imagery, drawn from victory on the field of battle, where an army advances over the corpses of the slain. It is a dramatic way of saying 'the righteous will be victorious'.

Verse 11 brings out the real meaning. When God removes bad governments, there are two good results:

1. The moral balance of society is restored, so that it again becomes worthwhile to live righteously, which is costly under tyranny.

2. God himself is shown as the true governor of *the earth*, the one to whom all rulers are accountable. Where there is oppression people say, 'Where is God?'. Where the oppressor is removed they say *Surely there is a God who judges the earth* (cf. Prov. 11:10-11).

Questions:
(1) If corrupt government is due to 'original sin' does this imply that only the regenerate are fit to govern?

(2) Does the psalm give us any guidance as to how we should pray for tyrannical governments?

(3) Can you think of any occasions in recent times or back in history when the truth of verse 11 has been demonstrated?

Psalm 59

David Under Siege

The background to this psalm, referred to in the title, is recounted in 1 Samuel 19:1-17. David had fled from Saul when he flung a javelin at him while he was playing to Saul on the harp. But Saul's jealous anger did not abate when David left him (1 Sam. 19:10). This time he pursued him by calling out and sending men to surround his house (1 Sam. 19:11). Being late evening they were to wait outside – to force an entry would have been to endanger the life of his daughter Michal, and Saul had not descended that far. So they were to wait for him to come out in the morning, then kill him. David spent the night, or part of it, in prayer, the general lines of which form this psalm, as the title indicates.

Verses 1-10a: David cries out to God
The cry *deliver* is a cry of distress, indeed the whole psalm breathes the emotion David felt at the time. His prayer *protect* is literally 'put out of reach', 'put me somewhere my enemies will not be able to get me'. The rest of the passage sets out the *reasons* for his request, the grounds on which he believes God should hear him.

(1) **The extreme hostility of his *enemies*.** They *rise up* in a literal sense, they are leaving their beds or chairs to pursue

him. The *evil* they are intent on is no less than his murder, for they are *bloodthirsty*. They are not executing him in a judicial manner but with great cruelty, for they are *fierce* (v. 3).

The immediacy of the psalm is even more apparent in verse 3 where he seems to be asking God to look out of the window with him at what is going on. What he can see (vv. 6-7) is Saul's men lying in wait for him. Evidently David did not leave his house that morning, so they went away empty-handed. They were back in the *evening*, however, like a pack of *wild dogs* who sleep by day and emerge at night ravenous for anything edible. In Israel dogs were rarely kept as pets; either they worked with sheep or ran wild. 'Dog' became a term of contempt used of Gentiles or Israelites who behaved like Gentiles. David justifies his description by pointing to their slanderous accusations and threats, for which he uses a mixture of metaphors showing the agitated state of his mind: they are like vomit, or dog's teeth or sharp swords. But when he comes to their arrogant defiance: *who can hear us?* he is sufficiently in control to recall that they are responsible to God who certainly does *hear* and will call them to account. Their threats are laughable to him.

(2) **His own innocence** which he expresses in verses 3b and 4a. All he has ever done is to try to serve his nation and his King. He has *no offence or sin* on his conscience – either against them or his God.

(3) **God's nature and his promise**. He is *the* LORD (v. 5), *the God* who is in covenant with *Israel*, who has undertaken to come to her aid, and who as *God Almighty* has promised to do so. While *wicked traitors* refers to those lurking outside, the call to God *to punish ALL THE NATIONS* (emphasis mine) seems to go far beyond this. Possibly he is conscious of danger from the Philistines, with whom they were still at war, so that he was being attacked on two fronts. Alternatively this phrase may have been inserted when the psalm was edited for congregational singing, as the title indicates it was. By that time David as king was responsible for protecting God's people from hostile *nations*, a responsibility which he could only discharge with God's supernatural aid.

Having recalled who God is, he can now entrust his case to him (v. 9). In spite of his military success, David knows he is vulnerable, but God is his *strength*. He knows too that his house is no castle, but God is his *fortress*. Above all God loves him (v. 10a).

Verses 10b-17: He recovers his confidence
Now he has got things into perspective he is sure that through God the tables will be turned and it will be he who does the *gloating* (v. 10b). He seems to be expecting some immediate blow to fall on his enemies for he asks God to hold back from sudden destruction (v. 11a). People soon forget their catastrophes, which do not deter the evil-minded for long. If the lesson is to be learned it would be better if the gang were broken up, went into hiding, were pursued and forced to *wander about* and eventually be *brought down*. He imagines their being placed on trial (v. 12), questioned about their slanders, threats, boasts, *curses and lies*; then condemned, sentenced and executed (v. 13a). The publicity in all this would make God known as the real ruler of the descendants of *Jacob*, that is, the head of God's Israel (v. 13b). The title of the tune to be used 'Do not destroy' suggests that this point (the way God will deal with his enemies) is uppermost in David's mind, above his personal danger.

This is borne out by what follows. The contrast between verses 14-15 and verses 16-17 is unmissable. His enemies assemble night after night, getting hungrier and hungrier like wild dogs who have not fed for days. When they are not *snarling* at David they are *prowling* impatiently and *howling* for his blood. *But* (v. 16) what is David doing now? Shaking in his shoes? Crying out in desperation? Not any more. The emotion he put into his prayer in verses 1-5 he now puts into his *praise* of God. He is sure he is in his *love*, that he who is his *Strength* is on hand, which turns his house into a fortress (v. 17). So his cry to be 'put out of reach' of these men (v. 1) has truly been heard. So *in the morning*, as his enemies slink away empty-handed, he lifts up heart and voice to God.

Such a composition as this was worth recording for later use, not only personal but corporate. This is why it is called *Miktam*, which probably means 'inscribed' and therefore 'recorded'.

Questions:

(1) How do you feel about David's prayer that his enemies should experience a lingering rather than sudden death?

(2) Does the punishment of Cain (Gen. 4:10-16) throw any light on the matter?

(3) Who are the enemies of the people of David's 'greater Son' today, and how should we pray for them?

Psalm 60

From Defeat to Victory

The title locates the circumstances in David's reign which occasioned this psalm. Battles with various Aramean (Syrian) tribes are recorded in 2 Samuel 8. Even more precise is the defeat of the *Edomites in the Valley of Salt* referred to in 2 Samuel 8:13, though there is a discrepancy in the numbers.

After the return of the ark to Jerusalem David wanted a more worthy building to house it, but God told him through Nathan that this was not a priority (see 2 Sam. 7). It was more important to establish David's dynasty in view of the hostility of the surrounding nations, who were still intent on bringing him down. The temple could wait for more settled times.

The advice proved wise, for it was not long before the Philistines rose up again and allied with Moab, Aram, Ammon, Edom and Amalek. David would not be able to fight on all these fronts. After some initial setbacks however, God stepped in and a great victory was won. This psalm recalls the struggle and ultimate victory.

The title calls 60 a *Miktam*, that is, a message from God *for teaching*. The theme of the message is indicated by the tune 'The Lily of the Covenant', meaning that it displays the beauty and fragrance of God's covenant with Israel, particularly his covenant with David and his house, the terms of which he has just spelled out in 2 Samuel 7.

Verses 1-4: On the point of defeat

The joyful confidence of David and the people when their
enemies were subdued and the ark of God was in Jerusalem
has now given way to consternation. We have seen in Psalm 2
how restless Israel's neighbours were under the yoke David
had imposed on them, and how they were conspiring together
to break it. Now they have succeeded and panic is widespread.
It is as if there had been an earthquake (v. 2) and everyone was
staggering around in a state of shock (v. 3). Since they had
attributed the former victory to God's favour, they can only
attribute their defeat to his *anger* and *rejection* (v. 1), though
why this was so they seemed not to know.

What verse 4 means is not agreed. If the NIV is right this is
a turning-point: God has raised his standard for the people to
rally to and go forward. Since there is no *but* in the original
and *to be unfurled against* is a paraphrase of a word which
simply means 'from the face of', it may mean that the *banner* is
raised to call them to retreat from *the bow*: the banks of archers
were too much for them and they must withdraw. This would
make verse 4 the lowest point of this event, hence the solemn
pause: *Selah*.

Verses 5-8: God steps in

But with God a low point *is* a turning point if it is used as a
basis on which to cry out to him. For it is *those who fear you*
who now find themselves cornered. God will not tolerate this
long, especially when appeal is made to his sovereign power
(*your right hand*) and his love for his people.

So we find he immediately answers: *God has spoken*. Perhaps
a priest in the newly-established *sanctuary* interprets the Urim
and Thummim on the ephod (which happened to David
more than once in his wilderness years); or perhaps a prophet
appears on the scene to speak in the name of God, speaking
'by his holiness' (as *sanctuary* may be translated). What he
says is that the places under attack are those he originally
gave to Israel and will restore to them – *parcel out* and *measure
off*. The places are on both the West bank (*Shechem* and half
of *Manasseh*) and the East bank (*Succoth ... Gilead* and the rest
of Manasseh). This counter-attack will be led by the tribe

with the largest number of fighting men – *Ephraim*, which is therefore called *my helmet*, and through the leadership of the tribe from which the kings came – *Judah* which is therefore called *my sceptre*.

Having done that, he will take the war into the enemy's territory: *Moab, Edom and Philistia*, whom he will again subjugate, as if they were domestic utensils like a *washpot*, or articles of clothing like a *sandal*, to be tossed carelessly aside. Thus he will *shout in triumph over Philistia*, the instigator of the revolt.

Verses 9-12: Confidence is restored
This does not mean that it will all be easy. *Edom* had a strong *fortified city* called Petra, built into the rock and seemingly impregnable (v. 9) So the boldness of verses 6-8 is shaken as he recalls that God seems to have turned from them. If God has *rejected* them (v. 10, cf. v. 1), how can their *armies* hope to succeed? So they again resort to prayer, putting their trust in God alone, not in human alliances as the enemy was doing (v. 11). This restores confidence, for *with God* can be done what man even at his most powerful cannot do (v. 12).

Questions:
(1) Are songs and hymns still a means of teaching, as they seem to have been under the old covenant (*Miktam* and Deut. 31:19)? Is this what Ephesians 5:19 means?

(2) Compare the situation of those in the psalm with a Christian's experience in the world, described in 2 Corinthians 4:8-11.

(3) Compare what cannot be done without God with what can be done with him (see Matt. 19:26; Luke 1:37).

Psalm 61

Longing for God's House

David wrote this psalm when he was a long way from home, though probably not as far as the NIV translation of verse 2 suggests: *the ends of the earth*. More likely earth should read 'land'. Since he was king at the time (v. 6) this psalm does not come from his time as an outlaw in the days of Saul. It may have been when he was on one of his campaigns against neighbouring nations or when he fled from Absalom. The emotions expressed here favour the latter alternative. The second part of the title should be singular: *a stringed instrument*, which may have been a lyre such as David himself played. This would be in keeping with the melancholy tone of much of the psalm.

Verses 1-4: He prays for restoration to God's house

The psalm begins with a plaintive *cry* (v. 1), for the word describes an audible noise full of emotion. He is seeking to gain God's attention so that he will *listen to my prayer*. He is still a long way from God's dwelling-place, for he was at *the ends of the land* (rather than *the earth*) (v. 2). He is physically and emotionally exhausted – *faint* , either because he has just fought a battle or because he has been fleeing from Jerusalem. He needs the comfort of God's presence, to be where he reveals himself – the tabernacle.

The metaphors he uses in verses 2b-4 are all drawn from the tabernacle and symbolise the comfort and strength to be derived from being there. In verse 2b he speaks of *the rock that is higher than I,* (possibly the Mount of Zion on which the tabernacle was built), signifying the strength it gave him; it was like a *tower* into which people retreat when the enemy comes (and David knew all about that).

In verse 4 he speaks of it as a *tent,* which indeed it was, but he may also be thinking of the tents of the nomads which were places of *refuge* for travellers, affording shelter, hospitality and friendship. At the heart of the tabernacle was the ark of the covenant with the cherubim and their outstretched wings, forming the horns of the altar where those fleeing for safety could find *refuge* (1 Kings 1:50).All this he *longs* to enjoy again. Yet in a sense he already does: the fact that he can still *call to* God all that distance away shows he believed God was not confined to Jerusalem but was accessible elsewhere. This leads to the next section.

Verses 5-8: David believes God is answering him
In verse 1 he asked God to *hear (and) listen;* now he knows he has done so, for his prayer had not been selfish but uttered in order to fulfill the *vows* he had made on his accession (75, 101), which he had probably repeated in his recent extremity. So he laid hold of the promise God had *given* him, that is, *the heritage of those who fear your name,* meaning the land and people God had entrusted to David in his covenant with him (2 Sam. 7).

Emboldened by this he prays for a new lease of life (v. 8). Whatever it was that took him away it was obviously a threat to his life, but God has spared him. The use of the third person in verses 6-7 does not mean these are someone else's words. The purpose of the continuation of David's dynasty over *many generations* was because the Messiah would come from David's line to set up his kingdom. Whether David was conscious of this or not, the Holy Spirit was putting this hope into his mouth. This gives meaning to verse 7: David was but a precursor of the one who would be *enthroned in God's presence for ever* (cf. Luke 1:32-33). This security, both for David and Christ, is guaranteed by the *love and faithfulness* of God. So the charged emotion of his 'cry' of verse 1 becomes the jubilant *praise* of verse 8, the spirit in which he pledges himself to continue.

Questions:
(1) Is God as real to you when you are away from your accustomed place of prayer as when you are there? (See John 4:21-24.)

(2) Do you find in Christ that sense of security which David found in the tabernacle? (See 2 Tim. 1:12.)

(3) Do you relate all your experiences, hopes and fears to the eternal reign of Christ? (See Rev. 1:4-6.)

Psalm 62

Rest in God Alone

This psalm comes from a time when David is virtually on his own, probably during his exile from his home and from the court of Saul. True, he had a band of faithful followers and Jonathan was doing all he could to effect a reconciliation, but David derives little peace from this. His comfort is that God is there and he *finds rest* in him *alone*.

The psalm proceeds very neatly in pairs of verses.

Verses 1-2: David is at peace with God

Literally, *my soul WAITS IN SILENCE on God alone* (emphasis mine) David is not trusting in the safety of his hideout, which could be discovered at any moment, nor in Jonathan's intercessions, which might not be successful, as indeed they were not altogether. These voices were *silent* and he is listening for God, for *God alone*. Because of this he is greatly strengthened in mind: God is his *rocky* place and will be his *salvation*; God is his mountain *fortress*, so that whatever happens his confidence will not be MUCH (rather than *never*) *shaken* (emphasis mine).

Verses 3-4: David defies his enemies

Outwardly things had not changed. Saul was still throwing everything at him, though militarily David was as weak as

a *leaning wall ... a tottering fence*. But Saul is obviously afraid
that David will grow in power and become a threat to him.
Jonathan had revealed that Saul knew of his anointing as
king (1 Sam. 23:17) and was doing his utmost to *throw him
down (and) topple him from his lofty place* as heir to the throne.
If force of arms will not achieve it he will resort to *lies*, flattery
and secret conspiring. Although David has said all this many
times, there is a note of defiance rather than complaint here,
as his question shows.

Verses 5-6: David encourages himself

Sensing that the thoughts of verses 3-4 were threatening to
disturb the peace he felt in verse 1, he calls his mind back to
God alone. In fact he takes himself on a stage further: God is
not only his *rock ... salvation and fortress* now, but his *hope* for
the future. So he is able to say, not merely *I shall not be* MUCH
shaken, but *I shall not be shaken* (unqualified). Saul's battering
ram will not break down the *leaning wall* because it is *leaning*
on God, his *rock*.

Verses 7-8: David encourages the people

What he has said to himself he now declares to the people,
with the addition of *my honour*, referring to his call to the
throne. This, like his present safety, *depends on God*, not his
personal ambition. From this secure position he addresses
his little band of followers. They are sharing his troubles, let
them share his *trust* in God. Let them not be inhibited in their
approach to God, but tell him everything they feel. *Pour out*
has the sense of 'empty' – do not keep a drop of your grief back
from him, for he is there for refugees who have nothing: *God
is our refuge*, he is father and mother to us. No doubt this part
of the psalm was appropriate when it was given to Jeduthun,
a director of music (title) for use in worship.

Verses 9-10: David adds a warning

Trust in God must be whole-hearted, with no vestige of
reliance upon human beings of whatever station in life. The
lowborn are (literally) 'sons of ADAM', man made from the
ground (Gen. 2:7); the *highborn* are (literally) 'sons of ISH',

man the husband (Gen. 2:23), the procreator of the human
race, the term used in such phrases as 'man of God'. However
great is our humanity it cannot bear the weight of trust when
weighed on a balance against God. For man is *only a breath*, he is
mortal, in fact he is sinful – *a lie*. This aspect is developed in
verse 10 with its reference to the fruits of sin: *extortion*, stealing
and covetousness. Where these things motivate men they are
living a *lie*, therefore *do not trust them*.

Verses 11-12: David simplifies his thoughts

What a great ending! In the midst of troubles coming from all
sides, of conflicting advice and not least of the many thoughts
buzzing through his brain, David centres on *one thing*, which
he has 'heard repeatedly' (as *two things* is a better rendering)
and which is *that you, O Lord, are strong*. Power belongs to
God, not to Saul nor to himself. This was not a trial of strength
between Saul and David, but a means of demonstrating that
God was in control. This power God wields lovingly (v. 12)
– not to destroy, but to build up; and justly, for he will *reward
each person for what he has done*. It is for God to decide whether
Saul is wrong and deserves punishment, or whether David is
fit for the throne he has been promised.

Questions:
(1) What points are made throughout the psalm which aid our
peace of mind? (See John 16:33; Phil. 4:6-7.)
    (2) How important is it for one who counsels another to be
on top of his own troubles? (See 2 Cor. 1:3-11.)
    (3) How far can a Christian be a person of 'one thing'
(vv. 11-12)? Is not life more complex? (See Luke 10:38-42;
Phil. 3:13-14.)

Psalm 63

Hope Triumphant

This psalm is similar in theme and spirit to the previous two: David is away from his house and the house of God, longing to be there but finding the very thought of God a great comfort. Like 61 it comes from the period of David's reign as king (v. 11) and may therefore be during his enforced exile due to Absalom's coup.

Verses 1-5: David longs to be with God
What he misses most of all is being able to meet with God in his house. Thus he sees in the arid region in which he is camping a reflection of his *thirsty soul*, indeed the thirst of his whole being, *body* as well (v. 1). This contrasts with what he experienced back in Jerusalem when he *beheld (God's) power and glory in the sanctuary* (v. 2), perhaps referring to visions he experienced, like Isaiah's (Isa.6).

'Absence makes the heart grow fonder'. So he is even more convinced that God's *love is better than life itself* (v. 3). Therefore even out here he will continue to *glorify* him with his *lips*. If he can do so at this time and in this place he can do it any time and any place – he will do it *as long as I live* (v. 4). Just as his body felt the longing of the soul (v. 1), so his uplifted *hands* reflect the elevation of his heart. Whether here or on Zion he will find his satisfaction, not in the delicacies of the table but in the praises of God (v. 5).

Verses 6-8: David holds on to God

He is winning the struggle, is less conscious of his absence from God and more conscious of God's presence with him. Even a sleepless night does not disturb him because he spends it meditating on God (v. 6). Whereas we might count the hours by the chiming of a clock, he would know what time of night it was by the changing of the *watch*, which would be three times. Although the *wings* of the cherubim in the sanctuary were not before his eyes, he feels as secure as if he were under their *shadow*, for the Lord is there, *upholding* him as if his hands were on him (v. 7).

In response David *clings to* him, like a child holding tight to a parent's hand (v. 8). What David is doing here is taking God at his word, for this is what he continually invited the people to do when he established his covenant with them (Deut. 10:20; 13:4.)

Verses 9-11: David is confident of victory

David is expecting many of those who had rebelled against him to be dead on the battlefield, left to the mercy of the scavenging beasts (v. 10), because they opposed his authority as king (v. 9), whether they are of Israel or foreign powers. For God has proved to him the certainty of his covenant promise to preserve him as king through his life, and his dynasty thereafter (v. 11). This was not a conflict between rivals for the throne, but between those loyal to God (those *who swear by (his) name*) and the *liars* who claim to be his covenant people but are not true to their word.

Questions:
(1) 'God thirsts to be thirsted for' (Gregory). Is it true that God rejoices when he finds us thirsting for him? (See Matt. 5:6.)

(2) Are those of us who are 'non-charismatics' right to despise lifting up the hands while singing God's praises (v. 4), cf. 1 Timothy 2:8?

(3) Can you see in verse 8 the two sides of the great 'doctrine of perseverance': that because God *preserves* us we *persevere* in faith? (See 1 Pet. 14-5): 'kept ... through faith'.

Psalm 64

Fierce May be the Conflict

God told David towards the end of his life that he was 'a warrior and had shed blood' (1 Chron. 28:3). It was true that David spent a great deal of his time battling against his enemies: first Saul, then the surrounding nations and finally his son, Absalom. Many of his psalms come from these conflicts, not least this one, in which the fierce hatred of his enemies emerges very vividly.

Verses 1-6 record his prayer to God for deliverance
David describes his prayer as a *complaint* (v. 1), that is, against the injustice with which he was being treated, which may indicate Saul or Absalom. Possibly *voice* means he uttered it aloud, as was the custom with *complaints*. As a godly man, however, he must do more than *complain* – he must pray. So he asks God to *protect* and *hide* him from the *conspiracy* (v. 2) against his *life*. For it is not just one man who is against him but a whole 'gang of criminals' as we might translate *noisy crowd of evildoers*.

In verses 3-6 he enlarges on his description of them in order to justify his *complaint* and back up his prayer. Before ever they attack him physically they are already assaulting him with their words, which are like *sharpened swords* and *deadly arrows* (v. 3, cf. Prov. 25:18), referring to their slanders and false accusations (possibly claiming he was planning a coup against Saul). They act like men waiting in *ambush*, trying to catch him unprepared, when he is not ready to reply and to prove he is *innocent* (v. 4). But they take care to stay out of the range of his counter-charges by ensuring their plot cannot be traced to them (v. 5).

So they congratulate each other on having come up with a *perfect plan* (v. 6), one which will succeed in destroying David without soiling their hands with his blood. The last sentence of verse 6 may be David's observation on sinful human nature as exhibited by his enemies, but it could be translated 'the mind and heart of man are impenetrable', meaning 'since we are keeping our plans to ourselves, shut up in our own minds, no one can get to know them'.

All this David is asking God to take into consideration – this cunning treachery against an *innocent man* (v. 4).

Verses 7-10 express his expectation of God's deliverance

The advantage of the *ambush* is the element of surprise – shots are fired before the victim can reach for his weapon. But such reckon without God, who is quicker 'on the draw' than the sharpest shooter (v. 7). This is not to be taken literally, as verse 8 shows. The weapons throughout the psalm have been words (v. 3), so the meaning is that God will expose them as liars and bring counter-accusations against them and so *bring them to ruin*. There will be no hiding-place for them, and the people's respect for them as officials under the king will be changed to scorn. Shaking the head was an oriental way of expressing disgust (cf. Matt. 27:39).

But David's expectations reach beyond his personal deliverance. This is God's victory (cf. 35:27-28); it happened not through David's power or skill but his prayer to God. It will thus encourage *fear*, praise and meditation on God and his *works* (v. 9). It will also restore the balance of justice (v. 10) – other innocent and God-fearing people will not worry lest they be the conspirators' next victims.

As with other psalms of this kind, David later issued this psalm for use in public worship: *for the director of music* title).

This shows it has principles relevant to all God's people – not only Jews under the old covenant, but Christians under the new.

Questions:
(1) Do you think it is acceptable for Christians to use prayer to 'complain' to God, or should we be above it (vv. 1-2)?

(2) What do verses 3-6 teach us about 'the devil's schemes' (2 Cor. 2:11; Eph. 6:11)?

(3) What does the psalm teach about the place of *expectant faith* in prayer (Mark 11:24; 1 John 5:14)?

Psalm 65

The Bounty of God

Although ostensibly *a song* of thanksgiving for harvest, this *psalm of David*, given to the *director of music* for public worship, chiefly glories in the richness of God himself. It might have been composed for the Feast of Pentecost when the new wheat or barley was offered to God (Lev. 23:15-22).

Verses 1-4: The God who hears prayer

Awaits (v. 1) is literally 'is silent', evidently the silence of expectation. It may mean that the people were assembled *in Zion* silently waiting to begin the service. Or it may mean they were waiting for God to answer their prayers so that they could begin to praise him. There is always an element of uncertainty in the Middle East as to whether the spring rains, on which the harvest depended, would arrive. The *vows* therefore were probably the pledges of praise and obedience to his covenant which they would *fulfill* when he blessed the land with produce.

Realizing God may withhold the rain because of their *sins*, they acknowledged how overwhelming these were (v. 3). But this did not deter them from praying and expecting a favourable answer, for they can say *you forgave our transgressions*. This great grace of God, both in forgiveness and prosperity, should encourage *all men (to) come to him* (v. 2), for 'who among the gods is like you, O LORD?', as they sang at the Red Sea (Exod. 15:11). But Israel is particularly *blessed* (v. 4), because they are chosen for special fellowship with God: they can come into his *courts* and *be filled with the good things of (his) house*, that is, enjoy his personal presence.

Verses 5-8: The God who controls his creation

But God's answers to prayer are not confined to growing crops. He performs *awesome deeds of righteousness* (v. 5), perhaps referring to the destruction of the Egyptians or the overthrow of the enemies who had troubled them during David's reign. So again there is a message for the nations, even those at *the ends of the earth* and across *the farthest seas*. Let them make this God their *hope* and they will avoid his judgments and enjoy his blessings. Look! He it is who *formed the mountains by (his) strength* (v. 6). *Mountains* were often objects or places of worship in the ancient world. Though these are stable the seas and waves are not and there is nothing we can do to control them (v. 7). But he can, *as he can the turmoil of the nations,* when 'ignorant armies clash by night'. Indeed, his *wonders* are in evidence across the globe, for everyone everywhere sees the morning dawn and the evening fade (v. 8). Only let them know who has caused it all, *fear his wonders* (stand in awe of him) and bring him *songs of joy*.

Verses 9-13: The God who gives bountifully

So comes the most beautiful harvest hymn ever written, to comment on which would be to try to gild the lily. At the Feast of Pentecost they saw the beginning of this process. But it gave assurance of what would surely follow. So, inspired by the Holy Spirit, David expresses his vision of the glorious climax of the harvest when God would *crown the year with his bounty* (v. 11). So those first 3,000 souls who came into the kingdom on the day of Pentecost (Acts 2:38-41) were the first fruits of the harvest of the nations, which is still being reaped today.

Questions:
(1) What do you know of waiting expectantly for God to answer your prayers and fulfill his promises? (See Ps. 27:13-14; 40:1-3; Rom. 8:23; Titus 2:13.)

(2) What do you know of God answering 'in awesome deeds', either in your own experience or in the world?

(3) Jesus spoke of the harvest of souls as something always happening, unlike the harvest of the ground (John 4:35-37). In what way is this true at the present time?

Psalm 66

What God Has Done

This *psalm* is certainly a *song*. Not all psalms are: some are laments and others prayers. The first four verses are all about 'singing to God' and praise is the theme all the way through. It was clearly written to celebrate a great deliverance corresponding to the Exodus (v. 6), one for which earnest prayers had been prayed and solemn vows paid (vv. 13-14). Some attribute it to the destruction of Sennacherib's army (2 Kings 19:35-37), others to the release from Babylon. It could certainly have been re-issued on those occasions, as no doubt were other psalms, but it also fits well with David's return to Jerusalem following the defeat of Absalom, although it is not even attributed to David.

Verses 1-7: Calling all nations!
A call to all nations to praise God (v. 1) is not unique (cf. 99, 100), for it is issued when he has done something which demonstrates his unique sovereignty. The **manner** in which he is praised should correspond to the **matter** for which he is being praised, v. 2. Since he has revealed *the glory of his name*, so *his praise* should be *glorious*. The particular *glory* they should acknowledge is the *power* of his *deeds* (v. 3).

Of course they do not want to do this, for it shames the faith they have in their own gods. Nevertheless God will settle for it if they just *cringe before* him, like a rebel reluctantly thrown down on his knees before his conqueror. For the day will come when even this will give way to more heartfelt praise (v. 4, where it is better to translate the verbs as futures). Here is a hint of the gospel and kingdom of Christ, when hearts will be changed and people will gladly 'turn to God from idols to serve the living and true God' (1 Thess. 1:9). But that's another story!

The band plays on (*Selah*) while this sinks in, then he enlarges on those *awesome deeds* which displayed his *power*. Let people take note of them (v. 5), for they are facts which cannot be denied. Let them recall what happened when he released them from Egypt (v. 6). The Hebrew reads 'there' rather than *come*, as if he is transplanting them back in time. However, he does not linger in memory lane, but comes up to date in verse 7: that same God has proved that *he rules* now and *for ever by his power*, that *his eyes watch the nations*. Let this be a warning against rebelling *against* him, as Absalom had done and Sheba after him. Another interlude (*Selah*) precedes the next section.

Verses 8-12: Calling all the tribes of Israel
From what follows in verses 9-12 it is clear that by *peoples* he means, not the nations of verses 1-7 but the tribes of Israel. They above all should *praise our God* (v. 8), for they were not mere spectators of his 'awesome deeds' but beneficaries of them. For what God had done for them was no less than to preserve *our lives* (v. 9) and to have kept *our feet from slipping*; that is, from slipping into a condition which would spell the end of Israel as God's special people. This shows how serious Absalom's rebellion was – far more serious than the threats against them from outside, for if a fruit's inner core is rotten, the whole must be discarded.

This explains the strong language of verses 10-12: their experience had been like *silver* passing through a furnace (v. 10b); like being shut up in *prison* away from normal life (v. 11a); like being doubled up under a heavy load (v. 11b); like falling on the battle-field and being trampled on (v. 12a); and like undergoing the ordeals of *fire and water* simultaneously.

If this did not actually happen, it appeared it was going to, and was only averted through God's intervention (v. 9). Why then did he allow it? To *test and refine* them (v. 10). David was frequently complaining of the corruption and lack of true godly worship in the land. God had taken note of this and acted. But now it was over and they were emerging into a new and better era: *a place of abundance*. It is appropriate they should acknowledge this, as they proceed to do now.

Verses 13-15: Calling on God
Although David speaks in the first person (I) he is speaking as leader of the whole nation. We have seen earlier in the Psalter how in exile he had longed to be in the house of God and had prayed to return. No doubt his prayer was accompanied by *vows*, commonly made *in trouble* (v. 14), *vows* of richer, purer and heartier devotion. Now in this celebratory service he is going to *fulfill (his) vows* (v. 13), by the *sacrifice of fat animals, rams, bulls and goats* (v. 15). Their number and variety show he was making his offerings as rich as possible. Also, they would be burnt offerings in which the whole animal was offered to God and none kept for the worshipper or even the priest to eat. Such great devotion calls for a solemn pause before the final part: *Selah*.

Verses 16-20: Calling all God-fearers
While this victory has chiefly been an occasion to praise God, it was also one to encourage his people. But this is only for those who *fear God* (v. 16), not for those who had been disloyal to him by supporting Absalom. To *fear God* is to be in awe of him, which does not mean terror but admiration of his greatness and goodness. In other words it is addressed to those who were entering into the spirit of this celebration and identifying themselves with David as he offered burnt offerings in thankfulness to God.

What encouragement does he offer the God-fearers? What is it *God ... has done for* him? He has *listened* to his prayer, *heard (his) voice* (v. 19), and not *rejected* his prayers or *withheld his love* (v. 20). In his extremity David had cried out to him, but at the same time not forgotten to praise him (v. 17). He wants to *tell* them all *what he has done*, for he can do it for them too. But the promise is not unqualified (v. 18): cherishing sin blocks the lines of communication with God. True, David had sinned, but he no longer *cherished* it; he hated it, confessed and repented of it. So his line to God was clear. The proof? *God has surely listened.* His return to Jerusalem as conqueror, not prisoner proved it.

Questions:
(1) Do you share David's vision of a time when God will be praised universally? (See Hab. 2:14.)

(2) Can you see any evidence in yourself or the church generally that God is testing and refining us (v. 10)? (See 1 Pet. 1:6-7.)

(3) Are you able to 'tell' your friends what God has done for you in the way of answered prayer (vv. 16, 19-20)? When you pray, do you examine your heart and seek God's grace from the love of sin (v. 18)? (See Matt. 6:12.)

Psalm 67

Salvation For the Nation

The harvest reference in verse 6 may indicate this psalm was composed for one of the annual celebrations of this event, such as the Feast of Tabernacles, also called 'The Feast of Ingathering' (Exod. 23:16), to be held 'after you have gathered the crops of the land' (Lev. 23:39). This psalm concentrates on the harvest theme (v. 6a), which should read *the land HAS YIELDED its harvest* (emphasis mine). But this is seen as a token of the total grace and blessing of God (v. 1), especially of his just rule (v. 4). Moreover, it has a vision of harvesting the nations to share in these blessings (vv. 2-5, 6b). The Title uses several phrases to emphasise the joyful way these sentiments should be expressed.

Verses 1-2: Israel's calling as God's priest to the nations
Verse 1 echoes the Aaronic blessing of Numbers 6:24-26, but is adapted for the whole congregation to pray for themselves by changing 'you' to *us*. This is asking for more than just a good harvest; it seeks the grace and blessing of God's personal presence and approval. As the Shekinah shone behind the veil, so the prayer is that he will be to his people like the glory and comfort of light and *make his face shine upon us*.

The *Selah* interlude may be to mark the change from the indirect third person *make HIS face shine* to the direct second person *that YOUR ways may be known* ... (in each case emphasis mine). For the psalm is going beyond the Aaronic blessing, which was for that nation as it crossed the desert to the promised land, when the thought of harvest was far off. Now that they are enjoying all this they can concentrate on their calling to be God's priests for the blessing of the world.

It is significant that words usually uttered by the high priest alone are taken on the lips of the whole congregation. For Israel was a priesthood (Exod. 19:5-6), it was to be God's witness to the world (Isa. 43:10-13). Indeed the concept goes back to the nation's founder, Abraham, through whom 'all peoples on earth will be blessed' (Gen. 12:3). Other nations were to look on Israel and see how blessed she was, with her fruitful land, her just laws and the personal presence of God (Deut. 4:5-8), so that not only *his WAYS may be known to them* but his *SALVATION also* – salvation from ignorance, idolatry and lawlessness (emphasis mine).

Verses 3-5: Their prayer for the nations to turn to God
Now they pray directly and specifically for this to come about. In verse 3 they pray for the nations to turn from idolatry and *praise you, O God*, so that the earth may be re-united under the one true God. Verse 4 encourages them to do this by speaking of what they will enjoy if God reigns over them, for if they turn to him he will not only be the object of their worship but the One who reigns over them. As ruler he combines the impartiality of a judge with the compassion of a shepherd who *guides*. For, as C. S. Lewis points out, the Hebrew concept of the judge is not only of the criminal on trial for a crime, but the plaintif seeking justice from his oppressor in a civil case ('Reflections on the Psalms', p. 15). It is the scenario of the poor woman appealing for justice in Jesus' parable (Luke 18:1-5). This is why *the nations (will) be glad and sing for joy* when it happens. With this in mind the prayer for them to turn to God is repeated (v. 5). For only as they acknowledge him as the one and only Lord will they enjoy his reign.

Verses 6-7: The present harvest as the assurance that God will bring the nations
The NIV gives the wrong impression in verse 6, supplying *then* and using the future tense *will yield*, instead of the past tense

(see the introductory paragraph). The meaning is not 'when the nations worship God *then* we shall have fruitful harvests', but 'the harvest we are celebrating is the token that God will bless us, and through us the other nations.' They could 'open their eyes and look on the fields' and see them 'ripe for harvest' (John 4:35) and thus know assuredly that *God WILL bless us* (referring to the original prayer of v. 1); and that he will answer their other prayer for the distant nations to *fear*, that is to revere him, praise him as the one true God and trust his righteous rule (emphasis mine).

Questions:
(1) How far are our churches fulfilling their role of being God's priest to the people of the world? (1 Pet. 2:9.)

(2) What nations do you pray for specifically when you pray for the spread of the gospel? Why not pray for them all, working through a book like 'Operation World' and using this psalm to give you the vision?

Psalm 68

May God Arise!

It is thought likely that this psalm was composed to accompany the entry of the ark into Jerusalem, after its long time away, first in Philistine hands, then at the house of Obed-Edom (see 2 Sam. 6:12). It opens with the words recited as the ark set out on its journeys (Num. 10:35) and refers later to the procession which brought it into its place (Ps. 68:24-25). David sees such significance in this that he recounts the whole history of the ark's journey from Sinai to this the final stage. The psalm falls into two main parts: verses 1-18 recount the story of the ark's long journey, and verses 19-35 reflect on the importance of the event being celebrated.

PART I
Verses 1-18: THE STORY OF THE ARK'S JOURNEY

Verses 1-3: How the ark left Sinai

From the time of leaving Sinai, whenever the people moved on, the ark would lead the way and Moses would cry out, 'Rise up, O LORD! May your enemies be scattered; may your foes flee before you' (Num. 10:35). The fact that they were now in Jerusalem proves the prayer had been answered. But the need was still there: in the desert Israel had been confronted by enemies, now she was surrounded by them. This is why

David echoes the prayer of Moses in verses 1-2. The presence of the ark in the city, however, meant God was as much there as he had been in the desert. Knowing this, they had an assurance that he would fight for them and they could be confident and happy (v. 3).

Verses 4-6: How God was present in the Ark
If we take the NIV marginal reading of verse 4: *prepare the way for him who rides through the desert*, these verses continue the theme of verses 1-3. In bringing his people from Egypt to Canaan God had shown his special care for the unprotected and victims of oppression, as they had been in Egypt (v. 5). They who had been *desolate* (v. 6 mg) and *prisoners* now had a home and a Father. However, remembering that this did not apply to all who left Egypt and that many perished in the desert through unbelief and disobedience, David adds *the rebellious live in a sun-scorched land* (and they died there too).

Verses 7-10: How the ark crossed the desert
Now he recalls in greater detail some of the mighty works God did when he led them across the desert to the borders of the land (v. 7). *Selah* occurs here in mid-sentence, as if he were saying, 'This is what happened – wait for it!' There were the phenomena at Sinai (v. 8, Exod. 19:16-20), expressed here poetically. There were *showers*, not just of rain but of manna and quails (v. 9, Exod. 16). In these ways they were sustained on the long weary journey; it was as if the desert were their *settled* dwelling (v. 10).

Verses 11-14: How the ark gave them victories
Several military victories are here condensed into a few lines. Verse 11 probably refers to the destruction of the Egyptians, accomplished by the *word (the* LORD *announced)* to Moses in Exodus 14:26. Celebrations for this victory were led by Miriam and the women (Exod. 15:20-21), hence *THOSE who proclaimed it* (v. 11, emphasis mine) is feminine. Verse 12 alludes to the *plunder* which they took from Egypt, but the plural *kings and armies* indicates that other victories were also in mind, especially those over Edom, Moab and Ammon, who blocked

the way to Canaan, and then over the Canaanites themselves. Verse 13 may refer to those who missed their share of the spoils of victory through sloth or fear, as the Reubenites did when Sisera was defeated at the time of Deborah (Judg. 5:16). Those who had taken part decked themselves in the *gold and silver* garments of their defeated enemies. Verse 14 alludes to the great victories over the Canaanite and Amorite kings under Joshua: the ground became white with the bleached bones of the slain, making it look like the snowy hills of Bashan, of which *Zalmon* was one.

Verses 15-18: How the ark has come to rest on Mount Zion

Talking of *Bashan*, Zion does not compare with the hills there for height and grandeur, yet God has passed them over and chosen for his dwelling the little hills on which Jerusalem was built. There may be an allusion here to the idolatry practised on the hills of Canaan, which God was judging through Israel (Deut. 12:2). So the ark has reached the end of its journey. *The* Lord, who revealed himself over the ark, had led them from Sinai with the vast angelic army which had fought for Israel, and established his *sanctuary* on Zion. The wars were over, the captives led in triumph and their spoils offered to him, for he *receives gifts ... even from the rebellious* (v. 18).

Here we see the abiding message of the psalm, for verse 18 anticipates the day when, having completed the work of redemption, Christ would make captives the enemies of all mankind and of God himself, and take his seat at God's right hand, to reign until his foes become his footstool. We have authority for this in Paul's quotation of this verse in Ephesians 4:8.

PART II
Verses 19-35: REFLECTIONS ON THE IMPORTANCE OF THIS EVENT

Verses 19-20: Praise to the God of the Ark

So the song of praise reaches its height: God has proved himself *our Saviour*. Though we have carried the ark, he has carried *our burdens*. Truly he is *a God who saves* – the history has demonstrated that over and over again. How many times had they been at a disadvantage from stronger enemies, yet *escaped from death* through their *sovereign* LORD.

Verses 21-23: The confidence this gives
Now we see the value of this long rehearsal of the ark's history: it gives confidence that he will defeat their present enemies and any that emerge in the future. *Heads ... hairy crowns* (v. 21) refers to the pride and vanity of those who threaten them. Verse 22 seems to assume they have fled from an awesome God to the mountains of *Bashan* or even out to sea. But God will *bring them* back and there will be a great blood bath (v. 23). Although this sounds like blood lust it is more likely to be retribution. It would be with words like these that their enemies threatened Israel. As so often in the Old Testament, the evil that men plan is visited upon them.

Verses 24-27: The great assembly gathers
The song is now taken up by those inside waiting for the ark to arrive and who now see *the procession* come into view. It is led by *the singers*, followed by *the musicians*, accompanied by *the maidens playing tambourines*, all of whom are exhorted to *praise God in the great congregation* that had assembled to celebrate this event. Then came the leaders of the tribes, led by *little Benjamin*, the smallest tribe but the one in whose territory Jerusalem was situated. They are followed by *Judah's princes*, as the ruling family. The rest would follow in geographical order, ending with the northernmost: *Zebulon and Naphtali*.

Verses 28-31: The conversion of the nations
Praise is followed by prayer – that God will do today what he did yesterday (v. 28). Prayer is followed by prophecy (v. 29), for these Spirit-led men expected God to answer their prayer. Now that God is established in his *Temple* (only the tabernacle at present) at Jerusalem, he will be honoured there with *gifts of silver*, brought by *envoys* from as far away as *Egypt* and *Cush* (Nubia). Egypt had once dominated Israel, but if they tried that again God would *rebuke* them (v. 30). *The beast among the reeds* is the crocodile, often used as a nickname for

Egypt, whose river was full of them (Ezek. 32:2). Similarly *bulls* are the heads of the nations, and the *calves* their people. This bringing of tribute to the temple in Jerusalem never happened and is prophetic of the conversion of those nations through the gospel, as a result of which they would come to acknowledge the God who had formerly dwelt in Jerusalem but whom they had despised at the time (v. 31). It is similar to Isaiah's prophecy in 11:1-4.

Verses 32-35: The God over the ark is the universal God
Not just Israel's neighbours but all *kingdoms of the earth* should *sing praises to the* LORD, for he is accompanied by a greater procession than that which brought the ark into Jerusalem: he *rides the ancient skies above*, he inhabits eternity and is everywhere accompanied by his angelic host. From there he speaks (v. 33b), from there he reveals himself and from there he shows his *power* (v. 34). This cosmic God is the One who has come to dwell in his *sanctuary* in Jerusalem, assuring *Israel ... his people* that he will *give power and strength* to them (v. 35). They have nothing and no one to fear now. *Praise be to God!*

Questions:
(1) What does this psalm teach about the value of knowing the events of the past?

(2) Compare verse 18 again with Ephesians 4:8: how does Paul alter the original and why?

(3) Look again at verse 28. Is Tozer right to say 'What God has done for others he will do for us'. If so, how can we recover this spirit of expectation today?

Psalm 69

In the Miry Depths

Of the many psalms which David composed under the oppression of his enemies, this is the longest and most deeply felt. The *enemies without cause* seeking to destroy him (v. 4) may have been Saul and his servants or Absalom and his followers. The reference to God's *house* in verse 9 favours the latter. Whichever it is, the curses he pronounces on them (vv. 22-28) are some of the fiercest in the imprecatory psalms. So intense are his sufferings they are a preview of Christ's. But David's curses stand in sharp contrast to Christ's reactions to his sufferings, when he prayed *for* not *against* his tormentors. Nowhere does the contrast between Old and New Testaments appear more clearly.

Verses 1-4: David is overwhelmed
David feels like someone on a river bed with his feet sinking into the mud and his head almost under water (vv. 1-2). He has cried to God until his throat is sore and his eyes weary. Yet, like Jesus later who quotes the words of verse 4 in John 15:25, he is the innocent party (v. 4).

Verses 5-12: David is suffering for the people
When he said in verse 4 that this treatment was 'without reason' and 'without cause', he meant that his enemies had no

just *cause* against him, not that he was innocent before God. He knows this was not so (v. 5), but if this were God's punishment surely his people *who hope in you* would not be suffering too (v. 6)? He claims that it is *for your sake* that he is suffering this *shame*, and alienation even from his family (v. 8).

What does he mean by this? Verse 9 shows us it is all about loyalty to God and his worship: *zeal for your house*. David's greatest achievement had been to set up God's sanctuary on Zion. He was also making plans for a permanent temple. All this would be abandoned if his enemies took over. What they were doing to him therefore was really directed against God (v. 9b). At this point David anticipates Jesus who quoted these words in John 2:17 when he cleansed the temple. Christ had come to re-establish the honour of God and purify his worship, of which this action is merely symbolical. But he knew it would cost him his life. Paul confirmed this by using the words of verse 9b in Romans 15:3. Verses 10-12 prove this principle. For when David responds to this treatment by giving himself to *weeping and fasting* before God they just mock him. In reality they are mocking God.

Verses 13-18: David gives himself to prayer

Convinced that this campaign was not God punishing him but was an attack on God's people, he boldly calls on God to intervene. He believes he is still in God's *favour* and *great love*, and can therefore expect his *sure salvation* (v. 13). So he asks to be rescued from this drowning experience (vv. 14-15). His plea is based on *the goodness of your love* and *your great mercy* (v. 16), on the fact that he is God's *servant* (v. 17), but about to drown.

Summoning all the arguments he can find, he uses a different word for *rescue* (v. 18), from that of verse 14, a word which has the meaning of 'ransom'. This, along with *redeem* recalls the escape from Egypt and the heavy price paid in blood for their freedom. What was achieved there is in jeopardy and calls for similar divine intervention.

Verses 19-21: David pleads his sufferings

He reverts to the subject of verses 9b-12 – the 'insults' he was having to bear because of his loyalty to God and his worship.

'Cannot you see what *my enemies* are doing?' he seems to be saying in verse 9b. That he is right to say this mockery is really directed towards God is proved by the closeness of his experience to that of Christ. Although not quoted in the Gospels, verse 20 in the KJV, was used by Handel in the Passion section of 'Messiah' because it was so true to what happened: they did mock him and none sympathised or comforted him. Jesus too was given *gall and vinegar* to drink (Matt. 27:34), though this was not to poison him (as David seems to think it was in his case) but rather to anaesthetise him against the pain.

Verses 22-28: David pours out curses on his enemies
This passage is only matched by the curses he called down on Ahithophel for his treachery (Ps. 109:6-15). Basically he is praying that his enemies will be dealt with in such a way that they will know what *he* feels like. Let *their* food be contaminated (v. 22); let *them* be struck blind and have to grope around in terror (v. 23); let *them* feel the power of God's fierce anger (v. 24); let *them* lose their position, as David had lost his throne, and have no one to succeed them (v. 25, cf. 41:5). Is this unjust in the light of what they were doing to him (v. 26)? Why should they not be justly charged for their *crime upon crime* (v. 27a)? But has he gone right over the top when he virtually calls for their everlasting damnation (v. 28)? Should we wish that on anyone, even the Hitlers of this world? Did not Jesus pray for the forgiveness of those who did to him far worse even than David's foes were doing to him?

What is true of 109 is true of this psalm, David is speaking not so much for himself as on behalf of God. He is upholding God's law which pronounced curses on those who broke it (Deut. 27:15-26). He is speaking as the Lord's anointed king, who had been placed on the throne by God himself, so that in driving him out they were rebelling against God. He is speaking as a prophet by the Spirit of God. To repeat the words of Augustine, quoted in the Introduction: 'these are not the words of one wishing that mischief may happen to his enemies; they are the words of a prophet, one who is foretelling in Scripture language the evil that must befall them on account of their sins.' This explains even verses 27b-28. The New Testament directions to us to 'love our enemies' and 'pray *for* them', not against them, is about their ill-treatment of us, rather than their enmity against God.

Verses 29-36: David gives praise to God

Verse 29 sums up his thoughts: yes, he is indeed still *in pain and distress*; but now he has great hopes that God will bring him through. For *salvation* is of the Lord (*your*) not of armies. So now he pours out his heart in praise, which is as full of feeling as his earlier complaint. His sufferings could *glorify* God, especially when he can *praise* him in the midst of them (v. 31). So it does not matter that he is not in a position to offer sacrifices. Indeed what he is doing *will please the* LORD *more*, for it is utterly free from formality and insincerity.

His followers too – *the poor* – will share this as they hear him praising God (v. 32). They will be encouraged to know that after all *the* LORD *hears the needy and does not despise his captive people,* who seem at the mercy of their enemies. Indeed, creation itself will witness it and join in (v. 34), especially when it is all over and the promises of God have proved true, when the damage done by Absalom has been repaired and the faithful are once again settled in their houses (vv. 35-36). For it is not these rebels against God but those *who love his name* who are the rightful occupants of *Zion* and *the cities of Judah*.

Questions:
(1) Can you accept the principle that the more faithfully you serve the Lord, the more likely you are to suffer at the hands of those who do not? (Rom. 8:17; Phil. 1:29-30).

(2) Do David's experiences here: of drowning, of unjustified attack and of mockery, help you enter more into those of Christ on the cross? (1 Pet. 4:12-13.)

(3) How well are you able, like David, to 'rejoice in sufferings' (Rom. 5:3; cf. Acts 5:41)?

Psalm 70

A Cry of Desperation

This psalm is almost identical to 40:13-17. This tells us two things.

Firstly, that it is not merely a bad copy of a former composition, but a fresh one to meet a new situation. Although the differences are only verbal, they are sufficient (at least 9 in 5 verses) to show that David was not copying his former words but re-using them in a revised form. The fact that he tends to change *God* to LORD and vice versa shows he was probably writing from memory. In fact the word in the Title translated *Petition* is literally 'for a memorial' or 'to bring to mind'.

Secondly, it shows that his present situation had strong similarities to that which had prompted 40. That had been one of his lowest points. He was still being pursued by Saul; he had just been expelled by the Philistines, with whom he had taken refuge; and he was about to be betrayed by the people of Keilah whom he had previously saved from the Philistines. He might have concluded like Jacob that 'everything is against me' (Gen. 42:36). He was 'bringing to mind' the tight situation he had been in then, in order to remind himself that he had escaped it; and possibly too reminding God and asking him to do the same again! For he is in just as much need as he was then, for this may, like 69, be connected with the the rebellion of Absalom. He prays almost, but not quite, the same prayer.

Perhaps his mind was in such turmoil that he could not find fresh words.

Verse 1. The psalm begins with an urgent cry to God: *Hasten... to save me*. The opening word is a significant alteration to 40:13 where the corresponding verse began 'Be pleased'. If his time in Keilah was desperate, how much more was this!

Verse 2 is unaltered apart from the omission of 'to take' in *seek my life*. The only significance of this is that it shows David was probably writing from memory. Absalom and his followers were trying to do just what Saul and his had sought to do – to kill him. Let God deal with them as he had with Saul, and frustrate their plans!

Verse 3 has *turn back* in place of 'be pleased', which again shows the greater urgency of this prayer. It is not enough they should feel *shame* – they should give up their campaign. Perhaps David has frightened himself by his prayer against them – he did not really want to harm his own son, but would rather he *turn back* from his enterprise and avoid punishment, which is just what God prefers (Ezek. 33:11).

Verse 4's only change is from 'God' to LORD. As before, it was not just David's life that was threatened but that of all those who were with him. The number of these had increased from the days when he led only a small band of others who were discontented with Saul's reign; now he led a whole nation, and there were still those among them who could be said to *seek God* and *love (his) salvation*. David felt the pure worship of God was being affected by this rebellion. If Absalom triumphed and David and his loyal followers were driven out, who would there be left to cry *Let God be exalted*!?

Verse 5's main change, apart from the reversing of the names of God again, is to substitute *come quickly* (the same word as that translated *hasten* in v. 1) for 'think'. What was needed was not just thought but action. *Delay* was dangerous.

Questions:
(1) When times are hard, do you go back to a similar situation in the past and recall how God resolved it?

(2) Consider how God's initiative in verse 2 is connected with man's response in verse 3 by comparing *be turned back* with *turn back*. Do these ideas clash or complement each other? Cf. John 6:44 with verses 45 and 53.

(3) In what circumstances may what happens to one person affect many others? (See v. 4.)

Psalm 71

An Old Man's Prayer

Here is an old man (vv. 9, 18) who has experienced adversity during his life (v. 20) but has always trusted God (vv. 5-6) and been an encouragement to others (vv. 7-8). Now he is in trouble again and his enemies will not leave him alone; but his faith holds fast (v. 14).

Verses 1-4: He appeals to God's salvation
In his previous adversities he has found protection in God, and as he faces the future he prays he will never have to be *ashamed* of trusting him. He believes that what God has been to him in the past he will be in the present: a *refuge ... a rock ... a fortress*. This is the advantage of a long experience of God – it gives the peace of assurance. The desperation of some of his earlier pleas is absent here, for he has learned a calmer trust in God.

This does not mean he can just assume that God will sort things out automatically. He still has to ask him for specific help in this particular situation (v. 4). But the fact that God has always heard him gives his prayer that much more confidence.

Verses 5-8: He appeals to his past experience
The man is able to look back on a life pockmarked with adversity. Even as a *youth* he had been afflicted, but he had put

his *hope (and) confidence* in the *Sovereign* LORD and survived. He goes back even further – to his birth and before, when he could not consciously trust God, yet God *brought (him) forth* into the light of day (cf. 22:9-10). He could not put this down to his faith; it was entirely of God, so the praise is his. This encourages him to believe it will be *ever* like this (v. 6).

But he is not saying all this just for his own sake, even though he is in dire straits again. He sees himself as a *portent to man* (v. 7). *A portent* is a warning sign, which shows he is not using his experience as an encouragement to the faithful so much as a warning to the faithless. Even then the meaning is ambiguous. He may mean: 'look what God did to my enemies and give up your rebellion, lest what happened to them happens to you', or, 'look what happened to me when I sinned and see how God has afflicted me.' What he adds, *but you are my strong refuge*, seems to favour the first sense: 'God put down my enemies but came to my aid.' This would fit the ascription of praise in verse 8. Yet even here the memory of his own sin would add to his sense of indebtedness to God, so perhaps there is a mixture of the two senses.

Verses 9-18: He appeals to his present plight

In spite of the confidence he has expressed there is still a question over whether God would continue his preserving ministry (v. 9). What if he only delivered him in his younger days because he had a purpose for him? But now that he is *old* and his *strength is gone* he can no longer be of use to God. So will God now *forsake* him and *cast (him) away* like an old shoe? His enemies thought so (vv. 10-11). They are just looking for an opportunity to strike the finishing blow. They do not expect any more divine interventions.

If this happened he would cease to be a *portent*, a warning to the enemies of God. For even though old, he was still in covenant with God (*MY God*, emphasis mine), as an Israelite (Exod. 6:7). So he is bold to ask God again to save him and destroy them (v. 12-14).

If God does this and demonstrates that age does not alter his commitment to his servants, the man will likewise show that age does not lessen his spirit of *praise* (v. 15). His life has been so full of divine deliverances it would take *all day* to *tell* of them. For they were more than he could count (*measure*). So this new situation and his assurance that God will act in it as he had ever done strengthens his resolve to *come and proclaim your mighty acts and ... declare your marvellous deeds* (vv. 16-17). It will therefore add to that long line of experiences which has proved the *righteousness* of God from his *youth* onwards to *when I am old and grey*. This is what *the next generation* needs to know – the *power* of God (v. 18). The righteous need it as an encouragement and the wicked as a warning.

Verses 19-24: He appeals to God's faithfulness
Deliverance from this latest trial will crown all God's faithful acts towards him (v. 19). He uses words which recall the crossing of the Red Sea (Exod. 15:11). This was to the Israelites what the resurrection of Christ is to Christians – typical of the way God raises his people from the depths to the heights. For what this man needed was a virtual resurrection, a Red Sea experience. He was at death's door in more senses than one: *the depths of the earth* (v. 20), meant either old age, illness or his enemies trying to finish him off. But when God acts again as he has always done, he will be restored to his former position of power, even more securely (v. 21). Anticipating this, he gives himself to the *praise* of God with voice and instruments (vv. 22-24). His song is of the *faithfulness* of God and his righteous redemption, because of which his enemies are as good as finished (v. 24).

Questions:
(1) As you grow older are you finding the number of your experiences of God's deliverance increases? (Ps. 103:1-5.)

(2) Do you look on these as ways to prepare you for greater trials in the future? (James 1:2-4.)

(3) What are the positive advantages of old age in terms of example, prayer and praise? (Titus 2:1-5.)

Psalm 72

A Coronation Ode

The first question is what does *of* mean in the title? Since it is the Hebrew pronoun normally used to denote the author, many take it to mean it was composed by Solomon. Others point out that verse 20 attributes it to David and that the Hebrew preposition can also mean 'to' or 'for', so that this is David ending his present contribution to the Psalter by seeking God's blessing on his son's reign. But whoever was the author it clearly concerns Solomon's accession to the throne (1 Kings 1:38-40). It is partly a prayer that he will govern justly and partly a prophecy of how God will bless his reign.

The language becomes so idealistic (e.g. vv. 5-11) that neither Solomon nor his successors did or could attain to it. It appears to merge into a vision of Christ's kingdom and has affinity with Isaiah 11:1-5 and Isaiah 60–62. Some dissent from this and explain the language by saying that, like the concept of kingship itself, it is borrowed from other Near Eastern coronation odes. More likely its inspiration came from God's covenant with David and his house in 2 Samuel 7. This volume will take it as partly Messianic, setting forth Christ as the ideal of sovereignty, a model for Israel's kings (or any other, for that matter) and the hope of his people under old and new covenants. The psalm sets down the foundation of such reigns.

Verses 1-4: Righteousness

Verse 1 is the prayer on which the whole psalm is based and highlights the chief function of any monarch – administering justice, so that his chief attribute should be *righteousness*. All governments are to govern justly (Rom. 13:3-4), but God's vicegerents are to govern with *YOUR justice* and therefore to be *endowed with YOUR righteousness* (v. 1, emphasis mine). Only on this platform will they proceed to *judge* (i.e. rule) *your people in righteousness*.

It is difficult to decide whether the prayer form continues from verse 2 onwards ('may he', NIV mg) or whether the verbs are futures, as in the NIV text: *he WILL judge*. If the latter is the case, it supports the idea that the psalm is looking on to the reign of the Messiah. This is certainly the case when it comes to the king's special duty to *your afflicted ones* (v. 2), which is to *defend* them (v. 4). Such may be *afflicted* because they are *poor and needy*, or because they are victims of *the oppressor*. Verse 3 shows that such a righteous reign is blessed with *prosperity*, which is said to be *the fruit of righteousness*. The righteous king will see that the *needy and afflicted* receive their fair share of this *prosperity*.

This particular ministry is very characteristic of Messianic prophecy (Isa. 11:4; 61:1-2), quoted by Christ in his Nazareth sermon in Luke 4:16-21. This does not mean that Christ came into the world as a social reformer. The Biblical concept of *righteousness* is basically that of a right relationship with a righteous God, which impinges on the whole doctrine of justification by faith as the gift of God, to believing sinners, of the righteousness of Christ. But the concept has social implications inasmuch as those who are righteous by faith and loyal to a righteous God will treat each other justly, especially if they have positions of responsibility. Those who live or govern thus will find their society prospers, that there is plenty for all and no need for poverty. It certainly shows that provision for *the poor* should be seen not as 'charity' but justice.

Verses 5-7: Blessing

Verses 6-7 develop verse 3 and recall what 'the Spirit of the LORD spoke' to David in 2 Samuel 23:2-4. The righteous ruler is a great blessing to his people. He is *like rain* which makes grass grow again when it has been *mown*, and *waters the earth* or 'the land', so that the crops grow. The consequences of this are: firstly, that the king himself is respected (taking the NIV mg of v. 5, 'is feared' as in the Hebrew manuscripts) throughout his reign, as are his successors; and secondly, that his people *flourish* and enjoy *prosperity* (v. 7). This was the case during Solomon's reign, probably the most prosperous in the nation's history.

The references to *the sun ... moon ... all generations* clearly go beyond any human king, even the Lord's anointed, and find their fulfilment in the reign of Christ. The *righteous*, those right with God who acknowledge ('fear') Christ, enjoy his blessings throughout their lives and into eternity.

Verses 8-11: Extensiveness
God had made promises about the extent of the territory Israel would possess (Gen. 15:18; Exod. 23:31). These words go far beyond this and make it virtually unlimited: *the ends of the earth* (v. 8). It comprises *distant shores* like Spain in the west (if *Tarshish* is Tartessus) and *Sheba and Seba* in the south (v. 10). This involves the submission of their *kings* and includes even nomadic people like the desert tribes (v. 9). Solomon saw something of this in his reign, for example, in the visit of the Queen of *Sheba* (1 Kings 10), but the words look on to the visit to the infant Christ of the magi from the east, who, if not literally kings, were men of power and influence. Their visit is usually taken as the first fruit of the coming of the Gentiles into Christ's kingdom (Matt. 2:1-2).

Verses 12-14: Deliverance
This passage is not a repetition of verses 2-4, but a development of verses 8-11. Verses 2-4 concerned the just government of Israel, whereas these verses extend that principle to the incoming Gentiles. When Christ comes to the nations through his gospel, he finds people *needy ... afflicted ... weak* and oppressed. He comes to *take pity* and to *deliver*, to *save (and) rescue* from all this. This goes far beyond the reign of Solomon or his successors; in fact the more the psalm goes on the more it seems to leave him behind and bring Christ into focus.

Verses 15-17: Loyalty

Such a monarch will be popular and loved by the people. They will wish him *long life*, bring him gifts, *pray for* him and *bless him* (v. 5). They will want to the see *the fruit* of his righteous government *flourish* (v. 16) and *his name* go down in history. To some extent this was true of Solomon, but we must not overlook God's warnings about the other side of kingship – that the king would expect people to work hard to promote his glory (1 Sam. 8:10-18), which in fact Solomon did, as they complained after he had gone (1 Kings 12:4). There were many who were not sorry to see him go and hoped for an easier life under his successor.

But this cannot be said of Jesus' reign over us. It is true he expects us to work hard and live sacrificially, to carry a cross, endure hardship and hostility. But we see this as a privilege in the light of what he endured for us. It is true too that he gave us some demanding duties, but because of his great love to us, which we reciprocate, 'his commands are not burdensome' (1 John 5:3), in fact they are our very life (1 John 3:24).

Verse 17b is the clue to this passage and to much of the psalm. It was what God long before promised Abraham: that the time would come when people of *all nations* will be *blessed* as was Abraham. That certainly did not happen during the reign of Solomon or any other Israelite king. For Abraham's blessing was the gift of righteousness through faith (Gen. 15:6), which has come to the world through Christ alone.

Verses 18-20: Praise

The chief fruit of Christ's reign is that it restores sinners to the worship of God. These words are a fitting response, not only to God's goodness to Israel through their chosen king, but to the prospect of such a reign as that of the coming Messiah. The *marvellous deeds* he will do outstrip all the achievements of the kings of Israel and Judah put together. For the spread of the knowledge of Christ the King would cause *the whole earth to be filled with the glory of God* (v. 19). On this note David ends meantime his contribution to the book of inspired praises (v. 20). Hereafter others will take up his lyre.

Questions:

(1) What does the psalm, especially verses 1-4, teach us about the social implications of the gospel? (Matt. 25:31-46.)

(2) How does the average government, with its glorying in such achievements as building programmes and military conquest, compare with the ideals of this psalm?

(3) In what sense or senses are we to expect Christ's reign in this age to be universal? What is in your mind when you sing 'Jesus shall reign where'er the sun does his successive journeys run'?

Psalm 73

Why is God Allowing This?

After the ark had been brought up to Zion and the tabernacle worship restored, David had set up a choir and orchestra under Heman, Ethan and Asaph (1 Chron. 15:16-22). These three also composed psalms, in which Asaph was the most prolific. Most of his compositions are collected here at the beginning of Book III (73–83). The remaining one (50) is in Book II.

Asaph had worked closely with David from the time of his accession to the throne, which was celebrated by Asaph in 75. He also composed psalms celebrating the victory over the Philistines (80 and 83), and over Syria (76). Clearly David shared, not only his experiences, but his deepest thoughts and feelings with this man. Perhaps, when he himself was not able to compose, through pressure of business or depression of spirits, Asaph came to his aid. In the present crisis, when David's grief and perplexity were too deep for words, Asaph expressed his thoughts in this psalm. Here we get to the heart of the matter: not what was happening but why. Why was God allowing the ungodly to prosper in the land?

The simplest way to follow the thought of this psalm is to observe the three occurrences of the word *Surely* (vv. 1, 13, 18) which introduce the main divisions.

Verses 1-12: Faith in God's goodness shaken

Verse 1 states the faith common to God's people – that *God is good* to them: he gives them food and drink, fruitful fields, peaceful homes and protection from their enemies. This has to be qualified since 'not all are Israel that are of Israel' (Rom. 9:6). God's promise is only for the *pure in heart*, those who are single-minded in their devotion to him and do not deviate either to idolatry or immorality. Many were going down that road at the time of writing, and were doing so with impunity.

So this faith in God's goodness was being severely shaken (v. 2). *The arrogant* and *the wicked* were enjoying the *prosperity*, God was being *good* to THEM (v. 3, emphasis mine). So, instead of despising and condemning *the wicked*, Asaph finds himself actually *envying* them. For it was the righteous whose lives were hard, since *the wicked* were enjoying *prosperity* at the expense of the righteous whom they oppressed.

Verses 4-12 are a long and detailed complaint about this treatment. The wicked are enjoying good *health*, and are *free from the burdens* of keeping body and soul together and from the diseases which befall people who live in poverty (vv. 4-5). This implies that the wicked were enslaving the righteous, who did the hard work while their oppressors lived on the fruits of it. The effect of this was to make them arrogant (v. 6), so that they felt they had the right to brutalise their workers. The illustration from *clothes* and jewellery hints at the finery they were able to wear now they were rich and free from manual labour.

The text of verse 7 is disputed. If the Hebrew text we have is correct (see NIV mg) it describes these overfed oppressors who *bulge with fat*. They think they are the greatest people that ever were (v. 7b), and that everyone else is contemptible (v. 8). They are greater than God himself and usurp his rule over heaven and earth (v. 9). The foolish people encourage this by their adulation (v. 10), making God an irrelevance (v. 11). His inaction proves he knows nothing about them. In summary (v. 12), they are getting richer and richer and do not have a care in the world.

Verses 13-17: The recovery begins

Asaph's mind follows the logic of the situation: *God is good to (the) pure in heart* (cf. v. 1); he has kept his *heart pure* (v. 13); but God is not being good to him, in fact he is continually being *plagued and punished* (v. 14). Therefore it is pointless living purely to God. Rather, it is better not to, since the example of the present generation of the ungodly shows that wickedness is the way to escape affliction and enjoy prosperity.

He is on the point of making this train of reasoning public (v. 15): *I will speak thus*, but thinks again and draws back. He suddenly realises this would be a *betrayal* of God's *children*. He had committed himself to the faith of verse 1. How could he go back on that and announce he no longer believed it? What he has thought in verse 13 has shocked him. He cannot say it; it would be irresponsible. He has seen what the consequences would be: upsetting the faith of those who were still loyal to him and to God.

But the problem has not gone away; he still thinks as he did, and now is in greater turmoil (v. 16). The word of God says one thing and his experience another. Who can *understand* this? His inner struggle was now more *oppressive* even than the national decline. If he could only *understand* what God was doing he could even accept this situation.

Asaph is a Levite with the right to enter the tabernacle, *the sanctuary of God* (v. 17). There his eyes are opened to the factor he had been overlooking. He been so obsessed with the present, so blinded by what was happening that he could not see what was going to happen. It was the *final destiny* of these men that must be put into the equation to make sense of it.

What was it about entering the tabernacle that made this difference? Perhaps it was the thought that it was only those who *kept (their) heart pure* and *washed (their) hands in innocence* who were acceptable there. The wicked could not follow him into the presence of God; they were not acceptable to him. So, whatever glory he was permitting them now, it would not last. They will have to reckon with him. This begins the road back to faith.

Verses 18-28: The recovery is completed

The next step on the road to recovery is the certainty of the fall of the wicked (vv. 18-20). Just as *surely* as God is good to his own, so *surely* does he judge his enemies. They will come to a sticky end, not just in the normal course of nature but as a deliberate act of God: *you place ... you cast* (v. 18). This can happen quite *suddenly* and totally: *completely swept away* (v. 19). The prosperous life has been but a *dream*. The reality is that they are under God's judgment. He does not really favour them; in fact he despises them (v. 20).

The immediate reference here is no doubt to some sudden judgment to be visited upon the miscreants. However, in the context of Scripture as a whole there is a hint of the final judgment of the wicked: *despise* is akin to 'contempt' in Daniel 12:2, which refers more clearly to the final resurrection.

The next step is the equal certainty of God's love for his children (vv. 21-23). Now he sees his doubt of God and envy of the wicked for what they are: *senseless and ignorant*. He had been thinking like an animal, not a human being, let alone a child of God The truth is that God has not forsaken him, but is *always with* him, held by his *right hand*. The feeling that his purity of heart and life were 'in vain' is as much a fantasy as the wicked's prosperity. This is the reality of the matter.

The final step is the equal certainty of a glorious end for the righteous (vv. 24-26). God holds his people's hands like a parent: he gives them both the assurance he is there with them and that they will make it home. Home for the believer is *heaven*, where God is, and is a better place than *earth*, where troubles must be expected. Because of these, *flesh and ... heart may fail*, we may give way to our weakness, our feet may slip (v. 2), but with him behind us we are lifted up and made strong. This will be *for ever*.

So to sum up, vv. 27-28: those who are *unfaithful* to God, who pursue their lusts and are indifferent to others and to God himself, are *far from* God and *will perish*. Because they do not obey God in this life they will not have him in the next life. But those who make *the sovereign* LORD their *refuge*, who trust him and the truth of his word (v. 1), are *near him* now

and will go to be with him then. So now, instead of that bitter
message he had been on the point of giving (v. 15), he can *tell
of all (God's) deeds*. Nothing had changed outwardly, but all
was different within.

Questions:
(1) Can you remember times when God's word has said one
thing and your experience another?

(2) How far is it true that non-Christians have a better life
materially than Christians? Is Proverbs 10:16 still true?

(3) Think what 'holding hands with God' (v. 23) might
mean for you.

Psalm 74

God Has Rejected His People

If this psalm follows 73 in time it would appear that things got worse before they got better. It may, however, refer to a different situation, since the trouble seems to have come from outside Israel rather than from the wicked among the people of God. Enemies have invaded the land and are in process of smashing up the temple. This did indeed occur when Pharaoh Shishak invaded during Rehoboam's reign (see 1 Kings 11–14; 2 Chron. 12). In this event it may have been either a son or a member of the 'school of *Asaph*' who wrote it. While it appears to be chiefly a lament over the devastation of the temple and a cry for God to intervene, he calls it a *Maskil* since it contains good advice to the godly on how to act in times of trouble. The psalm falls into two parts, in sharp contrast to each other, as in so many psalms written in times of trouble.

Verses 1-11: Doubt and indignation

If the psalm relates to Shishak's invasion, then Asaph sees what few others did, probably even the King – that these events were God's judgments on the increasing apostasy of his people, as the Chronicler was later to state (2 Chron. 12:1-2). The troubles had by now gone on for so long he felt the people were *rejected ... for ever* (v. 1). The question *Why?* seems unnecessary in these circumstances, but it is explained by the reference to the people as *the sheep of your pasture*. True, they had misbehaved, but what shepherd destroys his flock when they annoy him by their stupidity?

Moreover, they were his *purchased ... (and) redeemed inheritance* (v. 2). They had been bondslaves and a price had to be paid to free them: the ten plagues, the slaughter of Egypt's firstborn sons and their own precious lambs, and finally the Egyptian army and the Pharaoh himself. How could God throw away what cost so much? Further, he was letting men destroy his own house – *Mount Zion where (he) dwelt*. This is inexplicable in a wise, faithful, all-powerful God.

But perhaps he does not know what has been going on? So let him come and see for himself (v. 3). The words *Turn your steps* picture someone treading warily over the debris of a fallen building. But this is no ordinary building, it is God's *sanctuary*. The invader seems to have made a bee-line for the Holy of Holies, in order, not only to remove its treasures, but destroy God himself! Probably he expected to find a huge golden image of the Lord, as there would be of his own gods in his own temples. Disappointed, he smashed the place up.

Verses 4-9 describe what God would see were he to walk through *these everlasting ruins*. In *the place where you met with us* he would hear, not the joyful praises of his people, but the victory shouts which *your foes roared* at the tops of their voices (v. 4). He would see *their standards set up as signs* of their occupation of the whole citadel. They had fought their way into the sanctuary like men slashing their way *through a thicket of trees* with *axes* (v. 5). *With their axes and hatchets* they had cut the gold overlay from the panelling (1 Kings 6:21-22) to take it off as plunder (v. 6, 1 Kings 14:26). The wood of the sanctuary was then burnt as a deliberate act of desecration, to destroy the *Name* of God (v. 7). They believed that if they destroyed the *place where God was worshipped*, they would destroy their God and thus weaken the people (v. 8).

Let God observe this utter dereliction. They were left with *no prophets* to foretell when God would intervene and perform *miraculous signs* to confirm his intervention. Lacking this prophetic guidance, *none of us knows how long this will be* (v. 9). So he puts the question to God (v. 10), pleading, not their suffering but the dishonour being done to his *name*. *How long* can you go on letting *the enemy mock you, O God*? Can you let them *revile your name for ever*? The *how long*? question is followed by the *why*? question (v. 11). If God has observed what is going on, he is not doing anything about it. He is standing there like someone keeping his *hand* concealed under his cloak. Let him *take it* out *and destroy them*.

The change of mood that follows seems to indicate that God did hear and answer. Perhaps it is referring to the appearance of a prophet, who first of all laid the blame on the people and their leaders: it was because they had abandoned God that he was now abandoning them to their enemy. When the leaders accepted this, and 'humbled themselves', through the prophet Shemaiah, God promised that the devastation would cease, although they would have to become 'subject to Shishak' (1 Chron. 12:5-8). This answer leads on to the complete change of tone in part two of the psalm.

Verses 12-23: Confident expectation

God's promise of deliverance changes everything. *But you, O God* (v. 12), recalls David's restoration when he was at rock-bottom (22:19) and anticipates Paul's 'But God' in Ephesians 2:4. From the present his thoughts turn to the past. The present king was hopeless, but God was *king from of old*, the bringer of *salvation*, as he had proved many times in the past. He had done so at the Red Sea (v. 13). Egypt was popularly known as *the monster in the waters*. The Nile river had made them a great nation, and its waters were infested with the crocodile, whom they made into a god – Sobek or *Leviathan* (v. 14). But God *crushed* its power when Pharaoh and his army were drowned *in the (Red) sea*. Their bodies were washed up on its banks and became *food to the creatures of the desert*.

Nor was that all God did for his people. He opened up *springs and streams* in the waterless desert (Exod. 17:6) enabling them to survive that long perilous journey and reach the border of Canaan. When they faced the Jordan he *dried up the ever-flowing river* (v. 15). Nor is he just the God of one people and one time. He is the God who created all things (v. 16), which alludes to Genesis 1. He is also the God who, having created all things, governs them: he allotted lands to the families *of the earth* and *set* them within their *boundaries*; he ordered the seasonal variations, *both summer and winter* (v. 17).

These thoughts give him confidence to make his request to God instead of merely complaining and questioning (vv. 18-23). This confidence is shown in the grounds on which he bases his prayer for deliverance: firstly, the dishonour the *enemy* was doing to God's *name*, for both temple and people bore that name (v. 18); secondly, the treatment being meted out to his children – a tiny nation alongside Egypt, like a *dove* being attacked by *wild beasts*, so that his *people* were an *afflicted* people (v. 19); thirdly, God's covenant, in which he had promised them a land of freedom, peace and plenty, not one *where haunts of violence fill the dark places of the land* (v. 20), making them go about in fear, or hide in their houses trembling; fourthly, the enforced cessation of worship caused by the enemy occupation of their temple, leaving them *oppressed*, retreating *in disgrace, poor and needy*, so that they could not *praise (his) name* (v. 21). This was not what they or God intended when the Temple was built.

So he lifts up his prayer and calls on God to spring into action and fulfill his promises. It was *your cause* that was threatened and God himself who was mocked by *fools* who were being allowed to desecrate his sanctuary (v. 22). Their shouts, their *clamour (and) uproar*, were still filling his ears as he uttered this prayer (v. 23). Let God too hear it and not *ignore it*, but act against it.

Questions:
(1) What should we say when God appears to act out of character, against his promises and even his own interests? See Habakkuk 2:1-3.

(2) How do the words 'But God' get to the heart of the gospel? (See Eph. 2:4.) Have you experienced a 'but God' in your life?

(3) Translate the grounds on which Asaph prays for deliverance in verses 18-23 into arguments to use in praying for revival.

Psalm 75

Do Not Destroy

Here is Asaph in a very different frame of mind from Psalms 73 and 74. He is not preoccupied with the behaviour of the wicked and God's apparent unconcern. Far from it. He is rejoicing in the sovereignty of God over them, which he showed by punishing them and replacing them with righteous leaders. So he can now take as his tune Do not destroy, but hold back.

Verse 1: The people unite in thanksgiving to God
They had good cause to do so, since recent troubles were over and they were united under God. But the way this is expressed is interesting: *Your Name is near*, that is, the God who has revealed himself is with us again. This is the only explanation of the big change in their fortunes. But the reality of God's presence does not depend on special interventions. Just to recall his *wonderful deeds*, ancient or modern, brings him close. When God's people forget what he has done for them they soon lose touch with him, and vice versa.

Verses 2-5: God speaks to his people
Apparently a prophet or priest speaks in God's name at this point (*You say*), with a two-fold message.

(1) *Reassurance* (vv. 2-3). Recent events have not only been brought about by God, but in his *appointed time*. Whoever is king it is God who rules his people and *judges uprightly*. He may allow things to get out of hand (as they had for many years) to show that he it is *who holds its* (society's) *pillars firm*, who maintains stability when society seems on the point of collapse. This gives a deeper meaning to *your Name is near*.

(2) *Warning* (vv. 4-5). God's deeds of late and his more recent words should warn *the arrogant* not to *boast*. The disorders of the times have been due largely to ambitious, unscrupulous men, who had power; they were like bulls with powerful *horns*. But let them, or anyone else, take care not to *lift up (their) horns against heaven*, not to assert their power defiantly against God. He has proved what happens to such – some were already dead.

Verses 6-8: His people assent to God's words

The rest of the psalm probably represents Asaph's response to God's words in the name of the people. He takes up what God had said about *lifting up* (vv. 4-5) and uses it in verses 6-7, where it is translated *exalt*. It is God who chooses who will represent him on earth. He has power to 'hire and fire' leaders and kings, as he has proved by events from Saul's defeat to David's accession. Bulls may be powerful beasts with sharp horns, but he can *bring (them) down* and replace them with shepherd-like figures, who are gentle. *It is God who judges* who shall be up and who down.

Nor does this apply only to the ambitious. *All the wicked of the earth* are subject to him. If they persist in wickedness, they will find themselves drinking, not the sweet wine of the celebratory feast, but the *foaming wine mixed with spices* – hot, acrid and burning – which he will make them drink *down to its very dregs*.

Verses 9-10: The King resolves to rule accordingly

As for me: Asaph here appears to be speaking on behalf of the king, re-affirming his obligations as God's vicegerent. He will honour this God, *praise him for ever* and make no attempt to usurp his authority. At the same time he will be his willing instrument in controlling the ambitious and promoting the humble. The words *lift up*, which have been prominent since verse 4, are here used for the fifth time (if vv. 6-7 are included, where the same Hebrew word is translated 'exalt') and bring the psalm to an end.

Questions:
(1) Think of the place of memories in bringing someone close and apply this to remembering God's deeds (v. 1): in Scripture, in history, in your own life and especially in the Lord's Supper (1 Cor. 11:24-25).

(2) Compare verse 3 with Hebrews 12:26-28 and consider how much greater is our security under the Gospel.

(3) How would you apply the lifting up of the horns of righteous (v. 10) to these New Testament times (Matt. 23:12)?

Psalm 76

The Awesome God

Asaph continues in the same vein as in the previous psalm, rejoicing in the recent deliverance of Israel from their enemies. But his chief thought here is not the restoration of peace and order in itself but the greatness of the God who has given it.

Verses 1-2: God supreme on Zion
This great victory has confirmed that God is truly among them and has established his *dwelling-place in Zion* where the ark resided. The word for *tent* is not the word used for the tabernacle but one which means 'lair'. God guards his people from Zion like a lion. Calling Jerusalem simply *Salem* ('peace') hints at what God has achieved for his people and has been guarding – their peace.

Verses 3-4: The enemies defeated
Asaph, the author, recalls the way the victory was achieved, which was so obviously by God. The nations had come at them with *flashing arrows ... shields ... swords ... (all sorts of) weapons of war*. God has simply stepped in and broken them. The victory was won on the *mountains rich in game*, the mountains which formed the border of Israel and her neighbours. Where men normally hunted animals as their prey, God had hunted down

Israel's enemies, an expression which develops the idea of the lion and his lair in verse 2. Snow-covered mountains gleam in the rising or setting sun, but God was *resplendent with light more majestic* than they.

Verses 5-6: Silence after battle
After the noise and tumult of battle, all is silent. The soldiers, the *valiant men*, the choicest of the nations' *warriors, sleep their last sleep*; none will ever *lift his hands* to hurl a weapon again. *Horse and chariot* also *lie still*. Again it is emphasised that this is not due to Israel's military superiority but the *rebuke* of Israel's (*Jacob's*) God.

Verses 7-9: The Awesome God
The effect of this sudden decisive victory was to strike all who saw or heard of it with awe, fearing lest they too arouse God's anger and are similarly dealt with. This was God's *judgment* on these idolatrous and rebellious nations (vv. 8-9). He had called 'Be still' (46:10) and reduced them to silence. But what was *judgment* for the enemy was salvation for his *afflicted* people, who could now settle down under their king and worship their God.

Verse 10: The abiding lesson
What do we learn from all this? NIV regards the *wrath* as that of God *against* men, as proved by the late battle, through which he had *gained praise*. Others differ and the Hebrew certainly sounds like *the wrath OF man* (rather than *AGAINST*), suggesting he can use man's fierceness and cruelty to execute his judgments on them. By warring against his people they have lost their lives, which they would have kept had they remained at peace. 'The passions which excite men to rebel against God shall be used as instruments of coercion' (Alexander).

Some translate the second part of the verse 'the remainder of wrath you gird on' (cf. NIV mg.), which would make it mean the same as the first part. Alternatively it could be *gird IN*, that is, where they go to excess he restrains them. God later raised up the Babylonians to execute his judgment on Israel, but

when they went too far he brought them down, as he revealed
to Habakkuk in chapter 2.

Verses 11-12: A call to the nations
In the light of all this God's advice is: *to his own people* (v. 11a):
to re-affirm their loyalty to the God who has just saved them;
to the neighbouring lands: not to oppose his people, for in so
doing they oppose him. Let them believe that what he has just
done he can do again (v. 12) and therefore they should accept
that he is a real living God of power and come to his dwelling-
place with *gifts* rather than weapons.

Questions:
(1) In these gospel days, what corresponds to the 'Shekinah'
glory in the tabernacle (vv. 1-2, 4)? (See John 1:14, 18.)

(2) Are we to regard war as a judgment of God (vv. 7-10)?
(See Ezek. 14:21; Rev. 6:4.)

(3) What does the psalm teach us about the spiritual war of
Christ and his church against Satan and his servants, and its
ultimate outcome? (See Rev. 17:14.)

Psalm 77

Appealing to God's Holy Ways

In this psalm *Asaph* is back in the mood of 74; indeed it may have been occasioned by the same situation, when Israel's enemies were smashing up the temple. It was composed in co-operation with another of David's musicians – *Jeduthun* (1 Chron. 25:1-3) and has strong similarities with 74. Although written in the first person singular, it is not mere private grief; he is making Israel's troubles his own. This is in the tradition of psalms which anticipate the vicarious sufferings of Christ (Rom. 15:3).

Verses 1-9: Agony and perplexity
The depth of his sufferings is brought out in two ways in verse 1: that he could not keep them locked in his heart but *cried out*; and that he kept repeating his cry, which reads literally 'my voice to God ... my voice to God!'. He asks him for *help*, or at least for a hearing. This was not weakness or self pity; his distress was on behalf of the nation (v. 2). But since it is not his nation but God's, he *sought the Lord*, he *stretched out untiring hands*, not only by day but *at night*. He refused those who tried to make him rest by offering him *comfort*.

Even when he turned from pre-occupation with the troubles and *remembered ... God*, it did not help, but only made it worse: he *groaned* and his *spirit grew faint* (v. 3). For it only made him more aware that God had turned away and given them up to their enemies. The *Selah* pause reflects the faintness to which he was reduced which made him temporarily unable *to speak*. Then he continues to describe his nights (cf. v. 2): because of his sense of God's anger he could not sleep or pray, he was too *troubled* (v. 4). He sought relief by thinking *about the former days* (v. 5), as in 74:12-17, but his 'memories only brought torturing comparisons' (F. D. Kidner).

He even recalled those times when he had not been able to sleep for very joy and he and his people sang their *songs* far into the *night*, for God was near and they were celebrating his blessings (v. 6). Now these memories only raised questions (vv. 7-9). The big one is the first (v. 7): is this state of suffering to go on *for ever*? *Will the* LORD *never show his favour again*?

The confusion of thought lying behind this question emerges in verses 8-9. If *his love* is *unfailing*, how can it have *vanished for ever*? If his *promise* has *failed for all time*, how can he be a God of truth and righteousness? Can an eternal omnipresent God have *forgotten to be merciful*? If *he has in anger withheld his compassion*, there must be just cause for it. If the cause is removed, will the *compassion* not be restored? But excessive grief deprives us of the ability to think straight, particularly about God.

This time *Selah* marks a change of direction in the thinking, possibly also expressed by a key change or the use of different instruments by 'the director of music' (title).

Verses 10-20: Certainty and hope

Asaph had written like this in 74:12 and on an earlier occasion – perhaps Absalom's rebellion – in 73:21. This time he does not say 'But you, O God', but *Then I thought*, not in confusion but clarity. Instead of just comparing the present unfavourably with the past, he could make the past the ground of his *appeal*. For past glories were *the years of the right hand of the Most High*. This was the name which Abraham had given God after his victory over the kings of the east (Gen. 14:22). If Abraham's little band could defeat that larger army through the power of God, could not that same God throw off the Egyptians? The actual memories have not changed; what has changed is his attitude towards them. Instead of looking back negatively and nostalgically, he is doing so positively and believingly: *I will remember ... yes, I will remember.* He follows this train of thought and *meditates on ALL your works and considers ALL your mighty deeds* (v. 12, emphasis mine).

And so he does: verses 13-15 echo the Song of Moses after the victory at the Red Sea (Exod. 15:11-13). So often it is the recollection of this great event that restores faith in bad times. For it was no ordinary deliverance or victory. This was God showing how *great* he is alongside other *gods*, and how *holy* are his *ways* (v. 13). Unlike men and their gods, he can *perform miracles* (v. 14). He is not confined to one place, but can *display (his) power among the peoples*. This does not mean God was just showing off; he had a purpose (v. 15) – to redeem his people, *the descendants of Jacob and Joseph*, whom he had chosen and with whom he had made his covenant. This is the answer to those doubts about his faithfulness expressed in verses 7-9.

Now he has started down this road, there is no holding him back. He paints a vivid picture of the Red Sea crossing, almost as if he had been there (vv. 16-19). What he is most conscious of is the presence of God there: *The waters saw you, O God, the waters saw you* (v. 16); *your path led through the sea ... your way ... your footprints* (v. 19). The great storm which caused the sea to recede then return was his doing (vv. 17-18), his means of saving his people and destroying their enemies. As God went into and through the Red Sea with his people then, so he is with them now and will surely bring them through. What he did to the Egyptians then he could do again. The future too is secure, for he who *led (his) people like a flock by the hand of Moses and Aaron* will lead them on into the future (v. 20).

What a change of approach from the way he started out! But if he had not 'cried out' these things to **GOD**, would he ever have progressed from despair to hope? Let us be encouraged to express all our thoughts and feelings to him, whatever they are. He who can change our circumstances can change our attitude towards them.

Questions:
(1) How much do you identify with the present state of the church and the sufferings of Christians elsewhere? (See 1 Cor. 12:26; Gal. 6:2; Heb. 13:3).

(2) Do you ever so give way to despair that you call in question the basic attributes of God? Do you realise that in fact they are the answer to your problem? (See Ps. 16:8).

(3) Do you read about how God intervened in the past when the church had fallen into the hands of its enemy? Do these make you feel worse about the present or encourage you to pray for a repeat? (See Ps. 44:1; Hab. 3:2).

Psalm 78

The Praiseworthy Deeds of the LORD

Here is Asaph in historical mode. Perhaps he is developing the thought of 75 and 76. They have been delivered from their enemies and peace and order have been restored. This latest victory is now given its place in their history and the opportunity is taken to survey the mighty acts of God for them from Egypt (v. 12) to the present (vv. 65-72). That these were God's acts and not theirs is brought out by reference to their frequent failures and sins, which go back to the beginning (v. 9) and continue until recent times (v. 56).

Verses 1-8: Principles on which the psalm is based
When God brought the people out of Egypt he told them to be sure to tell future generations what he had done (Exod. 10:2, 13:8). Indeed the Passover was to be performed in the presence of their children so that they would enquire about its meaning and be instructed in this key period of their history (Exod. 12:26; 13:14-16) . Possibly this psalm was composed for use at one of the festivals or for a special victory celebration. Either way it would raise questions in young minds.

This is what the psalm's introduction deals with. Actions and words which would appear cryptic if not explained, *like parables and hidden sayings, things from of old*, are to be made clear. They were done to teach them both *the praiseworthy deeds of the* LORD ... (v. 4) and *the statutes* he decreed ... *and the law* he established (v. 5). Since he gave this for all generations, the fathers were responsible for instructing the next generation, a process to be repeated down the ages (v. 6).

But why these history lessons and dramatic demonstrations? Chiefly, to bring them to *faith* in God and lead them on in *obedience* to him (v. 7). If they did *not forget his deeds* they would *trust* him when they too found themselves in trouble, as their forefathers had. If they kept *his commands* before them they would be prompted to obey him

Along with this went another purpose: warning against the danger of forgetfulness. The subsequent history of their *forefathers* who came out of Egypt shows how they departed from faith and obedience (v. 8). It is these principles that are to be illustrated and proved in the body of the psalm, which draws on the story of the journey across the desert and their life in the promised land up to the time of David.

Verses 9-16: The Failure of Ephraim

The reason for singling out *Ephraim* is because of what the psalm is leading up to: transferring the leadership of the nation from Joseph (father of *Ephraim*) to Judah in the person of David, and of the ark from Shiloh to Jerusalem.

The unsuitability of *Ephraim* and the other northern tribes as compared with Judah appears soon after the conquest. For Judah made a fairly thorough job of driving out the remaining Canaanites in comparison with the other tribes who were half-hearted and *turned back on the day of battle,* even *though* well equipped for the task, being *armed with bows* (v. 9). The result was that whereas 'the LORD was with the men of Judah', to the others he said 'I will not drive them out ... they will be thorns in your sides' (Judg. 1–2:3). *They did not keep God's covenant* (v. 10), but entered into covenant with the Canaanites, so God gave them up.

The reason for their failure was their forgetfulness of what God had done for them when he brought them out of Egypt and across the desert (vv. 11-16). This emphasises the point of the whole occasion: keeping the words and deeds of God always before them so that they would persevere in faith and obedience (vv. 7-8).

Verses 17-31: Rebellion in the desert

This failure to persevere goes back even further than the settlement in Canaan – to the desert journey itself. He ended the last section by referring to the miracles God performed for them while crossing the desert. Now he shows how they failed to respond positively to these even while they were happening! When their food supply ran short, instead of humbly asking God for food and quietly trusting him to supply it, they challenged him, *they put God to the test* (v. 18), not believing he could really *spread a table in the desert* (v. 19).

When, in answer to their cries for water, God *struck the rock and water gushed out*, instead of falling before him thankfully and confessing their unbelief, they challenged him to give them *meat* also (vv. 20). While angered at their unbelief (vv. 21-22), he accepted the challenge and *rained down manna ... the bread of angels* (vv. 24-25). When they complained of the monotony of the manna and wanted meat, *he rained down meat on them like dust* (v. 27).

But he could not let it go at that. Their unbelief, grumbling, unthankfulness and testing God constituted *the sin (of) rebelling against the Most High* (v. 17), and must be punished. And it was, with a terrible plague (v. 31).

Verses 32-39: Mercy triumphs over wrath

But judgment had little more effect than kindness – *they kept on sinning ... they did not believe* (v. 32). True, after long years of suffering (v. 33), they did appear to *turn* and acknowledge him as their *Rock and Redeemer*, but it was only lip service, it did not come from the heart (vv. 36-37). So, unless he was going to wipe them out completely, all he could do was to be *merciful*, forgive *their iniquity* and not let justice take its full course (v. 38). They were after all only human – *but flesh – a passing breeze* (v. 39). So he persevered with them over that long period in the desert.

Verses 40-55: Sinful forgetfulness

Their basic trouble was that they failed to appreciate fully what he had done for them in bringing them out of Egypt: *they did not remember his power* (v. 42). They had been a weak, enslaved people in the hands of the greatest power in the world, power that the Egyptians attributed to their gods. But *the Holy One of Israel* was greater, and he humbled the Egyptians with those ten great plagues, most of which are mentioned here (vv. 44-51). Though they were just *like a flock* of sheep alongside the Egyptian army, they had a great Shepherd who *brought (them) out* and *guided them safely*. These unarmed weaklings saw the huge Egyptian army *engulfed* in the Red Sea.

Then in spite of the dangers and privations of the desert *he brought them to the border of his holy land* (v. 54), where again they faced fierce opposition from the *nations* in occupation. Yet they took them over and *settled ... in their homes* (v. 55). The point of all this is: if God did all that, why could they not trust him when lesser troubles rose, when nations who were nothing compared to the Egyptians came against them? When the crops failed and the land became barren, why did they not remember the desert which they had survived? Why must they compromise with their enemies and make treaties, or call upon pagan fertility gods to provide? The psalm was bringing all God's ancient deeds before them, so that they would apply the lessons to the present and future.

Verses 56-67: The rule of Joseph rejected

This brings the matter up to the time of writing, the reign of David and his transfer of the ark to Jerusalem. The northern tribes, dominated by Joseph, had proved unfit to rule and unworthy of housing the ark. So God *abandoned the tabernacle of Shiloh (and) sent the ark ... into captivity* with the Philistines (vv. 60-61), who had unleashed a fierce war on them (vv. 62-64). They had proved disloyal and faithless, unworthy of the position and blessing bestowed on them by Moses (Deut. 33:13-17), so *he rejected the tents of Joseph* (v. 67). The disasters they suffered under Saul, recorded by Samuel, are in mind here.

Verses 68-72: The choice of David and Zion

But he was not giving his people up altogether. He was removing the sceptre from Joseph and passing it to Judah, as originally predicted by Jacob (Gen. 49:8-12). At the time these promises seemed inconsistent with what he had said about Joseph (Gen. 49:22-26). Now all is clear. Joseph would be predominant for centuries, in fact he would have two large portions, Ephraim and Manasseh, with vast territories under his control. But eventually *he rejected the tents of Jospeh* (v. 67), and the sceptre passed to Judah in the person of David, remaining with him and his family 'until he comes to whom it belongs' (Gen. 49:10) – and we know who he was! The final proof of the change was David bringing the ark to *Mount Zion which he* (God) *loved* (v. 68).

Asaph who composed the psalm was David's contemporary, so he finished his record with David's good reign. It is not without significance that the metaphor used of God leading the people of Egypt (vv. 52-53) is that used of David ruling the people – the shepherd and his flock (vv. 70-72). David had spent his youth learning to be a shepherd, and learning what it meant that God was his shepherd (23). So God made him under-shepherd over his people, to hold that office until 'the good Shepherd' should come.

So not only could the generations of Israel look back to see how God's mercy had triumphed over his people's sin, but we too can see the bigger picture. How can we forget and fall into unbelief with all these stories of his power and mercy recounted to us, culminating in the life and death of Jesus Christ?

Questions:
(1) How can we Christians fulfill our responsibilities to the rising generation (vv. 1-8, cf. Eph. 6:4)?

(2) How often do we blame our memories when the trouble lies in an unbelieving heart? (see Heb. 3:7-19).

(3) How important is it for Christians to know the history of Israel? What does it teach us? (See Acts 7:51-53 [if possible read the whole chapter].)

Psalm 79

The Reproach On God's Name

This psalm is very much on the lines of 74 and 77, when Israel was in the throes of defeat and destruction at the hands of their enemies. However, there is more stress on prayer to God for deliverance from the invaders. *Asaph* is getting to grips with the situation, reasoning that God cannot let it go on and asking him to intervene on Israel's side.

Verses 1-4: Asaph's lament
As the devastation of *Jerusalem* continues, so does *Asaph's* complaint. But since it is addressed to *God*, it is phrased in such a way as at the very least to hint to *God* that damage was being done to him as well as to them. *It is YOUR inheritance the nations have invaded* (v. 1, cf. 74:2) and *YOUR temple they have defiled. It is the dead bodies of YOUR saints whom they have given ... as food to the birds of the air, and the flesh of YOUR saints which has been left to the beasts of the earth* (v. 2, emphasis mine). The reference here is to bodies left unburied, as verse 3b states. This is the supreme humiliation: to be so cast off there is no one to mourn over one's death and pay proper respect to one's body (Jer. 22:18-19).

Verse 3a has a touch of irony. Whereas in the past the *blood* of sacrificial animals would be *poured out* by the priests to cleanse the people and the place from being *defiled,* now it is the *blood* of the people that is being *poured out* by foreign warriors and is defiling the very place of sacrificial cleansing. All this adds to their shame in the eyes of *our neighbours* and *those around us* (v. 4).

Verses 5-13: Asaph's prayer

The prayer begins, as in 74:10-11 and 77:7-9 with a question to *the* Lord (v. 5). Certain assumptions underlie this: firstly, that God is aware of what is happening, yet not intervening; secondly, that this is the expression of his *anger* and *jealousy*, aroused by sin in the people; and thirdly, that God was able to stop it if he so willed. This is what Asaph must now persuade him to do. That God should be angry against sin and sinners he can accept. But surely it was more in keeping with his nature and promises that he should *pour out (his) wrath on the nations that do not acknowledge you* (v. 6). Granted, the behaviour of Israel lately has not been exemplary, and a division has occurred which is shutting off the larger part of the nation from God's altar, nevertheless other nations do not even know his *name*, far less *call upon him*. Further, they are trying to destroy those who do seek to do these things. This was not what God had promised, either through Abraham (Gen. 12:3) or Moses (Deut. 30:7).

The next argument he uses is the harshness of punishing them for what their fathers had done (v. 8, although there is a question whether instead of *the sins of the fathers* we should read 'our former iniquities', as in esv). True, punishment for sin was written into the second commandment (Exod. 20:5), but God was not obliged to enforce this, since he was a God of *mercy* and his people were *in desperate need*. He did not always punish his people for their own sins, let alone those of former generations. So Asaph feels he is well within the will of God to ask him to *forgive our sins* (v. 9). Since he had revealed himself as a God of *mercy*, would not forgiveness be *for the glory of your name*? It would enhance his reputation among the ungodly, whereas if he gave them up to idolatrous people, the nations would say, *Where is their God?* (v. 10, cf. Exod. 32:12; Num. 14:13-17). But they would not be able to say this if God came and avenged *the outpoured blood of (his) servants* by

sending the enemy packing and this was made known among
the nations. If this argument was not acceptable to God, surely
he could not refuse the pitiable *groans of the prisoners and those
condemned to die* (v. 11)? Surely his *arm* had *the strength* to
prevent further bloodshed among them?

His words have at least convinced *him*, for he waxes very
bold in verse 12 – perhaps too bold. Not only does he ask
God to do to their enemies what their enemies have done to
them, but to do it 'sevenfold' (ESV)! Is this the right spirit in
one who has just been pleading for mercy for his own people?
The answer lies in the second part of the verse, which is itself
consistent with verses 9-10, where he has been pleading the
dishonour done to God.

Evidently the invaders were not merely out for territory
– they had another agenda: to bring *reproach* on the Lord God
of Israel. Was the foreign king out to avenge the defeat of
an earlier one at the hands of Israel's God? Was he trying to
restore the supremacy of his gods over the Lord? Was this
why he especially targeted Jerusalem and the temple? If so,
Asaph, like David in the 'imprecatory' psalms, was acting as
God's prophet and pronouncing his judgment on them. This
is confirmed by verse 13. The destruction of the invading
army would release *your people, the sheep of your pasture,* who
will praise you for ever ... from generation to generation. This was
after all why God had chosen them, given them this land and
come to dwell in their temple (Isa. 43:21). So if he gave them
over to their enemies now, it would be his honour that was
chiefly impugned.

Questions:
(1) Is Christ as closely identified with the sufferings of
Christians and the church as the Lord was with those of Israel?
(Isa. 63:9; Acts 9:4; Heb. 4:15.)

(2) How do Christians pray for those who attack them
and their faith, physically or verbally? (Cf. v. 12 with
Matt. 5:43-45.)

(3) How do Asaph's words in verse 12 compare with Christ's
teaching and example on forgiveness in Matthew 18:21-35;
Luke 23:34?

Psalm 80

Restore us, O God

This psalm is in the same mood as 74, 77 and 79 and may relate to the same situation: an invasion of Israel by a formidable enemy such as Shishak, Pharaoh of Egypt (1 Kings 14:25-28). It is a prayer for deliverance set to a tune called *Lilies of the covenant*. *Lilies* probably symbolise love and the word for covenant here is not BeRITH but 'eDUTH, which means 'oracle' or 'revelation'. This indicates that the prayer is an appeal to God based on his pledged love to his people. It is styled in such a way that it could be used in later emergencies. The Septuagint adds 'concerning the Assyrian', showing it was re-used at the time of their invasion. So it is couched in the plural: *hear US ... restore US* (emphasis mine).

Verses 1-3: The people's desperate appeal
a. *Whom they appeal to*. God is described in two ways here: first, as *Shepherd of Israel*. This idea originally appeared in the mouth of the dying Jacob when he blessed the sons of Joseph – *Ephraim and Manasseh* (Gen. 49:24). The God who had cared for Jacob and his family was to *lead Joseph* (representing all the tribes) *like a flock* out of Egypt into their own pasture (cf. 77:20 78:52). Surely he would not now let them be devoured by their enemies? Secondly, he is described as the one *who (sits) enthroned between the cherubim*.

These are not baby angels but awesome supernatural beings, the guards of the gates of Eden (Gen. 3:24), later sculpted on the 'mercy-seat' in the tabernacle (Exod. 25:22), where God promised to dwell (1 Chron. 28:18). Thus God, while having the tenderness of the shepherd to his own, has the terrifying power of cherubim to turn on his enemies.

b. *What they appeal for* – for this God to *shine forth ... make your face shine upon us*. This is based on the priestly blessing of Numbers 6:24-26, the prayer for God's special favour. The earnestness of the appeal is emphasised by putting it in other words: *awaken your might, come and save us. Ephraim (and) Manasseh* are specified, being the tribes of *Joseph*, the leading and largest ones, representing the whole nation. *Benjamin* is important since Jerusalem, which they had just captured but abandoned, was located there.

The appeal is summed up in *restore* (v. 3), for the outcome of God's favour would be a change in their fortunes: they would have peace and stability, and be able to unify and re-establish the nation under its rightful king. This would lead to a restoration of their own love, worship and obedience to God.

Verses 4-7: The people's desperate state
That their desperate appeal was justified is seen here. Their present condition shows that, far from looking favourably on them, God's *anger* was smouldering (v. 4). When they had been on the point of recovering from internal troubles, outsiders had attacked them, turning their recent rejoicings into bowlfuls of tears (v. 5). Instead of regaining the respect of neighbouring nations they were a laughing-stock (v. 6). So the cry goes up again, *Restore us*.

Verses 8-15: The people's perplexity
The key word here is Why? (v. 12). It was not just that their condition was desperate, but it was contrary to all God had promised and done in the past. Again he refers to their origin; but instead of the flock/shepherd picture he uses

the *vine* image (v. 8). This was later to become prominent in Isaiah 5, Hosea 10:1, Ezekiel 15 and John 15, where Jesus used it of himself and his church. This image first occurs in Jacob's blessing (Gen. 49:24). The vine grew the grapes which provided the staple drink for hot, dry countries, and was an apt image for God's people. He had made them into a nation while in Egypt, then transplanted them to Canaan (v. 8), where they *took root and filled the land* (v. 9). A vine has a single root from which branches can extend without limit. The conquests of Joshua had vastly extended Israel's borders (vv. 10-11).

But the long wars with the Philistines had devastated the vine and exposed its riches to foreigners (v. 12). It was as if wild beasts had come and trampled on it and devoured its fruits (v. 13). So the appeal becomes even more impassioned in verse 14. This time it is based on the vine language. A vine is guarded and tended by its planter. When Jesus said 'I am the Vine', he went on to say, 'my Father is the gardener' (John 15:1). But the gardener had turned away from his vine and let the wild beasts in, even though his own *right hand had planted the root ... raised up a branch* (NIV mg) from it. The word *branch* was to become a Messianic word (Isa. 4:2; Jer. 23:5; Zech. 3:8; etc) and it begins to take on this meaning here, especially in what follows. Thus it is a powerful argument for God to work. If Israel prefigured God's Messiah, how can he let her be treated like this?

Verses 16-19: The people's hope

The parlous state they are in (v. 16) can be changed and they can again become a godly people (v. 18), but only if God will look on them, not only as his flock and his vine, but his son. Verse 17 has the king in mind – he is *the man at your right hand, the son of man* who represents God to his people and his people to God. Israel as a whole was God's *son* (Hos. 11:1), his first-born and heir, but the King was the figurehead. Like 'the servant of the Lord', *son* or *son of man* was one of the titles the Messiah was to take to himself to fulfill his mission to the world. All this is prefigured by Israel and was a powerful argument for God to *restore* and look again with favour on them (v. 19).

Questions:

(1) How important is it to you to begin your praying with a clear realisation of the One to whom you are coming? (See vv. 1-2, cf. Jer. 32:17-23; Matt. 6:9-10; Acts 4:24-26.)

(2) What do verses 4-6 teach us about being honest with God over our own spiritual state and that of the church? (See 1 John 18-10.)

(3) How does the whole psalm, especially verses 3, 7, 14 and 19 help us in praying for revival? (Cf. Ps. 85:1-7.)

Psalm 81

Sound the Trumpet

Here is Asaph in festive mood. Indeed the psalm may have been composed for use on one of Israel's feast days: Pentecost, Tabernacles or even the Feast of Trumpets, which began with the blowing of ram's horns (Lev. 23:23-24; Num. 29:1-6), referred to here in verse 3. This was held in the seventh month, Tisri, corresponding to our September–October, and was the highlight of the festal year. It was the first month of the civil year and believed by Israel to be the month when Creation took place. On the tenth day the great Day of Atonement was held, followed on the fifteenth by the Feast of Tabernacles.

It was therefore appropriate that the first day of this month should be marked by a feast at once joyful and solemn. The blowing of ram's horns was an expression of joy in what God had done in both the distant and recent past, and at the same time a summons to prepare for what lay ahead later that month.

It also coincided with the grape harvest, hence the word *Gittith* in the titles of Psalms 8, 81 and 84, which comes from 'Gath' and means 'wine-press'. It thus served as a thanksgiving for the provision of grapes for wine, which they would be making to store for the months ahead.

Verses 1-4: The spirit of the feast

The feast was celebrated with great fervour. Not only were they to *sing*, but also to *shout aloud to God our strength ... to the God of Jacob* (v. 1), as people did when greeting a great king on his return in triumph from battle. This was to be accompanied by whatever instruments were appropriate and available (v. 2). Above all they were to *sound the ram's horn*, as they had when Jericho fell with trumpets and shouting (Josh. 6:20). Israel used the lunar calendar, which meant that *New Moon* coincided with the first of the month, with full moon on the fifteenth, which was when Tabernacles was celebrated. So the Feast of Trumpets was not only a looking back to when they had gained entrance to the land, but on to the plenty they were to enjoy in it, celebrated in the Feast of Tabernacles on the fifteenth. Nor was this their own invention; it was all done on the authority of God himself (v. 4).

Verses 5-7: The substance of the feast

But this was not blind obedience, nor an excuse for an orgy. There were real grounds for celebration. For, like all the other feasts, this one referred to their release from bondage in Egypt (v. 5). It is probably better to read the third line as in the NIV mg: 'and we heard a voice we had not known', referring, not to the Egyptian language but to the voice of God, which they had never heard until he spoke at Sinai. It was then that he *established (the) statute* which included the celebration of this feast. The *distress* they had endured in Egypt is described in such a way as to make them feel something of what their fathers had suffered then: the *burden* of the bricks on their *shoulders*, and the weight of the baskets filled with straw which their *hands* had to carry (Exod. 1:11-14; 5:6-21). Such was their *distress* they had *called* out to God (Exod. 2:23) and God heard and *rescued* them.

But this was not all: he had done so, not merely because he pitied them but because he had a purpose for them – to mould them into a people who would know him. So he spoke *out of a thundercloud* at Sinai, giving them clear directions, which he enforced by his discipline when they failed in faith and obedience, as they had *at the waters of Meribah* (Exod. 17:7). An interlude – *Selah* – gives them opportunity for these things to sink in.

Verses 8-10: The message of the feast
God had listened to their cry in their distress, but would they *listen* to him? The words *warn* and *if you would but* throw some doubt on this, so the law is once again set before them in the shape of the preface to the Decalogue and the second commandment (vv. 9-10). Later in the month the whole law might be read at the Feast of Tabernacles.

But God's covenant at Sinai was not merely about their obligations to him but his to them. For it contained blessings as well as cursings, showing that the purpose of bringing them into the promised land was to enjoy its prosperity. This is beautifully expressed in verse 10c: *open your mouth* in my praises and your vows of loyalty, and *I will fill it* with the fruits of the earth.

Verses 11-12: The warning of the feast
But their history showed they had not listened, not submitted. They still hankered after *foreign gods* – as they had in Egypt, so subsequently had they in Canaan. So God let them have their way; *he gave them over to their stubborn hearts*. He had no need to inflict punishment, they brought it on themselves, for their entanglements with *foreign gods* involved them in the strife of those nations whose gods they worshipped.

Verses 13-16: The promise of the feast
But now it is a new year, a new month, and the opportunity for a new start. It is not too late for *my people to listen to me*. The offer is still on the table for him to *subdue their enemies* (v. 14). They could still see idolators come to *cringe before him* and suffer *punishment (which) would last for ever* (v. 15). They could still enjoy the blessings of fine *wheat (and) honey from the rock,* which was his original intention. Let them not miss this opportunity of knowing what it really meant to be the covenant people of God.

Questions:
(1) Do your memories of God's help in times past, especially your conversion, still move you to rejoice? (See 1 Pet. 1:3-9.)

(2) Look up Paul's use of the phrase 'gave them over' (v. 12) in Romans 1:24, 26, 28. Does this help you better understand the idea of 'the wrath of God' (Rom. 1:18)?

(3) The word 'listen' is used three times in verses 8-13. Does this truly describe what goes on between you and God when you read his word or hear it preached? (Heb. 4:6-13.)

Psalm 82

Who Judges the Judges?

This is a most unusual psalm: verses 2-7 are the words of God himself and only the first and last verses those of the writer. It reflects a time when the governing authorities are not doing their job: they are neglecting and even oppressing the poor and needy. This may come from the time when Absalom had seized power for his own ends, not the people's good. God knows what is happening and will reckon with the rebels; their days are numbered. On the strength of this, Asaph now challenges the wicked, targeting the rulers against whom he speaks the very words of God, for he is a prophet as well as a poet. Prophets were seemingly in short supply at this time, but God revealed his word to such as Asaph.

Verse 1: Asaph's Vision
In verse 1 the writer sees a vision of a *great assembly*, literally 'the assembly of God', a gathering God has summoned and over which he presides, in order to call to account *the gods*. Some understand this to refer to supernatural beings, as in Psalm 89:5-8 and Job 1:6, to whom God assigned authority over nations (Deut. 32:8; Dan. 10:13, 21-22). While this makes sense in itself, it hardly fits the charge brought against them of neglecting their responsibility to the weak and poor (vv. 2-4), who are in the care of men rather than angels. They

are therefore more likely to be local and national governors, regarded as God's representatives (Rom. 13:1-5). Jesus clearly saw these words as referring to human beings: John 10:34-35.

Verses 2-5: God's charges against the rulers

Verse 2: They were abusing their power. Any complaints brought against the wicked were quickly dismissed – not because they were not proven, but out of *partiality*.

Verses 3-4: They are turning their office upside down – defending the unjust and showing partiality to the wicked when they should be defending *the weak ... the poor and the oppressed* (v. 3). The rebels were falsely charging the latter and the judges were not delivering them *from the hand of the wicked* (v. 4).

Verse 5 is the most damning indictment: *They know ... understand nothing.* The law-makers and upholders are of all people supposed to *know* the law, what is right and wrong. But these men reverse right and wrong, they *walk ... in darkness.* So instead of upholding the fabric of state, which was based on the Law of God, they were shaking its very *foundations.*

Verses 6-7: God's verdict against the rulers

They have proved unworthy of their high office as God's representatives – *gods... sons of the Most High.* They are no better than other *men,* worse in fact. They are as bad *as every other ruler,* the kings and lords of the uncircumcised nations, whom the Word of God condemns for their corruption, pride and brutality. Israel's rulers will fall just like heathen rulers, as the prophets foretold and the Scriptures and history describe.

Verse 8: Asaph's prayer

With the very words of God ringing in his brain the psalmist bursts into a prayer that God will exercise the power he has just claimed (v. 8), not only over Israel but *all the nations,* for he is King of Kings and Lord of Lords. Here is a glimpse of the reign of Christ over the nations through the gospel (Ps. 72:8-11; Isa. 9:6-7) and his final judgment of men and nations (Matt. 25:31-32).

Questions:

(1) Does this psalm help you come to terms with the injustice and cruelty of some governments in the world today?

(2) What guidance does this psalm give you about praying for your government, and even exercising your vote? (See Rom. 13:1-5; 1 Tim. 2:1-2.)

(3) Should we Christians pray verse 8 with reference to Christ's return in judgment? (See Rev. 22:20.)

Psalm 83

Conspiracy

Once more Asaph is appealing to God to deliver his people from their enemies, as in 74, 77, 79 and 80. Here they have formed a large confederacy against Israel (vv. 4-5). A frequent practice in the ancient world was for a defeated nation to return with greater numbers, which was what happened after David's victory over the Philistines: see 2 Samuel 5:22-25. Often they brought in others by offering a share of the spoil. Josephus writes of a confederacy of the Philistines with Syria and Phoenicia at that time. If 2 Samuel 23:8-39 and 1 Chronicles 11:10-47 belong at this point then the exploits of Benaiah against Egyptians and Moabites show those nations were also involved, at least by sending mercenaries. Some think the occasion was in Jehoshaphat's time in 2 Chronicles 20, when Moab and Ammon headed a group which included Edom. Alternatively it may refer to the general hostility shown to Israel by the surrounding nations during its entire history.

Verses 1-8: The people's desperate situation
They begin by calling on God not to ignore what is happening (v. 1); not merely to look on and see his people crushed. The plea is based on powerful arguments:

> 1: that Israel's *enemies* are God's *enemies* (*your foes*, cf. *You* and *your*, vv. 3, 5).

2: that these *foes* are moving into action with pride and boldness: they *rear their heads* (v. 2), they are defying the Lord God himself.

3: that they have secretly and craftily conspired with Israel's neighbours, in order to attack Israel on every side (vv. 3, 5-8).

4: that they are intent on nothing less than genocide (v. 4), so that they may share Israel's good land among themselves (v. 12).

So they appeal not merely to their own safety and comfort but to the honour of God, which is bound up with the fortunes of *those you cherish* (v. 3).

Verses 9-16: The people's bold prayer

As so often in the Bible, a crisis prayer looks back to a similar situation in the past in which divine intervention brought about spectacular deliverance. Two incidents from the Book of Judges are alluded to here: the defeat of the Canaanites by Deborah and Barak with the aid of Jael (vv. 9-10, Judg. 4–5) and that of the Midianites by Gideon (vv. 11-12, Judg. 7–8). *Endor* (v. 10) lay at the foot of Mount Tabor where the battle against the Canaanites was fought. The point of these references is that both attacks were with a view to taking over the land (v. 12) and were reversed by God's intervention.

Recalling these events gave Asaph fresh boldness to ask for something similar in this dire situation. The language is very strong. He wants them blown away *like chaff before the wind* or *tumbleweed* (v. 13), which is something like the seedball of our dandelion which the wind blows everywhere! He wants them destroyed like trees in a *forest fire* (v. 14). He wants them scared to death as by a *tempest* (v. 15). But this is not mere vindictiveness. As with other imprecatory passages, the motive is God-honouring. These foreigners were defying God and opposing what was dearest to him (v. 3b). If God stepped in they would be made to feel *shame* at their behaviour and begin to *seek (his) name* (v. 16).

Verses 17-18: The people's ultimate desire

The thought of verse 16 is developed in this final passage. This was God's war and Israel's king faced it not by conferring with his generals but by enquiring of God (2 Sam. 5:23); not by working out a strategy or hiring a mercenary army but by obeying God's word. More was at stake even than the nation and its land. The question was 'Who is Lord? Who reigns *over all* the earth?' He is again speaking as the prophet of God and even foreshadowing the time when the power of the Gospel would challenge the gods of the heathen and bring them down.

Questions:
(1) With verses 1-8 in mind, who do you think 'God's enemies' are at the present time? (See Jude, vv. 3-4.)

(2) Looking at verses 9-15, what incidents in the history of the Church do you think are valuable for those who contend for the faith today?

(3) How do verses 16-18 help us guard against any spirit of vindictiveness against those who oppose the faith of Christ?

Psalm 84

Absence Makes the Heart Grow Fonder

The reference to *gittith* in the title links this psalm with 81. *Gittith* means 'winepress', for the grape harvest coincided with the Feast of Trumpets. But the approach to the feast in this psalm is very different from that of 81. The writer, one *of the sons of Korah*, recollects his feelings when away from the presence of God in his house. It is an 'absence makes the heart grow fonder' experience.

Verses 1-4: Longing to be where God is

To be where God is – *your dwelling place* – is what he loves most, for the word *lovely* basically means 'loved'. God's *dwelling* is *lovely* to him because he loves it (v. 1). So when absent from it in body he is more than ever there in spirit. This is not sentimental attachment to a building, for what he *yearns, even faints* and *cries out for* is *the living God, the* LORD *Almighty.* He uses many of the words available in Hebrew psychology to express this: *my soul ... my heart and my flesh* (v. 2). What he feels within (*yearns*) bursts out in a cry, perhaps of sheer joy – the joy he anticipates experiencing at the feast.

This is intensified by the reference to birds who *nest* in the eaves of the building (v. 3). Though they cannot feel as he does, yet they are there where he would be. This is not for the architecture but because it was there he met with the one he calls *my King and my God*. It is with him that true happiness (*blessed*) is to be found – not a happiness for selfish pleasure, but one which expresses itself in *praising* God (v. 4). All this intense emotion calls for an interlude: *Selah*.

Verses 5-7: Strength to endure the absence

These verses may suggest the idea of pilgrims going up to the feast. However, verse 5b best translates as 'in whose *hearts* are the highways', so that he may simply be spiritualising the idea of the journey to the feast. It is a different way of expressing the thought of absence and longing. During this period God gives him *strength* to endure it, in fact God's own *strength*. He compares this with those who *pass through the Valley of Baca* (v. 6), a hot dry place where only a few scrubby trees grow. But people dig for *springs* of water and find God responds with the *autumn rains*, which occurred in the seventh month, the one which began with the Feast of Trumpets. This too recalls the crossing of the Sinai desert (Deut. 8:1-8; Pss. 78:15-16, 11:48). So the nearer they get to *Zion*, the greater the *strength* (v. 7).

All this is testifying to his experience while away from God's house: although he misses and longs for the particular blessings of that place, yet God makes up for it by lesser though definite manifestations of himself. Thus his arrival at Zion is not so much a complete contrast as the culmination of a life of trusting God.

Verses 8-9: A special request

Now he has a particular request to ask of the God who is so good to him in his absence from his house. The words *listen ... hear* draw attention to the importance of his request. The *Selah* interlude underlines this, as it looks forward in this case rather than backwards. This is a prayer for the king, maybe originally David, but applicable to whoever was king at the time. For the prayer does not mean the king was in some sort of special trouble. He is simply asking God to *look with favour* upon him because so much depended on him.

Anointed one was the name by which the king was described and is identical to that for the Messiah, whom he typified. The need was not so much the king's as the people's, for he was their *shield* (v. 9). It is true that God is really their *shield* (v. 11), but he gave them a king as the one through whom he protected them. Their well-being was bound up with his. Festivals frequently gave special thanks and prayers for the king.

Verses 10-12: In touch with eternity

Either in reality or anticipation he has arrived at the *courts* of the Lord. The expression *one day ... a thousand* (v. 10), is expounded for us in 2 Peter 3:8, where it is a vivid way of referring to God as eternal, out of time. The thought is that to come into his presence is to come into contact with eternity and be lifted out of time. This is the reason for the sentiment expressed in verse 10b: the word *doorkeeper* rather suggests an official position, whereas the meaning is simply 'to stand on the threshold', that is, to be on the way in, or perhaps to be kept right at the back because of the crowds. But he prefers this inconvenient position to the comforts of *the tents of the wicked*, where he can sit or lie down in the bosom of the family. *The wicked* are not necessarily the desperately evil, simply those who did not have the inclination to go and worship God but preferred to stay at home.

But how can anyone be like that when they consider who he is and what he does (v. 11)! He is an energising, comforting, enlightening *sun* and a strong protective *shield*. To be his is to enjoy *favour and honour* far outweighing anything found among *the wicked*, however rich or important the owner of *the tent* may be. In fact those who are the Lord's lack absolutely *no good thing* they can need or even desire (23:1). For what he has found for himself is freely available to all, if they will but *walk* with him (v. 12).

Questions:
(1) Although Christians are released from bondage to buildings, what is it that should make us long to assemble together even more than the psalmist? (See Matt. 18:20.)

(2) Meditate on verses 5-7 as a picture of the Christian's life here on earth while longing to be in heaven. (Phil. 1:21-24.)

(3) Do you pray 'by the clock' or does coming to God lift you out of time into eternity and make you feel 'lost in wonder, love and praise'? (See 2 Cor. 3:18.)

Psalm 85

Praying for Renewal

This psalm comes from a time when the people had experienced a special *favour* from God (v. 1), yet things were far from happy and they still needed to be *restored* (v. 4). This would fit the early days of the return from captivity, when the euphoria of coming home had given way to concern over the magnitude of the task before them. They needed houses to live in and food to eat. But they were making little progress. 'Fear of the peoples around them' (Ezra 3:3) hampered their building work, and the infertility of the soil meant a shortage of food, resulting in physical weakness which in turn made them unfit for long hard work.

Above all, if God were to dwell among them again, he needed a house. They had made a start on this (Ezra 3) but the above problems had curtailed it. It was a vicious circle: if God were not with them how could they withstand their enemies, since their army was now non-existent? Also, how could they expect food from their fields since it was God who gave the increase? But if they were not protected and provided for, how could they build a place for God to live among them? Haggai the prophet urged them to get their priorities right and set up God's house first, or they would never break out of this cycle of woe. These concerns underlie this psalm.

Verses 1-3: What God has done

When life becomes turbulent it is good to look back to see how it was before things began to go wrong. This is what *the sons of Korah* (descendants of that school of poetry and music originally set up by David) do here, with their gift. God had proved his *favour* towards them when he *restored* them from Babylon (v. 1). This is the same phrase as that used in 126:1, 4 which can be translated 'turned our captivity'. God had sent them away because he was *angry* over their apostasy from him, so the fact that he had brought them back meant he *forgave (their) iniquity and covered all their sins* (v. 2). The word *covered* (cf. 32:1) refers to the blood sprinkled on the 'atonement cover' or 'mercy seat' of the ark (Exod. 25:17) which propitiated the wrath of God.

The *Selah* pause is appropriate here since these points needed to sink in. At the time of writing the sacrifical system had probably not been re-introduced. However, God was not restricted to ceremonies and his forgiveness was just as real as if they were in full swing. This meant they could not possibly still be under his *wrath and ... anger* which he had *set aside*, literally 'gathered in', and *turned from* (v. 3). Reassuring as this was, it left room for perplexity because of the present situation.

Verses 4-7: What they needed

In view of the above, how were they to interpret the present? It seemed as if his *displeasure* continued and his *anger* was prolonged. Was it to go on *for ever ... through all generations* (v. 5)? They needed another restoration: *restore us again* (v. 4). In fact the word *again* is not present in the Hebrew and it reads literally 'turn us', so perhaps it was their hearts that needed to change more than their circumstances. This could have been their response to the preaching of Haggai who reproached them for abandoning work on the temple in favour of their houses (Hag. 1). They had been convicted in their hearts that they had made their troubles an excuse. Now they ask God to 'turn' their hearts back to him.

This led on to the prayer that, as they turned wholly to God, so he would turn to them: *revive us again* (v. 6), is literally 'turn and revive'. For it was more than a change of heart on their part that was needed; God must turn to them, for there were things only he could deal with, such as granting fertility to the land and driving off their enemies. Let him do to them what he had done to the Babylonians. Their motive for this too is healthier – not just that they may *rejoice*, but *rejoice in you*, that is, come to him, not with complaints but praises. The clear thinking of 'the sons of Korah', already shown in verses 1-3, makes God's covenant the ground of this prayer (v. 7) for 'unfailing love' is 'covenant love'. The one they call to is *the* LORD whose *love*, shown to them in making them a people from the loins of Abraham and freeing them from slavery, not only from Egypt but from Babylon, is *unfailing*.

Verses 8-13: What God says

God always answers his people when they cry to him, if they truly *listen to what the* LORD *God will say* (v. 8). Even if he does not immediately and totally change things, he comes to tell us what he will do. The first person singular (*I*) may be the author speaking as a prophet, for the words of the psalms are just as inspired as are the words of the prophets. His reply is two-fold: a promise of *peace*, that is, according to the meaning of the Hebrew 'Shalom', total well-being in every respect; and a warning *not (to) return to folly*, which is basically a state of unbelief (14:1) tending to idolatry (idols were called 'follies' or 'vanities'). It had been *folly* that had caused their exile and it was *folly* that led to the abandonment of the work on God's house.

Let them remember they are *his people, his saints* and act accordingly: *fear him* (v. 9). They can be confident (*surely*) that *his salvation* from their present trouble will be *near* them and that God, their *glory* will again *dwell in our land* (v. 9). It is true that the Shekinah light did not return to the sanctuary after the exile, but this was probably because God was beginning to wean them away from outward signs and turn their thoughts to the One who will reveal the full glory of God, of whom Haggai spoke (Hag.2:6-11).

If they gave heed to this promise, now in anticipation and then in full realisation, they would experience the blessings of

God coming to *meet together ... and ... kiss each other*, the blessings of *love and faithfulness, righteousness and peace* – the whole panoply of God's grace (v. 10). As their *faithfulness* reached up to him, so his *righteousness* would *look down* on them (v. 11). This would go along with God sending *down from heaven* his blessing on their crops so that their *land will yield its harvest* (v. 12). Fruit of all kinds would abound: spiritual (v. 11), and material (v. 12). Verse 13 encapsulates the basic principles of all this: God himself comes in the wake of *righteousness*; when his people hear his voice, repent and reform, this *prepares the way for his steps*, that is, for him to come in the fullness of his blessing.

Questions:

(1) When things are collapsing all around you and God seems uninterested, do you make your redemption by Christ your bottom line? See Romans 3:21-26, where the purpose of the 'atonement cover' or 'mercy seat' is now fulfilled by the blood of Christ, assuring us that, however it may seem, the wrath of God is no longer against us.

(2) What does this psalm teach us about Revival in the church?

(3) What does this psalm, especially verse 13, teach us about the connection between revival and reformation?

Psalm 86

Poor and Needy

This psalm *of David* is called *a prayer*, which is basically what it is, although it does contain a wonderful ascription of praise to God in the centre (vv. 8-10). It comes from a time when he was not only being persecuted but was almost alone (v. 14), possibly when he and a handful of his followers went into hiding from Saul. Although it is an outpouring of troubles, the psalm is very carefully structured, which may indicate that he or another rearranged his thoughts when the poem was edited for worship. As the NIV layout shows, the seventeen verses are in five stanzas, symmetrically constructed thus: 4 - 3 - 3 - 3 - 4.

This makes verses 8-10 on God's uniqueness central. Flanking this are stanzas in which David encourages himself and his men. The two outer stanzas contain his cry to God in this desperate situation.

Verses 1-4: His plaintive cry

David comes to God as a virtual beggar: *poor and needy*, for he was an outlaw with no abode or means of support; and although he had some followers, they were in the same state as he. Yet he addresses God in the imperative – five times in four verses, and nine in the remaining thirteen! This is partly out of desperation, as a drowning man calls out 'Help!' not 'would someone be kind enough to assist me in my dilemma?'; and partly because of his close personal relationship with God, which dispenses with the need for polite language. He comes to God as a *servant* who is *devoted* to him (v. 2), not as one pressed into service. Thus his imperatives are not imperious, but humble, as his words *trust in you* and *I lift up my soul* (v. 4) reveal.

Verses 5-7: His self-encouragement
From what *he* is David turns to what *God* is, for only he can meet his *poor and needy* state. He recognises he is partly responsible for his *trouble*, but recalls that God is *forgiving and good ... abounding in love* and will hear his cry for mercy (v. 6) – ideas which echo Exodus 34:6. These thoughts give him confidence: *you will answer me* (v. 7), that is, 'you will not punish me for this tragic mistake'.

Verses 8-10: His vision of God
Because of the way he approached God in verses 5-7, David is given a vision of his glory. It was during such a vision that Moses heard God declare his love, grace and mercy to sinners (Exod. 34:6), words which are clearly in David's mind at this time (vv. 5, 15). This was not exactly the vision Moses had expected when he said 'Show me your glory' (Exod. 33:18), but it was better than a spectacular display of majesty. It had met the need of Moses and the people at that time, as it met the need of David at this time. Although the books of Moses would not have been accessible to David if he was on the run from Saul at this time, the story would be well-known in Israel, and David would no doubt have had the words by heart.

It is in his grace that God's uniqueness chiefly consists, though no doubt verses 8b and 10a comprehend the totality of his *deeds*. These prove him incomparable (8a) and unique: he *alone (is) God* (v. 10 cf. Exod. 15:11, an earlier experience of Moses). This is why David says, not *all nations should come and worship before you*, but that they *will*. This strikes a Messianic note. For the prophecies of a universal divine kingdom (of which there are several in the Psalms) in verse 9 were to come about through the sufferings of Christ. Of these David's life was in some respects a pattern, though as yet he did not realize it.

Verses 11-13: His positive prayer

So dazzled is David by his vision he seems to forget what he had set out to pray for, and looks beyond the present need to his life as a whole. He asks God to *teach* him how to live (*walk*, v. 11). To achieve this he must be single-minded and do everything out of *fear* of God's *name*, that is, trust and love. Then his whole life will be *praise* (v. 12). This he can ask with confidence, for God has already proved his love by saving him from lethal situations (v. 13).

Verses 14-17: His present need

He now comes back to earth. His desperate plight has not changed – the conspiracy goes on (v. 14). But over against this is the God of whom he has seen a vision, the God of Moses (v. 15). In the light of this he prays not merely for safety, but for *strength* to continue in God's service. *The son of your maidservant* means that he saw himself not as a bought slave of God but as one brought up in his house – more a father-son relationship than a master-slave one (cf. v. 2 and Paul in Rom. 1:1, etc.). So he does not ask for anything sudden or spectacular but only *a sign* that God will prove his goodness by taking David's part against his enemies.

Questions:

(1) Do you pray in the imperative mood ('Lord, help ... bless ... guide, etc') or the subjunctive (' I pray that thou/you wouldst/ would ... ')? Which is better? Does praying in the imperative only avoid grammatical difficulties or is there spiritual value in it?

(2) When you are in trouble do you only complain to God and call for help, or do you encourage yourself while the trouble continues (cf. Ps. 42:5)?

(3) Do you know anything about a 'vision of God'? What does it mean and how does it help?

Psalm 87

The Glories of the City of God

This psalm reflects the prophetic spirit of Isaiah. Indeed it can be seen as putting into song his prophecy of Isaiah 2:1-4, where he speaks of the glories of Zion in the Messianic age and how it would attract the nations of the world and bring about universal peace. It sets to verse and music the glory of the universal preaching of the gospel.

Verses 1-3: The glory of Zion as God's chosen city
Since verse 1 has only one line, some conjecture that line 3 of verse 5 belongs here, which would certainly fit logically. Be that as it may, the psalmist is glorying in the city that is being displayed to the nations. He draws attention to three features of Zion.

Firstly, that it is well founded or 'established' – *on the holy mountain*, that is to say, on the *mountain* where God dwelt. There was nothing marvellous about the soil, shape or position of Zion, it was simply that God was there; it was really he that was holy, not the *mountain*. In other words, she is founded on God himself – he is her strength.

Secondly, that he has set his love chiefly on her. If the question is raised, 'Why has God chosen to dwell there and nowhere else?', the answer is simply that he *loves* her. As to why *he loves the gates of Zion more than all the dwellings of Jacob* (v. 2), there is no answer, any more than there is to the question why he loved Israel above all other nations (see Deut. 7:6-8) or why he loves those he saves in Christ, except that it displays his grace (Eph. 2:3-6).

Thirdly, God has *glorious things* to say of *the city of God* (v. 3). Many have already been said by kings, prophets and psalmists. Now God is going to speak himself, so we observe a reverent silence (*Selah*) before hearing what he has to say.

Verses 4-6: Judah's enemies made citizens of Zion

Here is God revealing what he *will record* in his book, that is, whom he will number among his people. Notwithstanding his special love for Israel, he is to include people of other nations too, even her most implacable foes: Egypt (*Rahab*); *Babylon*, who was to become her conqueror; *Philistia*, the most persistently hostile of all her neighbours; *Tyre*, a powerful source of wealth and materials; and even *Cush*, representing the most distant nations. They *will acknowledge* him as Lord, forsake their idols and come and worship him (46:10; 47:9; 96:7-8).

This is looking far beyond the few who came from other nations to be Jewish proselytes, for these are described as citizens who were *born in Zion*. So astonishing is this declaration that it is twice repeated. In verse 5 it is spoken of as something that would be talked about: *it will be said*. And what *will be said* is that it will be true of many: *this one and that one* – some from *this* nation and some from *that*. If line 3 belongs here, it is saying that these converts will be as firmly *established* as his people as Judah herself is.

Verse 6 clarifies and intensifies the words *I will record* (v. 4) and explains what *establish* means: they are permanently included in his family, they are *born in Zion*, they are God's children. It was this thought that led Paul to refer to the true church as 'Jerusalem that is above ... our mother' (Gal. 4:26). Another pause follows these astonishing words of God: *Selah*.

Verse 7: Their delight in their new home

This verse shows that these Gentiles were not forced into worshipping God, but do so freely and gladly. They *make music, they sing*, as we all do when we are happy. And the theme of their song? The newness and freshness they have found in becoming children of God, after the dryness and dreariness of paganism, compared with which life with God is like *fountains*. This expression was translated into Christian language by John Newton in his hymn based on this psalm 'Glorious things of thee are spoken':

> Who can faint while such a river
> Ever flows their thirst to assuage?

Questions:

(1) Does the electing love and pure grace of God towards you humble and amaze you? (See Eph. 1:3, 6; 2:4-9.)

(2) Do you believe that people – individuals, communities and nations – who at present hate us and what we stand for can be included in the number of God's elect? (See Eph. 1:11-13, noting the word 'included' [NIV].)

(3) Is your connection with the church one of attendance only or of spiritual birth? (See John 3:3, 5; Gal. 4:26.) Do you have evidence of this in the experience of verse 7?

Psalm 88

In the Depths of Despair

Heman appears to have been a leader of a guild of musicians, to which Asaph and Ethan also belonged and to which the name 'Sons of Korah' was given. He may also have been one of the wise men of David's time whose wisdom was only exceeded by that of Solomon himself (1 Kings 4:31).Although called *a song* it is not the usual *song* of praise and triumph, but one of sadness and despair. So when the *director of music* included it in the Psalter he set it to the saddest of all tunes: *mahalath leannoth*. The first word is the name of the tune for Psalm 53 and resembles 'sickness'. But the addition of *leannoth* shows it is an even sadder tune, for the word is that used for poison, in fact hemlock, denoting his bitterness of spirit.

Verses 1-2: A despairing cry
In his loneliness, to whom can he talk but *the LORD*? He does more than talk: *I cry out*, as if God were far away, like his friends. However, faith has not completely gone, for he calls him *the God who saves me*. He is therefore right to call his *song my prayer*. Indeed the whole psalm is structured around prayer to God, each section repeating 'I call to you' (v. 9b) or 'I cry to you' (v. 13).

Verses 3-9a: A catalogue of miseries
In verses 3-5 he describes himself as one as good as dead.He may have been imprisoned in a hole in the ground – *the pit*

(v. 4). In verse 5 he appears to be alluding to those *slain* in battle who are hastily buried in the ground on the battlefield and not taken back to the rock tombs of the rich and honourable. Such are soon forgotten because no one knows where their bodies lie.

But there is worse, for the word for *grave* in verse 3 is 'Sheol', that place of darkness which God himself remembers *no more*. So his complaint is that he is not only *cut off* from his friends but from the *care* of God. Worse still, he attributes his woes to God himself (vv. 6-9): *you have put me in the lowest pit, in the darkest depths*. This is more than a deep dark hole in the ground, it is hell itself. This is why he speaks of *your wrath (lying) heavily upon me* (v. 7). He accuses God of drowning him in the depths of the sea. No wonder the editor has put a dramatic pause or musical interval at this point: *Selah*.

But he still has not quite finished the catalogue. God has gone so far as to leave him without any comforters (v. 8), so that his *closest friends* are far away, and in his excess of grief he attributes this to his shameful condition: he must be *repulsive to them*. Not true of course but excessive loneliness imagines all kinds of fantasies. There is no *escape* from this *confinement*, and all he can do is weep until his *eyes* become *dim with grief* (v. 9a).

Verses 9b-12: A slight recovery
Although he is probably unconscious of it himself, he is beginning to recover his spirits, to bounce back from the rock bottom he has hit. Notice the persistence with which he prays: *I call to you, O LORD, every day* (v. 9b), something Jesus encouraged and commended (Luke 18:1-8). So earnest was his prayer that his body came into action to express it: *I spread out my hands to you.*

This leads on to the arguments he now uses as to why God should do something for him. If he seemed before to have given up, he is now beginning to fight back. Some of the greatest prayers in the Bible are in the form of questions addressed to God (Gen. 18:22-32; Isa. 63:15-19). Jesus himself yielded to the arguments of the Syro-Phoenician woman (Mark 7:24-30). His argument here is basically: what use will he be to God if he goes on in this living death? All that is true of the dead is true of him in this Sheol on earth. The dead cannot witness God's *wonders* and respond with *praise* (v. 10). They cannot hear his message of *love (and) faithfulness* (v. 11). They know nothing of his *deeds* of providence and justice (v. 12). They no longer belong to God at all, for they are in the grip of 'Abaddon' (*Destruction*), that is, Satan, the Destroyer (Rev. 9:11). Can this be what God really wants?

We have to remember that all this is based on what had so far been revealed about death, which was very little, hence the constant reference to *darkness (and) oblivion* (v. 12). As C. S. Lewis wrote: 'It is difficult to know how an ancient Jew thought of Sheol. He did not like thinking about it. No good could come of thinking about it. Evil might' ('Reflections on the Psalms', p. 34).

Verses 13-18: A nagging question

Although he has recovered his spirits sufficiently to argue with God (vv. 10-12) and to continue pleading with him (v. 13), he is still stuck over the question *Why?* (v. 14). He can see no reason or purpose for what was happening to him. Somehow he seems to be unable to trust God, to grasp his hand in the dark, to believe he is working his purpose out and to find 'grace to help in time of need' (Heb. 4:16).

The remaining verses show what a dangerous condition this is: it exaggerates the trouble and gets it all out of proportion. He can see nothing in his whole life other than affliction (and) suffering (v. 15). From what we know of Heman as a prominent poet and musician in David's court, even if he were nothing more than that (which he probably was), this would deny his sweeping condemnation of his entire life.

And why should he conclude that his present sufferings were due to the *wrath (and) terrors* of God (vv. 16-17)? If this were happening because of his association with David, then it was down to the sin of man, not the anger of God. It would also mean David himself was under God's wrath. In his bitter *despair* he is so isolated that closest to him was *darkness*, which he ironically calls his *friend* (v. 18).

Such is the awful consequence of questioning and challenging God instead of trusting him. It is the story of Job again.

Questions:
(1) Does this psalm arouse your sympathies for Christians who are imprisoned for their association with Christ and his church? (See Heb. 13:3.)

(2) Does it show the danger of loneliness in which things prey on the mind and become disproportionate? Does this in turn show you the importance of strengthening your trust in God in order to counteract this danger (Ps. 13, especially v. 5 and Ps. 56:1-4)? Does it show you the need we all have for the Christian fellowship? (Heb. 10:25.)

(3) Does it make you more thankful to live in times when Christ's resurrection has changed fear of death into hope in death (1 Cor. 15:54-57)?

Psalm 89

The Revocation of the Covenant

This psalm reflects the language of the covenant God made with David regarding his dynasty (2 Sam. 7), which is probably the *vision* mentioned in verse 19. What follows is very similar to 2 Samuel 7:4-17. The reason this is made the theme of this long psalm may be that the covenant was under threat, as verses 38-51 say.

Ethan had been one of Solomon's wise men (1 Kings 4:31) and his psalm is called a *Maskil* (see Ps. 32) because it contains 'instruction' for God's people when they are experiencing perplexing times and God appears to have deserted them. It has similarities with Asaph's psalms (74, 77, 79) but being considerably longer it gets more to the heart of the matter: God's covenant with David and his dynasty (vv. 3-4, 19-37) which God seems to have revoked (vv. 38-51). But before that it glories in the God who existed before that covenant (vv. 1-18).

Verses 1-18: God's love and faithfulness

In spite of the dire situation, Ethan declares that the theme of his song will be *the LORD's great love* and his *faithfulness* (v. 1) – not only at this time but throughout his life and ministry, *through all generations* and even *for ever*. In fact he uses each of those two words, *love* and *faithfulness*, seven times. This is because his psalm is centred on God's covenant, which is founded on his *love* and *faithfulness*. Indeed they transcend Ethan's own experiences of them: *your love stands for ever ... your faithfulness is established in heaven itself* (v. 2) – before the earth was made and after it has gone.

It is as an expression of these two attributes that God *made a covenant with ... David* and his *line* that they would occupy *the throne* of Israel *through all generations* (vv. 3-4). The terms of this covenant are outlined in 2 Samuel 7:11-16. Although not called a covenant there, it is so called in 2 Samuel 23:5 (cf. Isa. 55:3; Jer. 33:20-21). The hold of David and his successors on the *throne* is as secure as the love and faithfulness of God. Yet at this time it is under threat possibly through Rehoboam's disastrous reign and Shishak's invasion. Ethan will come back to this later; meanwhile he will appeal to even greater works in confirmation of his theme. *Selah* marks this change of direction.

In verses 5-8 he declares that this God, who has placed David on the throne of Israel, himself occupies the throne of the universe. *The holy ones*, the supernatural beings, who assemble in the heavens, acknowledge him and *praise (his) wonders* in creation, providence and redemption (v. 5). There is none to *compare with him* even among the heavenly beings (v. 6). In fact, like his earthly creatures, they fear him, so *awesome* is he (v. 7). Although angels are *mighty*, their power does not compare with his, which is exercised not arbitrarily but in *faithfulness* (v. 8).

He gives examples to prove the point, taking first God's supremacy over *the surging sea* (v. 9). Subduing the sea was one of his first acts in creating the earth (Gen. 1:2, 6-10). But it has to be done repeatedly when its *waves mount up*. The ancients feared the sea and believed it was under the control of dangerous supernatural powers. The disciples' awe of Christ was never greater than when he stilled the storm on Galilee (Matt. 8:27).

This leads on to his reference to *Rahab* (v. 10), the monster of the Nile, also called 'Leviathan', possibly Sobek, the crocodile god. They were being invaded by *Rahab*'s subjects, the Egyptians. But Ethan recalls how God had *crushed* them when he struck the Nile and later overthrew them in the Red

Sea. This proves that *the heavens and the earth* are his and all that is in them (v. 11). Looking particularly at the earth (v. 12), he says that God reigns over all of it – lengthwise from *north* to *south*, and heightwise from *Tabor*, a low mount, to *Hermon*, which rises to 9,000 feet. The *arm* that brought all this into being is *endued with power*, it is *strong (and) exalted* (v. 13). Thus does he get the present situation into the perspective of a universal, eternal, omnipotent God.

But he has not finished, and, having spoken of God's rule, he now comes to its manner (vv. 14-18). God exercises his sovereignty in *righteousness and justice, love and faithfulness*, so happiness is to be found in submitting to him: *blessed are those who have learned to acclaim you* (v. 15). Literally this reads 'Blessed are the people who know the shouting', possibly a reference to the shouts of joy that accompanied the bringing up of the ark to Jerusalem (2 Sam.6:15), which would also explain *walk in the light of your presence*, describing the procession that followed the ark.

Although that place has now suffered damage, let them remember the glories of that day and continue to *rejoice in your name all day long* and *exult in your righteousness* (v. 16). For the God who came to dwell there is the God whose absolute sovereignty he has been praising. Let God be again what he was then – *their glory and strength*, let them believe they are still in his *favour* and he will *exalt our horn*, that is, recover our strength (vv. 17-18).

In all situations there is no better remedy than to turn our thoughts to the majesty of God and our relationship to him. This humbles us in times of triumph and revives us in times of defeat.

Verses 19-37: God's covenant with David

Ethan now returns to the matter in hand, which he introduced in verses 3-4, before launching into a eulogy on God himself – God's perpetual covenant with David and his dynasty.

Verses 19-29 probably refer to David's original call through Samuel, to whom God evidently appeared in a vision, not recorded in the historical books. This must have taken place either before Samuel told Saul he would be replaced by a better man (1 Sam. 13:14), or, more likely, when Samuel visited Jesse's family in Bethlehem and 'the LORD said (to Samuel about David), "Rise and anoint him; he is the one"'. It could be that Samuel recounted all this to David at the time and he in turn informed his inner circle after becoming king, so that it was eventually passed on to Ethan. Now Ethan is telling it back to God as an introduction to his complaint and prayer in verses 38-51.

God's promises to David go far beyond anything he ever said to Saul. Although a youth, David would be fully equipped for his task of leading Israel in its wars (v. 19). He was called and authorised by God himself: *I have found David ... I have anointed him* (v. 20). God would be with him in a way he had not been with Saul, so that he would enjoy supernatural strength (v. 21). Since none could *subject* God to *tribute* or *oppress* him, they would not be able to do it with David (v. 22). Instead, he would enjoy victory over *his foes* (v. 23). To verify this, God pledges his *faithful love* and his own *name* (v. 24). By this means God's original promise to Moses and Israel at Sinai of a kingdom from the Mediterranean to the Euphrates (Exod. 23:31) would be fulfilled (v. 25).

But to God David was more than an invincible warrior king,; he was his son and David would *call out to* him, *You are my Father, my God ... my Saviour* (v. 26). It was to be a personal, loving relationship. Others had fought and would fight God's battles without knowing this personal relationship David enjoyed. God goes further and calls him his *firstborn*, his heir, on whom he would bestow his inheritance, making him *the most exalted of the kings of the earth* (v. 27). David probably had these words in mind when he wrote Psalm 2:7-9. This is further reinforced in verse 28 where God speaks of his *love* for David. This covenant was not a mere legal arrangement; it was a personal commitment. Since God's love is *for ever* and *will never fail*, neither will his promise or David's *throne* (v. 29).

God's promises are conditional and here Ethan refers to the words of Nathan in 2 Samuel 7:11-16 regarding David's successors. For David was dead and his throne was occupied by his descendant. If the promise was to continue, then the kings occupying the throne must be to God as David had been. They must not *forsake my law* or cease to *follow my statutes* (v. 30), *violate my decrees nor fail to keep my commands* (v. 31).

The loving relationship between fathers and sons includes chastisement where necessary (v. 32), which was what was happening at the time of writing with Shishak's invasion. But it was fatherly discipline and did not mean his love had ceased or his *faithfulness* failed (v. 33). This was part of the covenant which he *will not violate,* because *his lips have uttered it* (v. 34). More, he has *sworn by his holiness,* his essential nature which cannot change, he the God who cannot lie (v. 35), that *his line will continue for ever* (v. 36). It will be *like the sun ... like the moon* (v. 37).

Why then did it come to an end at the exile, or why was it not restored on the return from Babylon? Because there was more to it than physical descent from David. The promise culminated in the Messiah, who was to be 'born of David's line'. For that long kingless period the covenant was merely on hold. It would be revived and come into its fullness in a remote descendant who would also be born in Bethlehem. This is hinted at in the term 'firstborn', used of David in verse 27 and of Christ in Romans 8:29; Colossians 1:15; Hebrews 1:6; 12:23; and Revelation 1:5. God did not violate his covenant, he fulfilled it more gloriously than in a mere succession of descendants of David, most of whom were unDavidlike anyway! All this needs pondering before proceeding: *Selah.*

Verses 38-45: God's seeming renunciation of the covenant
It is interesting to compare Ethan's approach with Asaph's, especially in 74. Asaph begins with his lament over the present situation and then recalls God's nature and deeds. Ethan proceeds the other way round. So, though both use the phrase 'But you' at the turning point, Ethan's is exactly the opposite of Asaph's. Ethan has set out the God of the covenant and the covenant of God. Now he has to say *But you* have gone back on it (vv. 38-39).

So this passage forms a strong contrast with verses 9-18. In verse 9 God was pacifying 'the surging sea'; in verse 38 he is unleashing his anger. In verse 10 he humiliated 'Rahab', but in verse 39 he degraded David's throne and *defiled his crown in the dust.* In verses 11-12 God rules over an unbounded area, but in verses 40-41 the enemy has *broken through* into his domain, so that, instead of being feared and admired by their *neighbours*, they are objects of their *scorn.* In verses 13-15 God was ruling righteously and making people glad, but in verse 42 it is their foes who are *exalted* and their *enemies* who *rejoice.* In verse 15 they were walking *in the light of your presence*, but now he has *put an end to (that) splendour* (v. 44). Whereas in verse 17 God had been their glory and strength, now their weapons were futile (v. 43). Far from the king's reign being everlasting (vv. 4, 29), it has been *cut short* (v. 45).

Verses 46-51: Ethan's prayer for God's mercy

The gist of Ethan's prayer is the same as Asaph's: *how long* is this to go on? (cf. 74:10; 77:7; 79:5). It is not the *event* of an enemy victory but its *duration* that is the problem. God had claimed the right to punish in the terms of the covenant (2 Sam. 7:14), but not to the extent of removing the crown from David's line for ever (2 Sam. 7:15-16). The chief worry of these men of God therefore was when it would end. His question is really a cry to God to quench his *wrath* and come out of *hiding* to their aid (v. 46).

To strengthen his plea he appeals to a number of aspects of the dilemma. Firstly, the shortness of his life (vv. 47-48). He and his people are but *men*, whose lives are *fleeting* (and) futile, who face *death*, from which they cannot save themselves. Secondly, he appeals to God's former favours towards them, which came from his *love* and his *faithfulness* to his covenant with *David* (v. 49). The twin themes with which he began in verse 1 – *love (and) faithfulness* – are still on his mind. Thirdly, he draws attention to the reproaches the nation is suffering (vv. 50-51). No doubt in using the first person singular here he is speaking as representative of the nation, even to the extent of talking as if he were the king himself: *your servant ... your anointed one.* For ultimately the nation stood or fell with the king, for it was he with whom God made the covenant. When he was *mocked* and subjected to *taunts*, the whole nation was brought into disrepute. Indeed so was God himself, for king and nation were God's *servant, (his) anointed.*

As the coming of Christ drew ever nearer, these phrases would come more and more to be used of the nation (Isa. 42:1, 19). Enshrined in this idea is the One who was to come to save the nation. The Messiah, the anointed one, was ultimately seen as one mocked and despised, reaching its height in Isaiah 53.

Verse 52 is the familiar doxology which ends each book, and was added when the Psalter was arranged in five parts.

Questions:
(1) How does this psalm help us see God's love and faithfulness as the essence of God's new covenant with us in Christ? (See John 13:1.)

(2) How do verses 5-18 show that the answer to our biggest problems lies in the character and works of God? (See Ps. 36:9.)

(3) What does the psalm teach about the Fatherhood of God in relation both to Christ and his kingdom, and to us as his sons? (See Heb. 5:6-8; 12:3-11.)

Subject Index

Scripture Index

Other Focus on the Bible Commentaries

FOCUS · ON · THE · BIBLE

Psalms 90-150

The Lord Reigns

Eric Lane

Psalms: 90 - 150

The Lord Reigns

Eric Lane

A Psalm is basically a poem set to music and sung. For centuries the Psalms would have been the most familiar part of scripture to people who had no access to books. They are not only an integral part of the shared experience of the church but they also communicate God's guidance to this world, reveal his character and encourage his people.

This volume continues his exposition with the last two books of the Psalms (90 to 150) - which includes the earliest Psalm (Psalm 90 – attributed to Moses), and the Psalms of Ascent (Psalms 120 to 134). Each of these two books ends with their own doxology

This collection of Psalms is ancient - as least as old as the second or third century B.C. It is not chronological, nor even grouped according to author. The style is predominantly praise but the Psalms also include prayers, complaints - and even curses.

This volume also contains an appendix, giving a suggested chronological order for the Psalms. All of which makes this a fascinating book to seek guidance from - with the experienced help of Eric Lane.

ISBN 1-84550-202-7
ISBN 978-1-84550-202-7

Christian Focus Publications

publishes books for all ages

Our mission statement –

STAYING FAITHFUL

In dependence upon God we seek to help make His infallible Word, the Bible, relevant. Our aim is to ensure that the Lord Jesus Christ is presented as the only hope to obtain forgiveness of sin, live a useful life and look forward to heaven with Him.

REACHING OUT

Christ's last command requires us to reach out to our world with His gospel. We seek to help fulfill that by publishing books that point people towards Jesus and help them develop a Christ-like maturity. We aim to equip all levels of readers for life, work, ministry and mission.

Books in our adult range are published in three imprints.
Christian Focus contains popular works including biographies, commentaries, basic doctrine and Christian living. Our children's books are also published in this imprint.
Mentor focuses on books written at a level suitable for Bible College and seminary students, pastors, and other serious readers. The imprint includes commentaries, doctrinal studies, examination of current issues and church history.
Christian Heritage contains classic writings from the past.

Christian Focus Publications, Ltd
Geanies House, Fearn, Ross-shire,
IV20 1TW, Scotland, United Kingdom
info@christianfocus.com

For details of our titles visit us on our website
www.christianfocus.com